Chicken Soup for the Soul®

the joy of less

Chicken Soup for the Soul: The Joy of Less
101 Stories about Having More by Simplifying Our Lives
Amy Newmark and Brooke Burke-Charvet

Published by Chicken Soup for the Soul Publishing, LLC www.chickensoup.com
Copyright ©2016 by Chicken Soup for the Soul Publishing, LLC. All Rights Reserved.

The publisher gratefully acknowledges the many publishers and individuals who
granted Chicken Soup for the Soul permission to reprint the cited material.

Front cover artwork courtesy of iStockphoto.com/Javarman3 (@Javarman3)
Front cover photo of Brooke Burke-Charvet courtesy of Jeff Katz
Back cover and Interior photo courtesy of iStockphoto.com/dsharple (@dsharple)
Photo of Amy Newmark courtesy of Susan Morrow at SwickPix
Interior photo of Brooke Burke-Charvet courtesy of Don Flood

Cover and Interior by Daniel Zaccari

Distributed to the booktrade by Simon & Schuster. SAN: 200-2442

Publisher's Cataloging-In-Publication Data
(Prepared by The Donohue Group, Inc.)

Names: Newmark, Amy, compiler. | Burke, Brooke, compiler.
Title: Chicken soup for the soul : the joy of less : 101 stories about
    having more by simplifying our lives / [compiled by] Amy Newmark and
    Brooke Burke-Charvet.
Other Titles: Joy of less : 101 stories about having more by simplifying
    our lives
Description: [Cos Cob, Connecticut] : Chicken Soup for the Soul
    Publishing, [2016]
Identifiers: LCCN 2016932380 | ISBN 978-1-61159-957-2 (print) |
    ISBN 978-1-61159-257-3 (ebook)
Subjects: LCSH: Simplicity--Literary collections. | Simplicity--Anecdotes. |
    Consumption (Economics)--Literary collections. | Consumption
    (Economics)--Anecdotes. | Contentment--Literary collections. |
    Contentment--Anecdotes. | Conduct of life--Literary collections. |
    Conduct of life--Anecdotes. | Anecdotes.
Classification: LCC BJ1496 .C45 2016 (print) | LCC BJ1496 (ebook) | DDC
    646.7--dc23

PRINTED IN THE UNITED STATES OF AMERICA
on acid∞free paper

25 24 23 22 21 20 19 18 17 16   01 02 03 04 05 06 07 08 09 10 11

Chicken Soup for the Soul

the joy of less

101 Stories about Having More by Simplifying Our Lives

Amy Newmark
Brooke Burke-Charvet

Chicken Soup for the Soul Publishing, LLC
Cos Cob, CT

Changing your life one story at a time®
www.chickensoup.com

Contents

❸

~All You Need Is Less~

❹

~Joyfully Unplugged~

❺
~The Joy of Sharing~

❻
~Less Is So Much More~

❼
~Joy on the Road~

8

~Count Your Blessings~

9

~The Joy of Starting Over~

❿

~Lessons in Less~

Introduction

We live in a society where most people are looking for the BBD (the Bigger, Better Deal) and not making an effort to nurture and enjoy what they already have. Making a commitment to prioritize what's most meaningful in one's life is imperative for living a life of fulfillment.

I'm surrounded by a world of privilege, excess, and fantasy. While I run a business and raise my four children, I also work in television and I come across many unsatisfied people who tend to miss the message of "The Joy of Less." That's why I was so excited to be a part of this inspirational collection of Chicken Soup for the Soul stories that help us focus on what really matters in our lives.

I believe in the power of saying "no" — "no" to too many material possessions, and "no" to schedules so crowded with "obligations" that we crowd out time we should spend with our families and our friends. We need to use the power of "no" so that we can say "yes" to the things that matter to us.

As a young woman, I shared my life with many people aiming to please others at the expense of being true to themselves and their own needs. I'll never forget the first time my boyfriend blew off a social dinner because we were jetlagged and simply too tired to pull it off. I was so relieved that we could skip what was potentially a four-hour dinner, but I was also mortified by his insensitivity to our hosts. I remember thinking how free he must feel to not be psychologically obligated to show up for someone else's event.

Rather than canceling, I have learned to say "no" up front. Now let me tell you, Hollywood is notorious for being flaky. I cannot stand people who say "yes" and then don't follow through. Being unreliable is unacceptable. There is an etiquette to saying no, which can be misinterpreted as being rude, but I believe in a good, honest "no."

I write my own story. I am responsible for the commitment to raise a connected family without guilt, and I alone control my journey. I often make compromises for my husband and family, but outside of that I do not do what does not serve me.

As a multitasking businesswoman and mother of four, I have chosen to conquer my work/life balancing act by saying "no" as often as I need to. Which means I don't have much of a social life! But my family life is so rewarding, and valuable, that I choose to put it first and let all other wish lists take a back seat.

I used to get anxious when looking at my calendar, calculating every full day and the endless events that filled it. I would furiously flip pages looking for an empty date that meant I would have some time to breathe. I placed my personal time last on the priority list. Then I turned forty and I grew up!

Saying "no" to many social events and other demands on my time, even optional ones that are for work, allows me to carve out my invaluable "me time." I need that for my sanity, and in order to do a good job doing what matters to me. I am often asked how I balance motherhood and my hectic life. I don't know if any woman honestly thinks she has achieved that perfect balance, but I am okay taking my life day by day and doing the best I can... and that means focusing on quality time. For example, I don't feel any guilt about passing on most invitations on school nights. On busy work days, I try my best to be home at night for my family. That means missing those fun "ladies' nights" with the other moms, and it means passing on nights out, even with friends I adore. They have to take second place to my family... and my own wellbeing.

The speed at which we move is so fast that we too often forget to hit the pause button. I spent much of my younger years going to places I had little interest in, socializing with people I didn't enjoy, and wasting time for other people's benefit. All of that compromised my personal gratification.

You'll read dozens of stories in this *Chicken Soup for the Soul* collection that will empower you to say "no" yourself. You'll see how other men and women did it, and you'll read about the consequences — which were always great! Most of our writers were pleasantly surprised by how well their "no's" were received, and by how well their lives went once they learned how to de-clutter their calendars.

You'll also learn about another kind of de-cluttering in these stories, and that is the how and why of reducing all the "stuff" that you have. It's a rare person who doesn't feel that he or she has too many material possessions, and we present you with dozens of stories that provide you with easy-to-implement tips for how to do it.

My own rule, the result of necessity, is "dig it or ditch it." If you aren't using it, if you haven't worn it in a year, get it out of your life. Give it to a friend, donate it to your church or a thrift shop that supports a good cause. Someone else will value the item that no longer fits in your life.

Keeping the clutter means someone else doesn't get the blessing of your unwanted item, and it also means you can't clearly see those items of value that really should remain part of your life. I love having a little space between hangers and being able to organize fashion choices. Having too much just isn't healthy. It's overwhelming, it hangs over us, and it slows us down.

So that's it. The Joy of Less. Less stuff and fewer commitments on our calendars. The joy of less isn't really about having less, it's about clearing the way to have more of what you love. It isn't about doing less, it's about doing more of what inspires you. It's about making room for meaningful things in your life and letting go of what does not serve you. By saying no you free up time and space for what serves you best.

Enjoy this collection. Be inspired. I know you'll come away filled with ideas and enthusiasm for the new life you'll carve out as you reduce the clutter in your life, literally and figuratively, and experience The Joy of Less!

~Brooke Burke-Charvet

Chapter
1

the joy of less

The Freedom of Less

Unit 91

If you want to make an easy job seem mighty hard,
just keep putting off doing it.
~Olin Miller

D ay after day, I drove to the Public Storage warehouses in Jacksonville, Florida in the oppressive heat and humidity. I punched a code in the keypad, drove in quickly when the steel gate opened and checked my rearview mirror to watch it lock behind me. I was alone in an unsavory part of town. I wound my way through the maze of narrow corridors between rows of numbered orange doors until I found Units 91 and 92. I slid the heavy doors up on their rollers and fought the feeling of panic. I was totally overwhelmed by the task at hand.

To even get into either unit I had to move articles nearest the front out to the parking lot. I started with a few smaller items: an electric heater, a vacuum cleaner, and some small end tables. To move larger pieces like bureaus or desks I slid cardboard under them to help slide them across the concrete floor, a few inches at a time, so I could shimmy by and size up the rear of the units.

I started with the stacks and stacks of packed cartons. Ideally the movers would have packed the tall bulky pieces at the back of the units and stashed the boxes close to the front. This had not happened. Their mission was to get it off the truck and into the storage units as quickly as possible. So now I looked at two 360-square-foot units packed floor to ceiling, with scarcely room for another bar of soap in either one.

Boxes. Boxes. Boxes. After opening one or two it became apparent that they had been filled indiscriminately in the last hours before our deadline to be out of the house we left in Maine. Tucked in with mixing bowls, cheese graters and soup ladles were packages of cereal, rice, raisins, sugar and nuts. To leave these items in storage in Florida's heat is to invite hordes of ants to an all-you-can-eat buffet. So my first item of business was to open every box that potentially had food items inside.

Because we had to drive from Maine to Florida, I had packed a carefully chosen selection of snacks: rye crackers, cheese, almonds, grapes, cherries etc. When we were ready to leave, I noticed, despite repeated instructions to all four men packing the truck, my basket was missing. They were just tightening the strap on the back doors, so with a shrug, I let it go. I found my basket six weeks later in Unit 92. A lizard had beaten the ants to the picnic.

> *I've given to friends and acquaintances just about anything they happened to admire when visiting our home.*

After unearthing the perishables, I went for the irreplaceable, the photos of my children, the originals of my poems, the essential papers indicating I had been born, married and having not yet died, paid my taxes every year. I culled the personal items from boxes stashed with everyday utilitarian items, toasters, towels and teakettles.

"Reduce. Reduce. Reduce." I repeated that like a mantra as I separated the contents into "discards," "essentials to keep" and "not sure yet." By the end of each day, hot, sweaty and exhausted, I would shove the items from the parking lot back inside the units until my next session. I would load my car with items I wanted or needed for our rented home and sigh over the still overwhelming loads in Units 91 and 92.

The work I did each day was hot, heavy and lonely. One afternoon I noticed a three-quarter-ton truck pull up to a unit close to mine. An older couple got out and went to work immediately loading things into their truck. My first response was gratitude for their company, even though we had not even spoken. A while later, when they had finished loading their truck, the man approached and said hello. "You got lots of stuff," he said. "Mind if I take a look?" He added, "In case you don't pay your rent," with a quick grin.

"Do you buy stuff?" I asked.

"We buy whole units. Cheap. When people don't pay their rent and the storage company gets rid of it all."

"I'll pay the rent," I said, "but I am looking to get rid of some of this." So I let him look around a bit, took his name and phone number and gave him my contact information. His wife called to request an inventory list of the items I wanted to sell. I said I had more sorting to do but would comply when ready.

Over the next few weeks I continued sorting, moving the items I would keep into one of the two units. I typed the inventory, affixing an estimated value to each item based on cost, replacement value and/ or Internet research. I submitted the list. They gave me a price and we set a date and time to meet at the storage units. They brought two trucks and a couple of big guys to help.

On a damp, misty morning I watched as belongings I'd had for years were loaded into a cavernous truck whose destination I did not know. The antique wardrobe with the beveled glass mirror, the pine secretary unit that used to hold my favorite books, the lingerie chests, bureaus, beds, a favorite corner china cabinet and on and on. Sofas, chairs, safes, lawn ornaments and assorted knick-knacks. The truck filled. Unit 91 emptied. I swept it out and went to the office to settle the paperwork. A few months later, movers would haul the contents of Unit 92 to the home we purchased in another city in Florida. The house would be more than filled.

In the three years since parting with all that stuff I have continued to make donations to Goodwill, I have dropped bags and bags of items at church thrift centers, and I've given to friends and acquaintances just about anything they happened to admire when visiting our home. I've tried to adhere to the policy of "one in, one out" when it comes to acquiring new items. We've downsized our home by several hundred square feet.

At the moment, there is nothing I need, and nothing lacking from my life. I no longer even think about all the items I got rid of nor do I miss any of them. I have no regrets, except that we moved all that stuff from Maine to Florida in the first place!

~Phyllis McKinley

The Pick-Me-Up that Doesn't Work

*We tend to forget that happiness doesn't come as a
result of getting something we don't have, but rather of
recognizing and appreciating what we do have.*
~Frederick Koenig

I was surrounded by piles and piles of clothes. Some showed signs of wear, others had been worn only once or twice, and a few still had tags. They held no appeal for me. Old or new, they had lost their luster and since there was no space left in the closet, they had to go. Spending hours sorting through the clothes and placing them in trash bags, I patted myself on the back for my efforts. In addition to de-cluttering, I was helping people. I shared clothing with friends who were ecstatic to get the text, "I'm cleaning out my closet." The rest went to charity organizations that would profit mightily from my barely used wardrobe.

We all cope with stress differently. A treat, a little pick-me-up, something to take the edge off the harshness of life. "You deserve it," the ads were quick to promote, knowing just the right thing to say. "Yes, I do," I thought. "It's been a hard day dealing with squabbling children, endless dishes and being the one to keep it all going." It was exhausting trying to keep the peace, and while some women might crave chocolate, I craved a place where there was no chaos and no one would expect anything of me.

A little trip to my favorite store usually did the trick. As I opened the door, scented candles ushered me in. Taking a deep breath, I could feel the stress fading away. No one here pulled on my arms or climbed on me like I was a jungle gym. In fact, they asked if they could help me. Here, I relaxed more deeply than any yoga meditation. As my shoes echoed on the wood floor, I could hear myself think in this beautiful place. I wandered around the store touching soft fabric between my fingers.

> *When I added up the amount of time spent purging the stuff, not to mention the buying, I realized I had been wasting the most precious gift I had been given… my life.*

This store represented everything I wished I could be. Neatly lined racks, evenly spaced hangers, and I wasn't the one who would do the cleaning. Store employees knew me by name, and I left with a shirt or a dress in a pretty shopping bag. Who am I kidding? There was never just one. The shopping bags burst with my finds. I left on a high, feeling as if I had done something truly meaningful. My world was not so bleak as I pulled into my driveway.

The problem was, it never lasted. Endless shopping trips later, I had a house full of stuff, most of which I neither used nor cared about. As I pulled the tie on the last bag of giveaway clothes, I glanced at the clock. I was shocked at how many hours had passed. When I added up the amount of time spent purging the stuff, not to mention the buying, I realized I had been wasting the most precious gift I had been given… my life.

A few days after my closet purge, a dear friend and I were having lunch. I learned she had been taking classes toward a master's degree. I walked away proud of what she had accomplished, yet wondering how she found the time to make this happen. Due to the amount of stuff in my house, sorting and picking up dominated my day. It dawned on me, if I had fewer things my whole life would be less cluttered. I could take the time I spent shopping and picking up to do something worthwhile.

Feeling inspired, I started that day. It took nearly a year to go beyond my own closet and go through everything in my house. I squeezed in a little time every day between carpool drop-offs and soccer practices. I went through every nook and cranny. I put to use my marketing degree and opened an online store, selling what I could and donating the rest. Things began leaving my house every day. Peeling away at the layers of stuff sitting around, with each decision to let go I felt only one thing... relief.

Wedding gifts that had not been used in a decade and a half were the first to see the door. Bulk items kept on hand "just in case" were the next to go. No toy was safe. I encouraged my kids to sell anything they no longer used, and I let them keep the cash. They learned a lot from the experience. Most of all they learned they had a lot of things they didn't care about. We cleared out an entire room of toys, consolidating them to a game room upstairs.

With that empty space I created a peaceful room where I could read and write. I no longer needed a store to calm my spirit. I often find my daughter curled up on the couch reading, a quiet place away from her rambunctious brothers. It was in this space I started to dream again. Not about what I could buy, but what I could do to make a difference.

Understanding I am better off without the clutter has led to a whole new way of living. I have more time to spend on the things that matter — lunch with my husband, playing with my children, a handwritten note to a friend, a volunteer opportunity. When the familiar need for a pick-me-up does creep in, I've discovered I can hit the gym or take a walk in the fresh air. Being physically active does far more to lift my spirits than any shopping splurge ever did.

This year for my birthday I received several gift cards. My family knows me well, so it didn't come as a huge surprise when they were for my favorite store. I have to admit, I was giddy at the prospect of a shopping trip. Some habits are hard to break. I determined though, before I set foot in the store, I would only use the value of my gift cards.

The store clerk greeted me by name. "It's been such a long time since we've seen you!" she said, nearly pulling me into a hug. For reasons entirely different than her intention, she could not have paid me a nicer compliment.

Checking out with my single item, she detailed the new fall collection arriving the following week. I mentally checked my calendar, debating which day I could swing by the store, and then I stopped. My face broke into a wide smile as she handed me the small bag. "Take care," I said simply, walking away knowing I would not be back no matter how gorgeous the colors were. There will always be more. Another collection to see. The latest, the greatest, better than the last... and I am better off without them.

~Katie Bangert

Going Places with Less

Don't settle down and sit in one place. Move around,
be nomadic, make each day a new horizon.
~Jon Krakauer

W alking along the trail with my husband, I took a deep breath and admired the view. Snowcapped mountains. Wildflowers blooming yellow, blue and red throughout the hillside meadows, their sweet scent carried in the breeze. A glimpse of a sapphire blue lake sparkling in the distance. We were in Glacier National Park, Montana.

One of the best, albeit scariest, decisions we made regarding our retirement was to sell our home of thirty years and travel across the country in an RV. Sounds great at first blush, but the reality of living in 350 square feet meant a drastic downsize. It would be quite a change for us. Oh, but our new back yard! We were downsizing with a purpose and we were excited to begin a new life chapter.

More than a year before our target departure date, we stopped buying anything except food. No more clothes. No more shoes. No more gadgets for the kitchen. It was actually quite freeing and easy to do.

As sad and difficult as it was, cleaning out my mother-in-law's home after her passing helped me. She was a borderline hoarder, purely as a result of her experience in East Germany during World War II, when she wasn't able to get simple things like sugar or coffee. While cleaning out her worldly possessions, I learned a very big lesson. Use it or give it to someone who can. All the excess things she had stored away — clothes, food, nylons, toys — were molded or moth-eaten and couldn't be used by anyone. It was so sad to realize the amount of her time, money and space that were wasted. She would have been sick had she known that everything would end up being thrown away. With that experience fresh in my mind, it was so much easier to make my own decisions on what to keep, give away or trash.

Slowly, we began downsizing. My husband and I each were responsible for our own "stuff," as were our grown kids. The downsizing was quite a challenge at first. It was easy to get rid of old Halloween decorations and the dated Christmas ornaments I had kept just in case we ever needed more for the Christmas tree. It got a bit harder when I was going through the boxes in the basement labeled "memories." There were my high school and college yearbooks, ribbons and a few trophies I had won as a child while on the town's swim team. When was the last time I even looked at those ribbons? And then there were the items I'd saved from our kids. The task at hand was to decide what to keep (in a storage unit), what to bring, what to give away, and what to trash.

Furniture was another story. We decided to just give it away. After family and friends took what they could use, we gave the rest to the young couple that bought our house. They were thrilled and we were happy to help this young family starting out.

As the downsizing momentum built, I tackled my photo collection — twenty-three shoeboxes to be exact. I could not bear to part with them so I scanned the photos into my computer and discarded the hard copies. What a feeling when that task was completed!

An avid and passionate knitter, I had accumulated lots of beautiful fiber for my creative pleasure. No. I could not give up even one skein. Or could I? This was one of the most difficult downsizing chores for me, and though I did well donating to various groups and fiber friends, I have a sizable stash to this day.

Fast forward to our current living conditions. We've been living in the RV for a year and a half and we want for nothing. We did a great job deciding what was necessary for our life on the road. There is not one item in our small kitchen that is not used. We have just enough clothes. Both of us have brought along our hobby supplies — yarn, computers and electronics paraphernalia. A few special pictures on the wall and a few select decorations make the motorhome into our "home sweet home." We even have a "garden" — several small pots of herbs we keep in our front window.

Because we are living so simply, there is much less to clean and no reason to shop. If it doesn't have a purpose or enjoyment factor, it doesn't come in the RV. It really is that simple. Instead of collecting things, we are collecting such unbelievable experiences. It's a magical life we are living right now. Granted, much has to do with being retired, but I strongly believe that some of the freedom we feel is a result of downsizing.

My husband and I enjoy nature and being outdoors. We have the opportunity to explore national parks, hiking and marveling at the world around us. Early in our journey, we had very poor TV reception, so we rarely watched TV. Now, even when we do have access, it is more of a decision to watch... not just a habit. When we do watch TV or a movie, we really enjoy it. Not being tied to the TV habit, we spend more time on our hobbies. My husband has even branched out into quadcopters and other radio controlled vehicles. His eight-inch telescope came along with us for those fabulous night skies. My yarn collection is diminishing.

We have a very rich and fulfilling life, just with less stuff.

This journey of ours does not mean Nirvana. We did not win the lottery. We are living on a budget. We have endured illness (including cancer) and accidents (requiring stitches) while on the road thousands of miles away from family and friends. Things have broken down. The windshields have cracked on the car and the RV. We've had a few disagreements on the road.

Though it wasn't easy to downsize, the result has been such a feeling of freedom — not being tied down by material things allowed us to experience life differently. It is nice to know we can winter in the Arizona desert and not have to worry about a big snowstorm in New Jersey and our home there. Can you hear the sigh of relief? That is what simplifying and downsizing feels like to us. Living uncluttered and unencumbered by material things. A nice feeling. We have a very rich and fulfilling life, just with less stuff. Simple as that.

~Susan Leitzsch

The Liberation of Liquidation

Reduce the complexity of life by eliminating the needless wants of life, and the labors of life reduce themselves.
~Edwin Way Teale

Annie and I had been living in a sprawling, three-bedroom, two living area house for over ten years. The house was a rental, but we had been in the place so long it felt like home. We'd originally intended to buy the place from the owner, who had passed away from old age. Now her relatives were ready to sell but we weren't ready to buy. It was time to move.

"You know," my sweet wife told me one morning after we'd gotten the news that it was time to move on. "We've spent over a decade mowing the lawn, trimming the hedges, pruning the trees, and all the other yard work that comes with living in a house. Don't you think that's enough?"

I nodded, standing next to her and pondering about paying rent on yet another house. All our children had grown up and gotten married, and my mom, who had come to live with us, had passed on two years before. I supposed we could rent a smaller house, but they seemed a bit hard to come by, and we weren't yet ready to buy our own house.

"Why don't we rent an apartment?" my wife said softly at my

shoulder. "There would be no mowing, no trimming, and no pruning to do."

I don't know," I argued, immediately thinking of living next to people who would be to the left of us, to the right, down below, and up above. "An apartment is not a house."

"A cozy, little apartment," my wife continued, "for just the two of us, a sweet little nest where we could be together."

> Everything we had slated to go into storage would be sold or given away instead.

"A small apartment would mean less cost," I conceded. Then I did a reality check and looked around. "But what would we do with all our stuff?"

And did we have a lot of stuff! We had rooms stuffed with stuff. The garage was stacked with boxes. There was so much stuff we didn't even know what we had.

"What are we going to do with all of our things if we move into a little apartment?" Annie asked. Then her eyes brightened. "Why don't we put what we don't need in storage and save it for when we buy our own house?"

So that was the plan. We found a wonderful apartment that was exactly the cozy, beautiful little nest my wife and I were looking for. It was only one bedroom, and so most of our things would have to be packed up and put into storage. That's when I got the bright idea to just let everything extra go. Everything we had slated to go into storage would be sold or given away instead.

"So you're serious," Annie said after I told her my idea. "You want to get rid of everything we can't take with us?"

"Why not?" I replied. I looked at all the furniture and boxes that wouldn't see the light of day for a few years. "What happens if we get to like apartment life, or it takes somewhat longer before we can afford to buy a house? Or what if we decide to wait until I retire? That stuff might be in storage forever."

"True," Annie replied. "We might not get around to it for a long time."

"Then again," I pointed out, "Let's say we stay in the apartment.

We'll get used to having less very quickly, and all that extra stuff will just be like an anchor around our necks. Why not keep the most important things, things that we treasure, and let someone else have the rest?"

Annie smiled at me. "I think I know who might be able to help."

So we hired a person who liquidated estates, let her take care of selling or donating three-fourths of everything we'd once thought we couldn't live without, and moved forward. Walking away from all the stuff we had acquired during our life together was hard, but it was also liberating.

Now, here in our tiny little nest, where it's just the two of us and those things that are dearest to our hearts, life is a different kind of adventure. In finally getting down to the basics, letting go of the need to have "stuff," Annie and I are better able to concentrate on our family and each other, and on living a life where what we have isn't as important to us as who we have in our lives.

~John P. Buentello

You Must Be Mistaken

*The secret of happiness, you see, is not found in seeking
more, but in developing the capacity to enjoy less.*
~Socrates

I was on the third telephone call that morning that required me to give someone descriptive information about the home we had just purchased. This conversation went pretty much the same as the two previous calls when we got to one particular question: "What is the square footage of your home?"

"485 square feet," I replied.

The person responded with, "Ma'am, I'm sure you're mistaken. You'll have to check your information again and give me the correct number before I can assist you."

"You must be mistaken" seemed to be the catch phrase of the day for me. I was hoping this wasn't a warning sign that we had made a mistake by purchasing what we thought was the perfect home for us.

Those phone calls made me realize we had done something out of the ordinary, or at least unique for our area, by purchasing a house of this size. Although not exactly prepared for what living in such a small house would be like, we were eager, ready and willing to accept the challenge. It was a new beginning for us. We were moving into this home with a sense of exhilaration that came from parting with the material things that were not necessary to our happiness. I was excited about having to expand my creativity to transform this small house into a comfortable, cozy, happy home.

Choosing to downsize is like all the other big decisions that we make throughout life. It has its advantages and its challenges. If I find myself getting a little frustrated with the limited space we have, I simply pause a moment and go through my mental list of the advantages that come with a small home. I don't have to go very far down the list before I realize that the advantages far outweigh the disadvantages. If you've been procrastinating about downsizing from your current home or are pondering the idea of giving small home living a try, assessing the advantages could be the encouragement you need to set the wheels in motion for a new and exciting experience.

We've learned the importance of what is referred to as the "one thing in, one thing out" rule.

I have a "less and more system" for assessing the benefits of living in a small house. The "less list" includes benefits such as less maintenance, less housecleaning, less money spent on insurance premiums, lower tax bills, lower utility bills, less clutter and less furniture and decorative accessories to buy. On the "more list" I include things such as more money, more time to engage in hobbies, and more opportunities to challenge my problem solving and creative home decorating skills.

My husband and I have learned quite a few lessons since moving into this house. Living in a small house keeps us looking up. We quickly learned the importance of utilizing vertical space for storage. Shelves and hooks are a functional part of our décor. We've learned the importance of what is referred to as the "one thing in, one thing out" rule. When you only have two tiny closets, you quickly learn to exercise restraint when buying clothes, shoes and other wardrobe accessories. When shopping, we now weigh the value and necessity of each potential purchase. Necessary items come home with us; unnecessary items remain in the store. Adding something new and unnecessary to our house would upset the organized, balanced household arrangement we've worked so hard to create.

Another lesson we've learned is that when you live in a small house, personal space becomes a highly valued commodity. We each need a space to call our own and we respect each other's personal space.

Our house is small and we've learned to limit what we bring in, with one exception. We happily share our small home with several pets. It seems that those we rescue understand that our living arrangement is compact and it's essential that they adapt to it. Animals are not concerned with the size of a house. They only notice the amount of love within the house. I continue to be amazed at how well our pets have adapted to the concept of respecting each other's personal space as well as the value of togetherness. I take that as further confirmation that rescue pets always seem to have an exceptional sense of gratitude for those who provide a loving forever home for them.

When I look back at some of the houses I've lived in, I realize they were larger than what I actually needed. Some rooms were seldom used and a lot of time and money went into the upkeep of those houses. I can honestly say that every part of our current home is used in a functional manner. We've learned the value of multi-purpose spaces, multi-purpose furniture and corners.

It's often said that life is filled with uncertainty. I don't disagree. However, we have discovered there are some certainties that come with living in a small house. There's certainly a sense of togetherness that can't be duplicated in a large house. It's certain that if we don't remain organized, clutter will rapidly overtake our living space. For me, I can always be certain that, when I compare the advantages to the disadvantages, small home living comes out the winner. Living in a small home has definitely lessened our need for material possessions. It has given us more time to devote to what matters most, which is time together, quality time with our pets and time to devote to our hobbies.

Small home living enables us to enjoy the things that nurture our souls instead of wasting time and money to satisfy an unhealthy appetite for material possessions. Adjusting to small home living and a simple lifestyle was easier than I would ever have imagined it to be. My only regret is that, even though we were ahead of the downsizing, small home living trends, I wish I had made this choice many years ago.

~Veronica Bowman

Farewell to My Diaries

Memory is the diary we all carry about with us.
~Oscar Wilde

I received my first diary when I was nine. It was pink and pocket-sized, with a gold latch and key. I started writing in it right away.

Fifty years later, I still keep a journal. On its lined pages I plan, dream, storm and mull. Journaling has been my partner all my life.

Over the years I amassed cartons and cartons of journals that I schlepped from town to town, state to state, and country to country. The journals are the record of my life. They're "me."

Once in a while, I would think of the dusty cartons taking up more and more space in one basement after another. Then I would imagine them gone, and a sense of freedom and weightlessness would come over me. I mentioned this to my sister, who has planted herself deep in the same plot of North Carolina soil for thirty-five years. "But you can't throw your journals away!" said Jane. "You can't! I'll store them for you!"

"What, ship them all to you?" I said, idly wondering which would be cheaper — USPS, UPS or FedEx. Any way I did it, sending them all the way from California would be an expensive embarrassment.

Keeping a journal is one thing; revisiting it is another. On the rare occasion when I descend into the cave of an old journal, I usually surface feeling morose, relieved to be back in the sunlight. All that drama! All that venting! True, every thirty pages or so I'll come upon an absolute pearl, and I'll think, "Gosh, I was brilliant!" But then, along with that comes, "But where did that brilliance go? How come I keep forgetting?"

I debated for years (all the while accumulating yet more journals) whether I should let them go. Always, I hesitated. I respect the value of documentation. Where would history be without records? And who knows, maybe one hundred years from now someone might come upon my journals and read with rapt interest what life was like in the 1960s, 1970s and 1980s, just as we read diaries of the pioneers, or Civil War memoirs.

Then I would imagine them gone, and a sense of freedom and weightlessness would come over me.

Plus, who would I be without my journals? On the other hand, letting go of them might set me free.

Back and forth I went. In one stage I tore out random pages from old journals and collaged them. But that only took care of a few pages.

Finally, somehow, I decided: for now, I'd keep all the journals up to age thirty, and out of the rest, pick fifteen to let go.

I gave my husband the fifteen journals, with the agreement that if within two months I had not asked for them he would "release" them (the phrase "throw away" made me wince). Out of respect for my earlier self, I tore out random pages and collaged them into my art journal. So who-I-was-then is grafted into my current life.

I never did ask him for the journals. I forgot all about them. So they have met their maker. Fifteen journals lighter, fifteen pounds lighter. Now I only have another sixty or so to go....

~Louisa Rogers

In Love with My Life

I find television very educating. Every time someone
turns on the set, I go into the other room
and read a book.
~Groucho Marx

The wood stove's cheery flames cast golden light that flickered across my family's faces. In the still of the evening, gathered in our cozy great room, I knew life didn't get any better than this. I turned the page and resumed reading out loud to my family. I had never felt so contented, calm, or in love with my life.

I hadn't always felt that way before we'd moved to the mountains and simplified our living space and belongings. We'd not only downsized, but we'd also cleaned out mental clutter as well, starting with eliminating live television! Right away, something wonderful had happened.

Although I'd never watched a lot of television, the emotions triggered by the stories I'd seen frequently remained in my thoughts for days or even weeks, weighing me down and making me blue. Now, I found myself in better spirits without the violence, disasters, worries, or sadness that the news stations and talk shows had broadcast. The family felt the same way.

Planning was easy now that our schedules no longer centered

around a weekly show. The squabbles over who got to watch what ended. In place of the constant noise we found quiet, clearing our minds for the things that mattered in life, especially each other.

An astounding change took place in our children. They didn't want or need the latest toys, cereals, gadgets, hair or clothing styles because they never saw them advertised on television. They had no idea what was popular. They became their own people, not some clone of the latest movie star or performer. Their creative outlets flourished as they hungrily pursued their own passions. The phrase "I'm bored" vanished.

Together we wrote and put on plays, read books, played games, made family calendars, did arts and crafts projects and plenty more. Enjoying nature, we had plenty of viewing time for the sunset, the sky, the stars, or the storm clouds that rolled through.

> *I can't help but wonder how many priceless memories never would have been made if we'd kept our television.*

If we desired, a VCR gave us the option of watching a special movie, but we controlled the viewing instead of aimlessly channel surfing.

Where family discussions had once centered on that day's news, or a show we'd seen, or fretting that something terrible we'd seen on TV might happen to us, we made our own news. We talked about our lives, our home and had in-depth conversations with each other. And at last our minds found peace as our family grew closer together.

I can't help but wonder how many priceless memories never would have been made if we'd kept our television — special times spent together in the great room, or snacking outside on a blanket, watching the stars, even our late-night trips up a mountain road in search of wildlife. I wouldn't trade those moments for all the sitcoms, talk shows, and movies in the world.

We've lived more than twenty years without live television. Our children are grown, but the question still pops up from inquisitive friends. "You don't have live television? How do you live without it?"

"We live much better than we did *with* it," I always answer, and that's the truth.

~Jill Burns

The Dream Home

Be grateful for the home you have, knowing that at this
moment, all you have is all you need.
~Sarah Ban Breathnach

"Nobody's ever home around here," my friend said, looking around at the large and beautiful homes in her new neighborhood. She had just moved to an affluent area in our town and I had come to visit her.

"What do you mean?" I asked.

"Well, everybody's working all the time. I guess they have to in order to be able to afford to live here," she said, smiling.

I looked around at the palatial homes, all new, with perfectly manicured lawns and vast amounts of square footage. I began to think about how nice it would be to live in one of them. My mind began to race with questions....

Wouldn't I feel better about myself if I lived here? Wouldn't I be happier? I began to think about our budget and how we could possibly stretch it to cover the monthly mortgage payments. As I envisioned myself in this beautiful neighborhood, I realized I would also need a newer car and a nicer wardrobe to fit in.

Soon the pangs of discontentment began to stir within me. I began comparing these dream homes to my humble one and suddenly other things in my life needed an upgrade, too. My car was not quite good enough and my clothes were in desperate need of an update. By comparison, nothing I had was good enough.

My house, after all, had been built in the *Brady Bunch* era of the 1970s when Jimmy Carter was still president. It was located in the more affordable, working class part of town. It met all of my family's needs, certainly, but it was paltry in comparison to the palaces lining this street.

But other questions nagged, too, forcing me to give my daydreams a reality check. If we lived here, would my husband's work commute increase so that he would be home less? What other areas of our budget would have to be slashed in order to cover a bigger mortgage payment? How much longer would it take us to pay off the mortgage? Would we be borrowing against our future, making early retirement an impossible dream? Would our travel opportunities be drastically reduced because we would be putting all our money into a house we could barely afford?

> *Instead of thinking of all the ways my home and possessions were lacking in comparison, I began to think of all the advantages I had in staying where I was.*

Reality began to set in as I started to add up the actual cost of living in one of these so-called dream homes. Instead of thinking of all the ways my home and possessions were lacking in comparison, I began to think of all the advantages I had in staying where I was. Because I lived in a more affordable home we could comfortably live on one income and I could be a stay-at-home mom. We could afford a couple of vacations each year without going into debt. We could save a good portion of our income for retirement and investments because all our money wasn't going to the mortgage payment.

I began to realize that there are different types of currency besides money and possessions. And that it didn't make sense to work more to afford a lifestyle I would have less time to enjoy.

As I drove back that evening and the houses got smaller and grew older with each passing mile, I began to realize that I already had my dream home. One that enabled me to have freedom from loads of debt while still meeting all of my family's needs. I didn't need a certain zip code or amount of square footage to make me happy.

As I pulled into my driveway that night, I felt peace and gratitude for all that I had, all the things that can never be bought.

~Suzannah Kiper

The Decades Long Dream

Heirlooms we don't have in our family. But
stories we've got.
~Rose Cherin

As newlyweds, my husband and I dreamed big. Not of money and mansions and expensive cars, but of something far more difficult to attain in today's society. We dreamed of simplicity.

On weekends, we'd leave our hectic city jobs behind, pack a lunch, and drive to the mountains, where we'd romp beside clear cool streams. Our favorite part of the day, however, was watching the Arizona sunset explode across the sky, spilling layers of crimson and gold onto the valley below. When darkness finally fell, we'd wait for lamplights to glow like fireflies from the windows of tiny cabins that peppered the night with their warmth. Leaning against a beefy Ponderosa pine, my idealistic young husband would draw me into his arms and whisper, "Someday, we're going to live in a little cabin in the mountains."

I'd sigh. "With a rocking chair on the porch?"

"Two." He'd grin. "For growing old together."

"For rocking grandbabies." I'd say.

"We'll have a Jeep." He was adamant about that.

"And get a dog?" I'd ask.

"Of course." He'd promise. "I'll build furniture and chop firewood."

"And I'll bake bread and write books."

We'd often fall asleep on a bed of soft pine, dreaming of that simple home in the mountains where we'd live happily ever after.

Life went on. I devoted my time to home schooling our three children while he devoted his days to earning a living in corporate America until a layoff, after twenty plus years of service, shook our world. But at the bottom of the rubble, our dream remained.

When a series of job related moves led us closer to family again, we bought a weekend cottage in one of our favorite places, the Ozark Mountain foothills. The old stone cottage was tiny, but it came with a mighty view from a ridge high above the river. Little did we know that within a year it would become our permanent home.

After twenty plus years of marriage, moving into a home with less than half the space required considerable downsizing. While the process proved to be cathartic, it was far from simple. Where does one begin?

Lives are not connected by objects but by stories about those objects.

For us, the first to go were gently worn clothes, coats, shoes and extra bedding. Missions and shelters covet such things. Our books were tougher to part with. Avid readers, we'd envisioned a wall-to-wall library complete with sliding ladder, but our cottage would only accommodate our very favorite reads. The day we discovered e-readers was transformative.

Photographs and artwork by family members went with us. I'd periodically swap them out, a bit like a museum that rotates its collection on display! Because storage is at a premium in micro kitchens, small appliances were replaced with multitasking gadgets, or not replaced at all. Nightstands doubled as dresser drawers. We added closet organizers, lots of hooks, and my cedar chest became our coffee table.

While deciding whether a possession would be moved into the cottage with us, one simple question determined its fate. "Where will we put it?" This was the litmus test for beloved trinkets and furniture alike. One piece of furniture caused quite a dilemma, but it also taught me an invaluable lesson.

For years, I'd grown up hearing my dad promise to fix the old black teacart that sat in our kitchen. Because it had come from my grandmother, I'd had an affinity for the fragile old thing. As a young adult I'd acquired the teacart, and for nearly thirty years we moved it from house to house all across the country. The wheels were broken, the veneer was peeling, the pins were gone, and the thing wobbled and tipped. My husband had promised to fix it, but he never got around to it. When my cousin saw the teacart in such disrepair, he also promised to fix it, but instead he moved away and the teacart remained.

When my kids were small, I felt the need to protect Grandma's teacart, so I kept it tucked safely in a corner, away from their rambunctious play and Hot Wheels. By the time our younger son had grown, the teacart had become a liability rather than an asset. He promised to fix it for me too, but then he got married and started a family and had repairs of his own. I propped the teacart behind a couch to protect our grandchildren from getting hurt on the splintered old relic. When the time came to decide what would go to the cottage and what would not, I wasn't sure the old thing would survive the cut. I mentioned my dilemma to my dad.

"Then why try to move it?" he asked.

"Because I don't think I can bring myself to leave behind a family heirloom."

"Heirloom?" he chuckled. "Are we talking about the same teacart?"

"The old black one of Grandma's that sat in the kitchen."

"That never belonged to your grandmother, honey."

What? Was my dad's memory slipping? "Dad, I don't think I heard you correctly."

"The broken teacart belonged to a neighbor of my parents," he explained. "The old guy died before he could fix it, so your Grandpa promised to fix it for the wife. But then Grandpa passed away, so your grandmother brought it to me to fix. Before I got to around to fixing it, we lost Grandma, and then the old thing ended up at your place. Never was a very good design. Cheap veneer, too, from what I recall."

I didn't know whether to laugh or to cry, but I'd learned a life changing truth that day. Memories are not made of things, but of relationships. Lives are not connected by objects but by stories about those objects. Appreciating family heirlooms can be a wonderful thing, but allowing possessions to possess us is not. The next day, I called a local charity that helped recovering addicts repair donated items to sell at a resale shop.

"Sure, lady," they promised, "We'll fix it."

I prefer to believe they kept their promise and the old teacart found a good home. But in the eternal scheme of things, it doesn't matter. The Bible reminds us to lay up our treasures in Heaven, as everything else is just hay and stubble, no matter how sentimental.

The adage "less is more" proved to be true on our journey to a simple life. We have a big family that enjoys getting together, and many out-of-town friends visit often. Our solution for overnight guests? Sofa-beds, air mattresses, and sleeping bags. Our cottage was tiny, but we packed everyone in, often bursting to the seams with love and laughter.

During a record-breaking snowfall, we bought a Jeep. The following spring we adopted a rescue Lab. I wrote while my husband tinkered in his woodshop. Simplicity is what we'd yearned for; richness is what we were bestowed.

~Julia M. Toto

10

Going Naked

Whether I'm wearing lots of make-up or no make-up,
I'm the same person inside.
~Lady Gaga

I t didn't happen quickly. First, I stood in front of a mirror for several long minutes staring at my naked face. There was not a trace of make-up on it. And I was about to meet the outside world this way.

I'd been wearing make-up since my mother finally allowed it in the ninth grade. First it was just lipstick — a shade called "Pixie Pink" that made me feel like the most grown-up, glamorous creature on the planet.

As the years went by, I experimented with other delights like eye shadow, eyeliner and — the big one — mascara. Things got better when I mastered the art of getting that sticky stuff on my eyelashes, not in my eyes.

Ordinarily, I wouldn't think of going to the supermarket without at least some make-up. I'd spend at least five or ten minutes each day in front of the mirror putting on various products that promised me miracles. I have dozens more of these products rattling around, virtually unused, in drawers and closets.

I would probably think twice about going to the library, the cleaners or even the gas station without hiding behind some make-up.

But recently, I had seen two TV shows that got me thinking.

One was a documentary about the men and women who chose

to go back in time and live as folks had in pioneer days. They had no creature comforts, no conveniences.

And what did one woman weep about during those first few weeks? Her loss of make-up.

Then one of the talk shows did a segment on three women whose cosmetics were taken away for a week. Their reactions ranged from mild hysteria to a sense of release and relief.

It all gave me pause. I figured this was as good a time as any to try liberating myself from the shackles of cosmetics.

My husband, who is still basically clueless about what is in those jars and tubes, thought it was a terrific idea.

> *I figured this was as good a time as any to try liberating myself from the shackles of cosmetics.*

My daughters couldn't believe I'd actually leave the house without eyebrow pencil.

And my fifth grade granddaughter proclaimed all make-up "yucky" and told me she'd never, ever wear it.

Well, I did it. On a recent day, I went to the mall in pants, a blazer, fairly fashionable boots — and not a drop of anything else on my face or lips.

Initially, I felt exposed. Utterly vulnerable. And in my view, I looked like I was dying.

Miracle of miracles, nobody stared. Or gaped. Or even seemed to notice.

The saleswoman in the department store was happy to sell me four blue bath towels. The man behind the counter at a jewelry store to whom I handed a necklace to repair didn't look away in horror.

I even got brave enough to walk into the hair salon, where beauty is a sacred rite, to schedule a haircut appointment. There, the receptionist did seem to do a double take. Still, I held my head high and scheduled my next trim.

By day's end, I'd almost forgotten that I was moving around in the world minus my mask. Back at home, my husband stared a bit, then asked me whether I was feeling all right. He'd forgotten, of course, that this was Experiment Day. To him, I just looked weary.

Okay, what have I learned?

First, that I can do it. I can leave home without even a trace of lipstick. Nobody cares.

Next, that I am definitely a woman who looks better with make-up than without it. Perhaps it is decades of training my eye to see myself that way. Maybe it's the hype I've absorbed from a culture in which women spend billions to gild the lily.

Finally, I've decided that every once in a while, just to test my own confidence, I'm going to come out from hiding and go *au naturel*. Uncomplicate at least one part of my overloaded life.

It's probably good for the skin.

And it's surely good for the soul.

~Sally Friedman

Chapter 2

the joy of less

The Joy of No

11

Eating Lentils

Nobody can go back and start a new beginning, but
anyone can start today and make a new ending.
~Maria Robinson

I practiced law in the 1980s. That was the era of *L.A. Law* and business suits with "power shoulders." My department at the law firm was major and complex litigation, and business was booming.

I did a lot of traveling — flying into Denver for a week of hearings, days of depositions in New Jersey, document production in Philadelphia, and months of trial in Los Angeles. We flew first class and stayed in luxury hotels. After growing up in a rural, blue-collar family, the first to earn a college — let alone professional — degree, it felt like I'd really "made it."

I realized I could buy an expensive purse or briefcase if I saw one I wanted. So I did. I never quite got over my childhood frugality, but I did treat myself to good haircuts. And I shopped a lot on my lunch hours, buying high-end clothing at department stores.

I'd worked hard for my career, graduating at the top of my class, but I hated it. I'd enjoyed the study of law, but I didn't enjoy practicing it. The adversarial, competitive aspects of litigation wore me down. The stresses of decision-making on multi-million-dollar lawsuits kept me awake at night.

As I rode public transit to work, I retreated into reading a book, trying to forget where I was headed. I became a clock watcher, longing to leave the office and be on my way home. Friday nights were wonderful. Saturday nights were sad, because I knew my weekend was already half over.

I felt trapped by velvet handcuffs. How could I walk away from something I'd worked so hard for — which people told me I was good at? How could I give up such a high salary — one my father could never have dreamed of? How could I tell my husband the sacrifices we'd both made were no longer enough motivation to make me stay?

My cat Sammy seemed to sense my misery. We'd inherited the red-point Siamese from my husband's aunt when she passed, and I'd been there for him during his protracted grief. Now, he was there for me when I came home at night, settling his warm bulk into my lap with a comforting, rhythmic purr.

> *I was a ball of anxiety, but the day I quit that job, I felt a lifting inside me.*

My low point came when Sammy started to lose weight and his coat became rough looking. The vet said he had feline leukemia. In those days, there was no vaccine, and the disease was terminal. Adding to my grief, we were in trial in Los Angeles, and I flew out every Sunday night and didn't return till the following Friday night. I felt like I was abandoning my faithful little friend in his darkest hour.

After we lost Sammy, my desire to leave the firm became overwhelming. Arriving in Denver late one night, with a massive head cold, all I wanted to do was crawl into bed. My boss was holding a strategy meeting in the next room, along with a junior partner and our local counsel. When he asked if I wanted to join them, I pled my need to sleep off the worst of my cold.

It was already eleven on the East Coast, but out here, only nine. I fell asleep to the rumble of voices through the wall. That was when I became sharply aware that my boss should logically have been my role model — the success I was aspiring to. But I knew I didn't want to be the person who had to chair a meeting late at night, with people looking to me for answers. That's when I definitely knew I was living somebody else's dream, not my own.

From that moment on, my actions were governed by my plan to escape. We paid off our mortgage early and drove our older, paid-off cars. I crunched numbers constantly, trying to figure out how to survive without my income. Nothing else I was qualified to do — or could bear to think of doing — paid nearly as much money as practicing law. My only other training was as a writer — a notoriously ill-paid and unpredictable profession.

After six years, I made partner. Among the perks was a travel junket every year to a legal conference any place I chose. I never took it. Maybe subconsciously, I didn't want to have people saying I'd taken advantage, only to quit shortly afterward. Neither did I take the free, luxury leased car. I wanted to own my own transportation, and not have to worry about being forced to turn my lease in and suddenly having to buy a car in order to make my getaway. When my fellow junior partners took out big mortgages for sprawling five-bedroom showplaces in upscale neighborhoods, we just stayed in our old farmhouse with its worn siding. Consciously, we tried to travel light — and debt-free.

As a young mom, I took the longest-available maternity leaves, and sobbed for weeks before I had to return to work. I missed my children and knew they were missing me, too. But no matter how many ways I crunched the numbers, they still didn't work. Things would have to go. We'd have to cut our eating out, and the traveling we loved so much. No more browsing for beautiful purses and clothing. Even so — with vet bills, swimming lessons for the kids, math tutoring, etc. — it would be tight.

But when my girls were six years old, and my son eight, I finally quit. It had been nearly twenty years. My husband knew my desperation, and one day, just said, "Do it. You can't keep going through life this way."

I was a ball of anxiety, but the day I quit that job, I felt a lifting inside me. I started smiling a lot. A few other young partners confessed they wished they could do what I was doing. One of them cornered me to ask, "How are you doing it?"

"Living in an old house. Eating rice and beans. Driving old cars," I said.

I told him the story of the old man who lived on lentil soup. Another man felt sorry for him, and gave him this advice: "If you bow down to the king, you won't have to eat lentils anymore." The old man smiled and shook his head. "If you would learn to eat lentils, you wouldn't need to bow down to the king."

My friend smiled sadly and shook his head. "I like my BMW."

I smiled back. "Luckily, we like lentils."

~Katie Drew

12

Mommy, Your Head Is Wrong!

While we try to teach our children all about life, our
children teach us what life is all about.
~Angela Schwindt

It was a busy day, but as a single mom with a full-time job and two young children to care for, this was nothing unusual. I had just gotten home from my job as an elementary school teacher and I had less than thirty minutes to feed the kids and shuttle them to their afterschool activities.

Both of my children were sitting at the table, not so patiently waiting for dinner to be served. The kids had been bickering since I'd picked them up from daycare, and I was feeling a bit irritable from refereeing.

I was dashing back and forth from the kitchen to the dining room, ferrying bowls of food on each trip. As I leaned over my three-year-old daughter to place a bowl of green beans on the table, I realized that she was staring at me.

"What's wrong, Julia?" I asked. "Are you okay?"

She shook her head, eyes wide, and continued to stare at my face.

I reached for a paper napkin, assuming the spaghetti sauce had splattered on me. But before I could wipe my face, Julia grabbed my arm. "Don't, Mommy. Don't touch it," she said urgently.

"Why not?"

"Because your head is wrong."

"My head is wrong?" I asked. "How could my head be wrong?"

She nodded vigorously. "It's wrong, Mommy. Up here, it's wrong." She touched my forehead gently with her chubby fingers.

My hand followed hers. I felt my forehead, which at that moment, was a mass of stress-induced wrinkles.

Julia nodded again. "See, I told you. Your head is wrong."

I chuckled and tried to ignore the less than subtle reminder that I was indeed getting older. "It's not wrong, sweetheart. Mommy's head just gets like that when I'm really busy."

"Well, when you're busy, your head looks mad," she insisted.

> Jordan said, "Mom, I like it better this way. Staying home sometimes feels good."

"But Mom is always busy," piped up my six-year-old son, Jordan.

I began to explain that I always had so much to do, but I stopped short. In my children's logic, if busy equals mad, did that mean that I always looked angry to them?

What a scary thought.

I sat down at the table, dinner quickly forgotten. I rubbed the deep grooves on my forehead and looked at each of my children.

"What are you doing, Mom?" Jordan asked.

"Taking a break," I answered softly, knowing that the three of us clearly needed one. After thinking for a moment, I asked them if they would be okay with skipping their activities that evening. "Let's stay in tonight and just be together," I suggested.

"Can we play Go Fish?" Julia asked.

"Of course," I said, giving her a hug.

"Can we watch a movie and eat popcorn?" Jordan asked.

"Absolutely," I answered with a grin.

That night, the three of us relaxed and spent time together. We played games and hung out, something we rarely did during our hustle and bustle weeks.

During a game of *Connect Four*, Jordan said, "Mom, I like it better this way. Staying home sometimes feels good."

I smiled. "You're right."

"So I was thinking, do I have to sign up for soccer again next year? Because I really like playing hockey better anyway. And I think one thing is enough for me."

I laughed so hard that tears filled my eyes. "I've been thinking the same thing for months, but I didn't want to disappoint you," I said.

Jordan grinned. "I won't be disappointed. I'll feel better because I'll have more nights like this one."

As I hugged my son, I could feel a burden lift from my shoulders. "More nights like this one is exactly what we need," I said.

At bedtime, while I was reading a story to Julia, I caught her studying my face once again.

"What now, honey?" I asked, almost afraid to hear the answer.

She smiled and touched my forehead. She said, "Mommy, you fixed it. Your head is right again."

I smiled back, grateful that my priorities were finally straightened out as well.

~Diane Stark

13

From Super to Serene

Nothing is less productive than to make more efficient
what should not be done at all.
~Peter Drucker

My goal was to be Super Mom. I cooked elaborate meals and decorated snacks. I made costumes and devised holiday games. I took my little ones to "Mommy and Me" classes and never missed any of our kids' ballgames, band concerts, or plays. Like most parents, I drove them to lessons, practices, rehearsals, and club meetings, helped with homework, and provided a welcoming atmosphere for their friends. Since I also worked a regular job while finishing my college degree, I often stayed up into the wee hours of the morning catching up on laundry, cleaning, and details for the coming days.

My husband and I spent plenty of family fun time with our children, too, enjoying hiking, sports, and board games. There were also vacations to plan and out-of-state relatives to host so our kids could have time with extended family. Every activity was a joy that I didn't want to miss.

My "super" mindset extended beyond home. I was a "yes" person, always agreeing to help anytime and anywhere volunteers were needed. Field trip chaperone and classroom assistant at our kids' schools. Sunday School teacher, summer vacation Bible School teacher, and cook for the seniors' dinner at our church. Fundraising walk organizer, donation collector, volunteer recruiter, newsletter writer, and public relations associate at one charity after another. I wanted do my part to help people and improve the world. Sometimes I was the one who had to make the calls asking for volunteers, and I knew scheduling people to lend a hand could be difficult. So, whenever I was asked to help, I said "yes."

I made lists and kept a detailed calendar. The demands on my time were becoming overwhelming. Sometimes I just didn't have the energy to give each endeavor my best. As a perfectionist, I had a hard time accepting that. I couldn't stand the thought of letting anyone down. Rather than eliminating some duties, I looked for more efficient ways to get it all done.

"I'll sleep next year!" became my mantra.

One day, yet another call came from one of the nonprofits where I was involved. "Hey, I need to add somebody to our event planning committee. Wondering if you'd do it."

This time I hesitated. How could I take on another responsibility?

> *Sometimes it's okay to say no and step aside, so that someone else gets the chance to step up.*

"You know, I have so much on my plate right now, I'd rather you find someone else for the committee, if you can," I explained. "But call me back if you have trouble."

"Oh, that's okay. I'm sure I can get someone else. You're the first person I've called. I just started at the top of the list."

It was as if a bucket of water had just hit me in the face. How could this not have occurred to me before? My last name starts with A! Everyone always called me because I was first on the list.

And I always said yes. By trying so hard to do my part, had I inadvertently prevented people further down the lists from being offered the opportunity to do theirs? Should I stop trying to be more efficient, and simply... stop?

From that point on, it became much easier to decline when I felt I was already doing my share. I even realized that there was no need to be Super Mom. My kids would do just fine with Serene Mom.

Sure, my greatest joy is still in doing things with and for my children. But happiness also comes from seeing what they accomplish when they take on some chores and responsibilities for themselves. I also still love to volunteer. I do what I can to help others. However, I no longer exhaust myself by overdoing it. Now I can commit my efforts more fully and energetically where I do participate. And I can enthusiastically appreciate the successes of others.

I gained a new perspective on my place in the scheme of things. Sometimes it's okay to say no and step aside, so that someone else gets the chance to step up.

~D.S.A.

14

Silencing the "Should" Monster

Half of the troubles of this life can be traced to saying
yes too quickly and not saying no soon enough.
~Josh Billings

Women have it tough. Maybe it's biological. Perhaps it's just plain insanity. But women, in general, have this deep desire to be everything to everyone all the time. We want to be the fantastic wife, amazing mother, loving daughter, caring sister, dependable employee, and supportive friend. The list is endless and exhausting. Every single day, I am surrounded by amazingly smart, strong, and independent women who are "shoulding" themselves to death.

Let me explain.

We think we should be Superwoman. We should keep a sparkling clean house and cook dinner for our families every night. We should plan themed birthday parties for our kids with twenty of their closest friends. We should be community volunteers throughout the week and bring homemade dishes to church functions on Sunday. We should pick out the perfect baby/birthday/graduation/wedding gift and then attend all those events with smiles on our faces. And we should do it all without asking for help from anyone.

Is that realistic? Absolutely not.

But more importantly, it's unhealthy.

Unrealistic expectations on our energy, time, and emotions can lead to anxiety, depression, guilt, and low self-esteem. Frazzled isn't just a state of mind. It's a reality. And it's a reality that leaves us feeling physically exhausted, mentally drained, and emotionally unfulfilled.

As wives, mothers, daughters, and employees, we fight the "should" monster every day. Of course, there will always be things that must be done. But what about the things we don't have to do? I don't always have to do the grocery shopping. My husband can help with that. I don't always have to go to the funeral of an acquaintance. I can send a card or flowers instead. I don't have to pick out the perfect birthday gift for a niece or nephew because kids love gift cards too. I don't have to bake a homemade dish for a church dinner when something from the grocery's deli will be just as appreciated.

Now, I do my best to silence the "should" monster by doing the things I want to do and politely declining the rest.

We have to learn to give ourselves a break.

And, if we don't want to do something? It's absolutely okay to say no.

Let me repeat that. It's absolutely okay to say no. In fact, it's a necessity, because the truth is we can't do it all. We can't. Not if we want to keep our sanity.

I went through a period a few years ago where I was dealing with anxiety issues, and a lot of it was caused by the fact that I was spreading myself too thin. I was always the dependable one. The reliable one. The first to volunteer for anything.

Why? Because I "should."

While dealing with my anxiety, I spent some time with a therapist who asked me a question that still resonates with me to this day. During one of our sessions, I mentioned that I was dreading a particular event. She wondered why I was going if I felt this way.

My answer? "Because I should."

My therapist looked at me and very simply asked, "Why should you do something you don't want to do?"

I explained that while I didn't want to go, I felt that it was expected of me. She said, "That's why you're dealing with anxiety. You're trying to make everyone else happy. What about you? Are you happy? You can't be, because you're trying to juggle all the things you have to do with the things you feel like you should do. You have to start being a little selfish with your time. You have to learn to say no."

I honestly couldn't imagine such a thing. But I gave it a shot. I started saying no when it was possible, and you know what? The world didn't spin off its axis.

Now, I do my best to silence the "should" monster by doing the things I want to do and politely declining the rest. I delegate as much as I can (my husband honestly loves grocery shopping). I volunteer for things because I want to and not because I feel obligated.

It's not always easy, and I still struggle with feeling selfish from time to time, but I'm a happier, calmer person.

And that's the way it should be.

~Sydney Logan

15

The Challenge

When in doubt, choose change.
~Lily Leung

In January 2014, my sister, Carole, announced she was challenging herself to stop buying any new clothes, handbags, shoes, or jewelry for a whole year. "The rules are you can't buy anything from a shop, even if it's hugely reduced," she explained. "You can buy anything — even new — from charity shops, go to secondhand shops, boot fairs; you can make things, you can be given things, you can swap things. The only things you're allowed to buy new are underwear and tights." She looked at me. "Of course, you wouldn't be able to stick to that, Den."

She knows I enjoy a shopping spree once in a while. Not every week, or even every month, but my friend Gill and I love a shopping day in Tunbridge Wells, particularly when it's the new season, and between us we normally come home with a few bags.

"I'm going to do it, too. In fact," I said recklessly, "I'm adding no make-up to the rules."

Carole shook her head. "We'll see how long you can keep it up. I'll give you a month."

I told Gill what I intended to do and she laughed. She was sure I'd succumb long before the year was up. In fact, I don't remember anyone saying "Good for you" or giving me the slightest encouragement.

I have to admit at first it wasn't easy. Once, I almost forgot. I was wandering around the cosmetic counters in Hoopers department store.

Many of the cosmeticians knew me and were eager to demonstrate their latest lines and colours. A gorgeous scarlet lipstick caught my eye, but I remembered in time and told them about The Challenge. Although intrigued, they were obviously sorry they hadn't made a sale.

"We'll probably see you before long," they chirped as I smiled and nipped out of the doors and on to the safety of the High Street.

Except, of course, the High Street was the least safe place to be when one is committed to The Challenge. The clothes in some of the shop windows were mouthwatering. They were presenting their spring collections and I could just picture myself in some of the outfits.

You're getting older, I told myself. You won't be able to wear this sort of thing in a few years. Enjoy them now. But I steeled myself and hurried by.

The strange thing was, I kept receiving items of clothing from women who didn't even know I was participating in The Challenge. A friend of my sister's gave me a gorgeous slinky black silk evening dress by Laura Ashley which she couldn't get into; another friend sent me some lovely sweaters and blouses she could no longer wear. Items seemed to come to me. I must say, if you do The Challenge you need to cultivate friends and family who are prone to putting on a bit of pudding!

I knitted an evening jacket, which my sister sewed together. It has become my favourite item of eveningwear. I call it "the cobweb," as it's incredibly delicate, yet warm and cosy, and I feel very proud when people compliment me on it.

One day I glanced in the window of our local hospice shop. A pair of black high-heeled court shoes were pointing toward me with my name on them. I just knew they would fit perfectly.

"How much are they?" I asked. I could see they were brand new.

"Ten pounds. They'd be eighty in the shops."

I gladly handed over a ten-pound note and can confirm I've worn them loads, and even though the heel is fairly high they are extremely comfortable.

Gill was curious as to how I was managing.

"Actually, it's not that bad once the shock wears off," I told her. "And

I realise how much time I spent window shopping, looking through rails and never seeing what I wanted, trying on things in the fitting room, taking things back… there's more time to do other interesting things."

My friend looked doubtful. So you can imagine my surprise when a few weeks later she said, "I'm going to take up The Challenge."

I hadn't tried to persuade her to do this. I thought that as a dedicated fashionista she'd be the last person to give up shopping.

"I know some people think I'm all lipstick and handbags," she smiled, "but I'm determined to do it."

I reacted the same way as my sister. No chance, I thought. But I didn't say it. I just said that her husband Peter would be pleased.

"He won't notice."

"He will when he looks at his bank statement," I said with a grin.

Gill really did astonish me. She kept it up for more than a year, and has only recently bought a couple of new things. But nothing like she would have done.

> Now, when we go to London, Gill and I are much more likely to wander round museums and art galleries instead of shopping.

"I realise I don't find clothes shopping as much fun as I used to," she said.

"We've all got too much. That's why Carole decided to do it in the first place."

"I took this skirt out of the back of the wardrobe," she pointed to her pretty leaf-printed skirt, "and I bought the jacket (it was black and lacy) for a summer funeral years ago and had not worn it since. They seemed to go well together and it was like introducing two old friends."

I fervently agreed. In the last year we've both donated to charity shops the clothes that we no longer wear that still have plenty of life in them. And I managed to get Gill into a charity shop for the first time ever when I spotted a fabulous black sequined flapper dress in the window. She tried it on at the back of the shop, stepped out looking terrific, and wore it at a New Year's party. Everyone adored her "new" £12 dress.

Now, when we go to London, Gill and I are much more likely to wander round museums and art galleries instead of shopping, and it's been no hardship at all. We used to do the culture stuff as well, but a London trip didn't seem complete if we didn't come back with a few bits.

On saying that, I belong to the University Women's Club in Mayfair. In September they're having an evening fashion show put on by the Harvey Nichols department store. Gill and I have already got our front row seats booked.

Well, you can't be good all the time, can you?

~Denise Barnes

16

Practice Makes Perfect

*It's your place in the world; it's your life. Go on and
do all you can with it, and make it the life
you want to live.*

~Mae Jemison

"Time to practice piano!" I shouted up the stairs. I must have hollered that sentence a thousand times. My son started playing piano in kindergarten. I realize that it's a bit early, but he comes from a musical family and piano lessons are a tradition. Besides, he's very musical.

I'd beam with pride during his piano recitals as his little fingers sailed across the keyboard playing tunes by Mozart and Schumann. "That's our son," I'd whisper to my husband, as he'd dismiss me with a "Shush, be quiet."

Although I'd revel in my son's musical accomplishments, the fact was that he would rather have been spending his time playing baseball or making videos with his friends. Every week, as the piano instructor arrived at our door, I'd coax (or bribe) my son to go downstairs for his lesson. "Don't keep John waiting. The sooner you start, the earlier you'll finish. I'll buy you a Starbucks oatmeal cookie; just go down there." He'd reluctantly leave his room (and his action figures) and start his lesson.

James loved his action figures. He used to create stop-motion videos of his action figures battling each other and upload them onto YouTube. He was passionate about film and animation.

Like my husband, my son is not a complainer. He took his piano lessons religiously every week and—although I had to constantly urge him to practice—he never complained.

As he got older, however, school became more intensive and homework required more time. It was hard to juggle it all. I remember thinking that my friend who had a daughter in middle school was pushing her unnecessarily with too many activities, like tap, ballet, and hip hop, but I wasn't looking at my own situation, which was very similar.

James's short films became more and more interesting as he matured and his passion for filmmaking never seemed to tire. It was obvious that he found joy in filmmaking, not in piano, and I realized one day that in order to be really good at something, you have to let other things go.

And so, as much as it surprised me to utter these words, I did: "I think James should give up piano."

My husband (a musician) looked confused. James was the soloist in the jazz band at school

> *Between school-work and sports… it's just too much. No one can do everything!*

and had played well year after year. He had perfect pitch to boot. "Why would you suggest that?" he replied.

"Because it doesn't make him happy. Making videos makes him happy and he can't do everything! He has too many activities. Between schoolwork and sports… it's just too much. No one can do everything!"

And so, after some thought, my husband asked the key question, "Does he ever sit down and play piano just for fun?"

"Never," I answered.

That settled it.

His recital was a couple of weeks away and we didn't say anything to James until it was over. On the way home in the car, we asked nonchalantly if he'd like to discontinue piano lessons.

There was silence for a few minutes. Then he answered. "Let's not schedule any lessons for the summer. I'll decide in September." His answer was so mature it knocked my socks off.

By the end of the summer, after many sunny days of tennis (which had replaced baseball) and filmmaking, he brought up the subject of piano.

"I'd rather not take any more piano lessons, if that's okay."

It was more than okay! It would free up time during the school year to do what he really loved.

Music is what I (and my husband) had wanted for him, but it's not what he wanted. I wasn't listening to the real music… the music of my son's heart!

I have never had to yell the word "practice" again. He naturally follows his passion. James is blooming as a young film editor and making friends along the way.

Last year, his short film came in second place in a tri-state film festival and today he is shooting a music video for an aspiring singer with passions of her own. The song is called "Believe" and is being co-directed by American Idol contestant Robbie Rosen.

The song lyrics remind the listener to stay positive, not give up, and believe.

I believe that God has his own plans for my son.

And I believe that He gave my son the passions of his heart in order for him to become the person "He" wants him to be. Not the person "I" want him to be. He's well on his way and I love watching him as he practices being himself every single day.

~Mary C. M. Phillips

17

Too Much of a Good Thing

*Happiness is not a matter of intensity but of balance
and order and rhythm and harmony.*
~Thomas Merton

Dancers occupy the lowest rung on the ladder of the art world. Patrons will occasionally pay visual artists and musicians for their work, singers and actors can rake in the big bucks, but dancers? Forget it. There are very few financially viable career opportunities for those of us who choose to dance.

So when I received my first job offer, fresh out of grad school, I was overjoyed: a full-time position as Arts Education Director at the Children's Studio School in Washington, D.C. Never mind that my commute was going to be an hour in each direction. I had a job!

Then, before I even started work, I was offered another position: part-time instructor of modern dance at the University of Maryland. I had to commit to spending my Saturdays on campus, but my office hours were flexible. This would not conflict with my full-time position at the Studio School. As long as I put in the required forty hours per week in D.C., I was golden. Now I had two jobs!

You may not believe it, but my good luck did not end there. I soon received a phone call asking if I was interested in another part-time faculty position: Goucher College needed a Dance Education Specialist to teach a course that fall. I was the perfect candidate, having just completed a master's degree in this exact subject. How could I say no? That's right, I ended up with three jobs!

However, in order to put in enough hours at my full-time job, I had to get up before the crack of dawn, drive an hour in the dark, and sweat through eleven-hour days at the Studio School. On Tuesdays and Thursdays, I drove an additional hour and a half to teach my education course north of Baltimore. After fighting the tail end of rush hour traffic all the way home on the Beltway, I'd collapse into bed, often too tired to even eat dinner.

Did I mention I was newly married? My husband and I were living together for the first time after enduring a two-year separation while I attended grad school in New York City. And I decided we really needed to adopt a puppy to make us feel like a family. If you have ever owned a puppy, you already know the fluffy balls of fur are irresistible but practically as much work as a newborn infant. Many sleepless nights ensued. There was much crying and whining. Some of it from the puppy.

When I examined all the commitments I had made, I realized not only was I stretched way too thin, I was receiving very little enjoyment from most of the work I was doing.

As I battled through that fall semester, I began to wonder where the joy had gone. Here I was, living the life of my dreams. I was in love with a wonderful man. We had a house, a yard with a vegetable garden, and a beautiful little puppy. I had not one but three fabulous and highly coveted jobs in my field. And yet, I was angry and irritable during the vast majority of my waking hours. My husband and I fought over everything from the dishes to the laundry to the training of our pup. My fuse grew shorter and shorter until it took almost nothing to set me off.

On a particularly bad Thursday of a week that felt longer than a month, I had scheduled a hands-on teaching experience for my education class. The students and I showed up at the on-campus daycare center to share a carefully planned creative movement lesson with a group of four-year-olds. Disaster is the only word to describe the fiasco that took place: children running in all directions, knocking over desks and chairs, ignoring suggestions, climbing on top of each other and rolling on the floor like a troupe of crazed monkeys. In order to control the chaos, I was reduced to screaming at the top of my lungs, a very big no-no for an education specialist! The gaping mouths on my students' shocked faces told me in no uncertain terms, I had stepped over the line.

Driving home that evening, the light finally dawned on me: I had too much of a good thing.

When I examined all the commitments I had made, I realized not only was I stretched way too thin, I was receiving very little enjoyment from most of the work I was doing. I was stressed to the breaking point, spending too many hours driving on crowded highways, rushing from one place to the next, not to mention the constant worrying about the little details that inevitably slipped through the cracks. I couldn't do my best at any of these jobs, and that included being a wife and a puppy mommy.

So I quit.

In fact, I quit the full-time position at the Studio School. I completed the single-semester commitment at Goucher and ended up with only one job, and a part-time job at that. But as it turned out, one part-time job was plenty for me.

Now, instead of sitting for hours in traffic, I was able to sit in my claw foot tub and enjoy a good soak. Instead of skipping dinner, I harvested fresh tomatoes from my garden and made spaghetti sauce. My husband and I had time to hike with our puppy and even throw a dinner party on occasion. In other words, I had a life. Not just a career, but an actual, fulfilling life.

I discovered too much of a good thing can be a very bad thing. But in the end, I found the perfect balance for me.

~Liz Rolland

18

There's a Limit

*Being able to say "No" is a necessary ingredient in a
healthy lifestyle.*
~David W. Earle

A real Good Samaritan. That was me. Need a ride to the doctor? I'll be glad to take you. Does your dog need to be walked while you're on vacation? No problem. Would you like someone to talk to about your troubles? I'm here for you.

I thought of myself as the true definition of a friend and was more than happy to put the needs of others before my own. After all, what are friends for?

Judging by how often my phone rang, it seemed that my reputation as a ready, willing, and able helper was common knowledge among those in my circle. Relatives, co-workers, neighbors, and even casual acquaintances all seemed to have my number — literally and figuratively speaking. I didn't mind, really, if I had to put some of my own responsibilities and needs on hold. It felt good to do good for others. Besides, it was the right thing to do. And I was okay with that until one afternoon when I received a call from an acquaintance of my dad's.

This man I barely knew phoned to inform me that I was to chauffeur him to a medical appointment he had made for the following Tuesday. I sighed and checked my calendar. Then I told him as nicely as possible that I couldn't help him that day. I had a morning appointment with my brother, an afternoon business meeting, and then I needed to stop at the pharmacy for a friend who was recuperating from knee surgery, followed by a stop at the supermarket to buy milk and bread for her and her children. If I was lucky, in between I might find a few minutes to wait in the drive-thru line at some fast food joint and eat lunch in my car. "No," I told him, "I just can't do it." His reaction wasn't very kind and the conversation ended with the threat of some really bad karma on my part for not helping an elderly fellow in need.

That phone call was my turning point.

I took a closer look at my calendar. I was averaging fourteen good deeds a month. That meant that almost every other day I was running somewhere for someone. Clearly, some things in my life had to change. I stepped away from the calendar, eyes finally opened, and took a closer look at myself. Dark circles shadowed my eyes. Well, I'd known for a while I didn't feel like my usual energetic self. Instead, I felt weary and worn, and sometimes, resentful too. Really resentful. Like the time I got not one but two late-night distress calls in the same week and the time I realized I was "picking up a few groceries" for someone who could have just as easily shopped for her own provisions. Obviously, my Good Samaritan routine was wearing on me.

> *My schedule had put me on a hamster wheel where I ran circles for the benefit of others.*

Yes, it was time for a change. By being overly generous with my time I was not honoring my own needs or myself. Instead, my schedule had put me on a hamster wheel where I ran circles for the benefit of others. And was it really for their benefit? I started to wonder. Or, was I actually doing those I sought to help a disservice by allowing them to become dependent upon my kindness and not allowing them to learn to care for themselves? It was time for me to change. But how?

I brought my concerns to my friend Lucille, another busy woman. With a job, a husband, three kids, two grandchildren, and an aging father who needed her, I knew she had a lot to do every day. Yet, she somehow managed to maintain balance in her life. Despite the fact that she worked full-time, her house appeared well cared for, she had time to socialize, and in most cases, got a good night's rest — things that were lacking in my own life. How did she manage all that? I asked her.

She gave me her secret in one word: limits. You have to set limits, she told me. Don't run every time someone calls. Instead, ask the person some key questions: *Is this an emergency? Is someone else available to help you? Is this something that can wait?* And, the question I knew I should have been considering all along: *Is this something you could do for yourself?* "Certainly," Lucille said, "if someone is in a bind, by all means help them. But don't become a doormat. Set limits."

Now I consider those logical questions before jumping to another's aid and the benefits have been great. Thanks to paring down the favors I do for others I have more energy, sleep better at night, and even gained enough free time to pursue a hobby or two. Though I was fearful that cutting back on my kindness would have been met with disapproval from my crowd, those friends, relatives, and acquaintances quickly lost their sense of entitlement and started showing some real appreciation for my help when I chose to give it. Now, sometimes, they even help *me* when I'm in a bind. And that, perhaps, may be the greatest benefit of all.

~Monica A. Andermann

19

An Idyll of Idleness

*Children will not remember you for the material things
you provided, but for the feeling that you
cherished them.*
~Richard L. Evans

We had so many plans. We would take our visitors to the movies, to the park, to a toy store, to a place where they could play miniature golf.

We would also try to schedule a visit to the science museum and maybe the aquarium, too.

We would cram all of this into the two-day visit of our youngest grandchildren who had cleared their own incredibly busy calendars for some Grandma-Grandpa time.

Seven-year-old Emily and six-year-old Carly arrived toting suitcases into which they had stuffed what seemed to be all their earthly belongings. Coloring books and crayons, electronic gizmos, toys of all sorts and descriptions. In other words, loads of "stuff."

Along with marveling at the accumulation of excess baggage, I also noticed that these two tiny girls looked exhausted. Downright spent.

Small wonder. Like so many modern kids, they have activities that seem off the charts. What were we thinking?

I took my husband aside, and in a hurried kitchen conference, we decided to make a drastic change in those carefully outlined plans. We would scrap them all.

We would do… nothing. Absolutely nothing. At least it would

be a novelty.

And if our grandchildren balked — if they viewed the formless two days as cruel and unusual punishment — we'd make up for it the next time.

Step One: everyone into pajamas. Yes, pajamas. So what if it was four in the afternoon — and broad daylight? It would set the mood.

Initially, Emily and Carly exchanged knowing glances, the "Boy, they're crazy!" looks. And who could blame them? Our usual visits were dizzyingly active, and this was clearly at the opposite pole.

But soon enough, the suitcases had been emptied, and pajamas were the uniform of the moment. For Grandma and Grandpa too. It felt downright decadent.

> *Our idyll of idleness had clearly been the perfect early summer balm that this tired little girl needed.*

"So what do we do now?" Emily, always the pragmatist, demanded to know. And she soon found out.

We sat around in the family room, dug out a deck of ancient cards and played Go Fish! Never mind who won.

Then we made a great big meatloaf, with our granddaughters beating egg whites until they were like shaving cream — their great-grandmother's secret for a delicious loaf. I loved watching them as they took turns mixing the ingredients in the biggest bowl we own, and then concocting a ketchup sauce to pour on top of the whole lopsided loaf.

Dinner took an hour instead of our usual fifteen minutes. That was because we sat around the kitchen table and told silly stories, with Grandpa illustrating them with cartoons. I didn't rush to clean up because I've finally learned that the dishes can wait — but kids sometimes can't. It's a lesson I wished I'd learned with my own daughters.

Our "glamorous" evening consisted of watching the *Dr. Doolittle* video that our grandchildren had seen at least three times, but still loved, and then eating popsicles at the kitchen table.

Bedtime, sometimes a struggle, wasn't this time. Our visitors were happy, sleepy and delighted to hear me tell the story of Cinderella, hamming it up of course, just like we used to do before life's complictions got in the way.

We spent the next day playing a fierce game of Frisbee in the yard, having peanut butter and jelly sandwiches outside under a tree, and taking two walks. We also colored, finished a multi-part crossword puzzle, and polished off a pepperoni pizza.

We laughed a lot, sang a few nonsense songs, and watched the girls' favorite Nickelodeon shows.

When it was time to return our overnight visitors to their parents, they honestly didn't want to leave. "Do we have to?" Carly asked woefully. Our idyll of idleness had clearly been the perfect early summer balm that this tired little girl needed.

Of course, we assured Carly and Emily that we'd definitely do absolutely nothing again soon.

And I think they understood, perhaps for the first time, that doing nothing is actually… quite something.

~Sally Friedman

20

Saying No with Passion

*Passion is energy. Feel the power that comes from
focusing on what excites you.*
~Oprah Winfrey

I have always believed in giving back. As a single mom for most of my adult life, I didn't have the option of doing that by writing a check; instead, I volunteered for every worthwhile cause that crossed my path. When my son got to school age I signed up to be a room mother, a classroom volunteer, a Cub Scout leader, and a Sunday school and Bible school teacher. Some of these activities I enjoyed, some not so much. Then my two daughters came along and the activities tripled. As a lawyer, I was deluged with requests to serve on boards and participate in charitable activities. And there was my church — with various committees asking for help.

How could I say no, if it was for a worthy cause? I found myself overcommitted and resenting the time that all of my charitable work took away from my alone time and my time with my kids. Still, I continued to volunteer for everyone who asked. There were so many people who needed help. Then one day at lunch I shared my dilemma with a good friend.

"You need to learn to say NO," she said.

"How do I do that? How do I ever decide which cause is more important?"

"It's not about which cause is more important. They're all important. It's about finding your passion."

"My passion?"

"Find that one thing that means the most to you personally and then volunteer in that area. You'll see that you enjoy it more and resent it less, thus making you a much better volunteer."

It made sense. But what was my passion? I cared about a lot of things. I slowly began to search for the answer. I loved my kids and definitely had a passion for spending time with them, so I limited my volunteering to their various activities. My children became a convenient excuse. "Sorry I would love to help you out but I'm busy with _____." (Fill in the blank with one or more activities of my children.)

This plan worked remarkably well until the day my youngest went off to college. Guess what? All of those people I had put off with my kids as an excuse came out of the woodwork. Even though I had more time to volunteer, I again felt overwhelmed. My mind kept returning to that idea — find my passion. I took a class on discovering one's passion and did a lot of thinking and praying about it. One day it hit me. I had enjoyed my own children at all ages from birth on, but

> *Find that one thing that means the most to you personally and then volunteer in that area.*

what I really loved were those high school years. For me, there was just something special about that age group. They were old enough to not be watched constantly, but young enough to be open to new ideas. They were excited about life and full of energy: half adult, half child. So I looked for ways to become involved with high school kids.

These days when I'm asked to volunteer for other organizations, I can politely decline without feeling guilty. My answer is simply, "I have a passion for high school youth and that is where I spend my volunteer time."

It has been nine years since my youngest left home and I have spent thousands of wonderful, happy hours with youth, watching so many of them move on to be successful, caring, responsible adults. I have formed lifelong relationships with amazing people. I have a blast doing it and best of all I never resent the hours I spend. I am no longer overwhelmed. Those kids keep me young at heart, which is a gift in itself.

Whatever your passion may be, find it and you will be a better volunteer. And you'll be able to politely say no, guilt-free.

~Jill Haymaker

Chapter
3

the joy of less

All You Need Is Less

21

Living the Dream

*The human spirit needs places where nature has not
been rearranged by the hand of man.*
~Author Unknown

On 9/11/2001, my husband came home early from work to tell me that he had joined the military. He could not stand idly by and not do his part to protect our country. Since we had already been talking about the possibility of moving to a more rural location, he thought that this would be the perfect opportunity, since his new military pay would not be enough to cover our existing home's mortgage payment.

We sold our house, and my children and I moved to a different state in order to live with my parents while my husband went through his military training. While my husband was away, I searched for our new home. We both wanted something that would be a child's dream home and property — a rambling house with plenty of places in which to play hide-and-seek, a large yard, plenty of climbing trees, a creek, and woods that could be explored. We had noticed that most of the children in our old neighborhood spent the bulk of their time glued to electronic devices. We wanted our children to instead be able to experience the joy of creative play.

Unfortunately, our budget was extremely small, and any properties that met our criteria were far too expensive. Finally, my real estate agent suggested that I take a look at a property that was possibly going to become available. She warned me that it would need a lot of work, but said that it did meet all our requirements.

So, we drove to the mountains, to a quaint little town so small that its town center, marked by a four-way intersection, only boasted a post office, an inn, and a laundromat. At the edge of town, she pulled over in front of an old, white farmhouse.

For me, it was love at first sight.

Despite the obvious signs of neglect — overgrown grass, broken windows, and peeling paint — the house was charming. It was two stories and had a wrap-around porch, which was edged at the top with gingerbread trim — the exact sort of porch that simply begged for rocking chairs and lemonade.

The inside was a mess — the house had been vacant for three years and had sustained a lot of interior damage from burst pipes — but the structure was sound, and the layout of the home was perfect, with lots of nooks and crannies for children to roam and hide, an enormous farmhouse-style kitchen, and plenty of room for visiting friends and family. The yard was exactly what I had wanted. The house sat on over five acres of apple trees, berry bushes, fields, and woods with plenty of climbing trees, and was bordered on the back by a creek.

> *Throughout their childhood years, my children were constantly exploring the outdoors, splashing in the creek or building forts in the woods.*

I knew this was our new home.

We have lived here now for over thirteen years, and I cannot think of a better place in which we could have raised our children. Throughout their childhood years, my children were constantly exploring the outdoors, splashing in the creek or building forts in the woods. During the winter, they would create extensive snow tunnels and fortresses, and then return indoors in order to thaw out with hot chocolate in the farmhouse kitchen. Their creativity was endless. To this day, despite the fact that my daughter is now grown and my son is a teenager, both of my children would rather engage in a crabapple fight or try to catch crayfish in the creek than be glued to an iPad or iPhone.

My husband and I also have learned a great deal from living here. In light of our deliberate choice of a simple, frugal lifestyle, we learned how to perform home repairs ourselves — fun things like plumbing, electrical work, framing, and flooring. We learned how to build sheds, playhouses, and furniture, and how to make beautiful items out of scrap material. Because of our rural location, we learned how to care for farm animals and how to create and manage a large garden, which provides healthy food for our family. Due to our choice to heat our home with a renewable resource, firewood, we learned how to operate chainsaws and log splitters. In order to make our food budget stretch, I learned how to purchase staples in bulk and then cook as much as possible from scratch, using as much produce from our garden or wild crafted from our fields as possible.

Although I know that our lifestyle choice is not for everyone, I cannot begin to explain the joy that I have felt while watching my children chase each other in the back yard, seeing them playing with the farm animals, or giving each other rides in the wheelbarrow (something which has not stopped, even though my son is now 6'5"). I look at them and see two young adults who have not been caught up in consumerism, but instead are throwbacks to previous generations of people who preferred relationships over material things. That is something that will continue to benefit them — as well as the people around them — for the rest of their lives.

Our move to a rural location in order to simplify our lives has also given me a lot of personal pride for the skills that my husband and I were able to develop — skills that benefited us as well as others. But, more than that, I have a deeper appreciation for my family — our slower pace of living has fostered our sense of belonging as we share life together.

While the events that led to this lifestyle change were tragic, I am grateful that for us some good has come out of that tragedy — the ability to live our dream.

~Marybeth Mitcham

22

The Undecided Pile

*Self Storage: When you care enough to just hide the
stuff from his bachelor days rather than
throwing it all away.*
~Author Unknown

"There's a car under there?" I stared at the five-foot
pile of junk that filled one entire bay of the garage.
"Yeah, a VW Rabbit. I'm going to get it running
and sell it as soon as I have time," said my soon-to-
be husband, Jimmy.

"How long has it been there?"

"Ten years."

For the first time, I realized the full extent of the project to move
both our households into the house we'd just closed on. I was already
having trouble making decisions about my own belongings even though
I had considerable experience with downsizing from my frequent moves.
And Jimmy! My God, had the man never thrown anything away in
his entire life?

We had started our packing project with good intentions and
mutual consideration.

"What's in that box?" I'd asked.

"My grandmother's dishes. No one else wanted them when she died."

They were really ugly and chipped, but our relationship was still
new enough that I hesitated to object to a family memento.

After a day at his house resulted in only a piddling pile he was willing to give up, we moved on to my apartment.

"How about this?" Jimmy asked, nudging a wicker basket.

"All the programs from the plays I've gone to over the past twenty years. I thought they'd make a great collage someday."

He started to say something but apparently thought it prudent to let it go.

After a few hours I realized that, at this pace, we'd never be ready to move by our deadline, so we agreed that it all would go in the attic, with the stipulation that as soon as we settled in, we'd ruthlessly go through it piece by piece. Maybe have a yard sale.

"But the Rabbit goes!" I said.

He was wise enough to realize he'd won the war, and easily agreed to offer the car to a single co-worker with a junk-filled back yard.

Our move was accomplished; fifteen years passed. New stuff came in, old stuff went into the attic, or the cabinets, or the too-large closets, sometimes into the basement. I was fairly confident there was room for at least two vehicles in the garage since I never saw Jimmy's van or truck on the street, but I preferred to stay ignorant of what might be stored in the rest of the space. We occasionally talked about that yard sale, but somehow never found the time.

Then we decided to retire and follow our dream of buying a motorhome and wandering around the country having adventures. We took a year to plan our escape down to the tiniest detail. Or so we thought.

"They made a bid on the house, but if you accept it, they want to move in a month from now," announced our real estate agent.

We wanted to jump up and down and shout "Hallelujah!" The one element we'd had no control over was how long it would take to sell our house, and here the third couple to look at it actually wanted it! Thank God our motorhome was ready to move into. We were in the home stretch.

Thus began the most challenging period of our marriage. Jimmy was still working every day, so I went through the house room by room, with the exception of the basement, the attic and the garage, which we would handle together. I began by assigning each item to either the "keep" pile, the "thrift store" pile, the "junk pile, or "undecided." Eventually it became obvious that the largest pile of all was the "undecided." I invited friends and relatives in to take what they wanted, but still that "undecided" pile filled an entire room — two rooms after Jimmy and I finished with the basement and attic. The garage turned out to be the easiest. Jimmy agreed to sell most of its contents to the new buyer of the house, who apparently didn't have enough garage junk of his own.

"We just can't keep it all," I wailed, as we looked at the huge piles of "undecided" stuff on our last Sunday evening.

Jimmy looked up from the box of Grandma Sowder's ugly dishes. Was that a tear in the corner of his eye?

"Okay, listen," I said, knowing a quick solution had to be reached. "Let's just rent a second storage unit, move all this stuff in, and once we get into the motorhome, we'll sort through it, keep what we want and sell the rest at a yard sale."

> *"There's a car under there?" I stared at the five-foot pile of junk that filled one entire bay of the garage.*

Well, our site at the RV park didn't have a yard, did it? Besides Jimmy had sold his truck and van, so how could we move the stuff out of storage?

Six months later, off we went, heading west for the beginning of our adventure, one substantial monthly payment automatically deducted from our checking account for two large storage units. I only thought about them when I balanced our checkbook at the end of the month.

Then one day the manager of the storage facility called. A junk dealer was offering five hundred dollars cash for the contents of our "undecided" unit. Jimmy balked when I told him.

"If you can name five things that are in it, we'll keep it." I said.

"Uh, Grandma Sowder's dishes. And I think there's a table, uh, maybe some pots and pans?" He held up his hands in surrender. "Okay, we'll split the five hundred."

Every couple of years, we go through the remaining storage unit while visiting our hometown, and over the years we've downsized to the smallest unit available. It's been surprising how little most of the stuff we'd deemed keepers seems to matter anymore. All that remain are family documents, a few antiques, and some artwork we still can't relinquish.

The reasons people hold on so tightly to stuff they don't use is because they think they might need it someday, or because it reminds them of a person or a time from their past. Maybe it gives them a sense of security, of safety in a world that sometimes feels too large, too impersonal, too lonely. Jimmy and I have learned that most stuff can be easily and cheaply replaced if you need it, and is quickly forgotten when out of sight. And those forever memories are carried with us in our hearts, not our attics, and are all we really need. How often do you actually dig Aunt Helen's teapot or Grandpa Jack's old derby out of the attic and think about the departed? More often it's an old song, the smell of fresh-dried lavender, the taste of rhubarb pie — catching you unaware — that triggers memories and brings those loved ones back to you for a brief moment.

We still constantly fight the impulse to acquire, but it's now kept under control by the limitations of our space. And to our surprise and delight, having only as much as we actually need gives us as much of a sense of freedom as does living in a home on wheels.

~Sheila Sowder

Good Riddance

*Material blessings, when they pay beyond the category
of need, are weirdly fruitful of headache.*
~Philip Wylie

There's nothing like the sudden loss of a parent to put one's life, and one's priorities, in perspective. My dad had passed away four months ago and my husband Eric's dad had a serious illness. We decided it was time to move closer to family.

So one night, after dinner, while we were all still sitting around the dinner table, Eric brought up the subject, with only two words: "We're moving." The statement hung in the air for a moment, with none of us speaking, before he continued. Holding up a calendar, Eric added, "We're planning on moving at the end of May, back to Fairhope." There was another second or two of silence in this sudden dinner-turned-family-meeting.

"It's only January," fourteen-year-old Sarah said, after giving twelve-year-old Gus a "back me up" look. "Why the rush? And what about your jobs?"

"I do international work," Eric said, "so I can work anywhere. As for your mom, she's a teacher and a writer; she's pretty mobile, too."

After a little further discussion, both kids were on board to prepare for our move from just outside Nashville, Tennessee to Fairhope, Alabama, 520 miles south. Although Sarah had been right in saying that we had months to get ready, we had a large house that was filled to the brim with possessions. We had four months to empty a four-bedroom house with a five-car garage, guest quarters downstairs, and a 150-square-foot basement storage room. The house would have to be fairly empty by the first of May for us to put it on the market and have it sold by the end of that month.

We laid out a plan: everyone was to pack a box a day, label it, and tape it up for a storage space we had rented in Fairhope. This box-a-day plan sounded simple, but every day there were decisions about what we really, truly needed for everyday living, because the boxed items would stay in storage for several months until we found another house.

And so the months flew by, with our house becoming more streamlined and less cluttered. Some items were destined for storage, and twelve vanloads of stuff went to Goodwill. By the first of May, with so many possessions removed, we discovered something we had not anticipated: we were suddenly less stressed about taking care of the house. Eric noticed it first. "Do you know," he asked me, "we're not spending nearly as much time dusting, moving and generally

> *Rather than our "owning" possessions, after a time, they "own" us.*

taking care of things?" His eyes took in the living room, empty now save for the television and sofa. "Our life is simpler."

"Yeah," Gus chimed in. "I kind of like it this way."

We all seemed to feel a sense of lightness, without all those possessions.

As we drove to Alabama it occurred to me that none of us truly owns our possessions. Every item you have must be cared for, kept clean and, sometimes, insured. Rather than our "owning" possessions, after a time, they "own" us.

By the time we got to Fairhope, offloaded our truck and collapsed onto our blow-up mattresses, we knew it was time to downsize. With most of our things in storage, we first looked for a house that would accommodate us and no more — no guest quarters, no huge garage. The minimalist bug had bitten us, and hard.

We moved our basic necessities into the new, smaller house, and after a few weeks, all four of us went to the storage unit, planning on taking all that to the new place. But a funny thing happened: once we opened the door to the storage unit, nothing inside appealed to us.

For example, the chairs in need of reupholstering didn't need to come out; I'd had them for years and had never touched that project. The huge roll of upholstery fabric was there, too, still in its original wrapper. Parts of bed frames were there, still in need of repair. Filing cabinets, full of papers we'd not even looked at in years, lined the walls. Boxes of hundreds of books and dozens of pounds of research papers from my writing projects stood nearly to the ceiling. Boxes of stuffed animals and toys the children hadn't even wanted or played with were stacked near the entrance.

We all stood there, eyeing all the possessions that had consumed so much of our energy. We eyed the mountain of "stuff" again, and then, nearly simultaneously, we all said, "It's all going to Goodwill." That was eleven years ago, and we haven't missed any of it. And now, when we're rearranging items such as furniture or artwork, we pretend we're moving again, and that usually lightens our load a bit more.

~T. Jensen Lacey

Giving New the Boot

*I love charity thrift stores. Amazing one-of-a-kind
pieces at terrific prices, and all the money you spend
goes to a good cause.*
~Lara Spencer

"Look what he's done!" My eight-year-old daughter and her six-year-old brother were returning from their first day of the new school year. Rhys had left the house wearing grey high-tops and Levis and a crisp blue and grey football shirt, all purchased especially for the occasion. "Look!" Ceily repeated theatrically, flinging her arms toward her brother's incomprehensible state of disrepair.

His new shoes were suggesting at least six month's steady wear. The Levis, although they still retained most of one knee and surprisingly all of the other, clearly posed the question as to how much longer this would be the case. The blue and grey football shirt? Well, obviously Rhys had painted with black and orange and red; and, clearly, there had not been enough paint smocks for the entire class.

"Oh Rhys!" I said. Not surprised but, nonetheless, disappointed. "However, did you manage...?"

"It was a rough day," he interjected, "and the clothes were squeezy and stiff."

"Stiff... squeezy," I repeated. "Well, you know that your kindergarten clothes don't fit anymore, so I guess it's shorts and a T-shirt tomorrow until I see if I can do anything with these..." and I paused, considering what I should call the once pristine outfit.

The following day, I relayed the story to my sister. "We had a good talk after he was in bed — his dad away and us not having a lot of money, trying to make ends meet as they say…. Of course, we've had this conversation before and I'm sure that the next time he won't wipe painty hands on his shirt; he'll use magic marker on the buttons or something like that. It's never the same thing but it's always something."

"Have you thought about buying his things from the thrift shop until he gets a little less impulsive?"

The thrift shop? The core of my being gave a violent shudder. Granted, I had peered in the store several times and once I had even seen a window display that seemed rather attractive. But dress one of my children from the thrift shop? What if another child or another parent recognized the clothing? What if someone saw me in there?

> *Eventually I found myself checking the thrift shop before I purchased new clothing or kitchen cutlery or even hinges for the bathroom cabinet.*

When both knees of the Levis disappeared and I had to turn the pants into shorts, I decided, at the expense of my misguided pride and ego, to explore my sister's suggestion.

"Cool!" said my son when he saw my bargains. "Man! These are exactly like Dooley's." I said nothing.

The year wore on and both children's clothes wore out; and, eventually, I brought home two sweaters and a pair of jeans for Ceily. They were in excellent condition. And then one afternoon in spring, I found the perfect lightweight skirt and shirt for myself. "Why not?" I thought. "They're like new and anyway, who's to know?"

With time, my two children discovered first fad and then fashion. But me? Well that perfect lightweight skirt and shirt led to a perfect pair of jeans and then to a perfect sweater. Eventually I found myself checking the thrift shop before I purchased new clothing or kitchen cutlery or even hinges for the bathroom cabinet.

I had joined the community of and discovered the comradeship of the surprisingly large number of truly dedicated recyclers. Together, we relished the thrill of the hunt and of putting the secondhand boot to our throwaway society. We found ourselves wearing each other's shirts and jackets and instead of hiding, we acknowledged and took pleasure from the fact that we were supporting the local hospital thrift shop and at the same time proving that new was not always nicer nor was it always necessary. For sure, less could be more in many, many different ways.

~Robyn Gerland

25

Increasing My Income by Getting Rid of My Junk

I am learning… that a man can live profoundly
without masses of things.
~Richard E. Byrd

Each month it had become harder to cover my expenses with my retirement check. As I sat at the kitchen table with my manila folder marked "Bills" and began writing checks, I became angry with myself. I had been paying for a storage space in Detroit, Michigan for how many years? I looked at the statement start date: nearly fifteen years? Jeez! When I first moved to California, I thought I would soon be sending for all my "stuff." Now here it was fifteen years later and I still hadn't shipped my belongings to the West Coast.

I realized that I was hanging on to those things more for the sentimentality and not because I really needed that garage full of packed boxes and egg crates stuffed with record albums. It was time to get rid of it. I looked at the bill for my storage space and a chill ran down my spine. Over the years, it had quadrupled. When I leased that spot, I had no idea they had the right to increase my storage fees annually. What had started out as a reasonable rental amount was now costing me a third of what I was currently paying for my apartment. Ridiculous! It just so happened I had booked a flight to Detroit to attend an annual weekend jazz festival. So, I decided to use that trip to get rid of those things in storage.

A few weeks later, I stood staring into a garage sized storage space piled high to the ceiling with junk. My nephew and his teenaged son stood by my side.

"Wow, Aunt Dee," they both muttered, overwhelmed by the magnitude of things stuffed into that storage space.

We started going through the boxes of knick-knacks, bathroom towels, bedroom sheets and comforters, kitchen curtains, pots and pans. I'm an avid reader and there were boxes of books galore; magazines that went all the way back to the 1950s; clothes I would never fit into again. We made piles to give away to a church that housed the homeless and protected battered women. Each evening, I drove to that church with a carload of clothing and household goods. They itemized the donations and I received receipts that I could use as tax write-offs. The eradication had begun, happily with some of my junk going toward a good cause.

One entire wall of the storage space was stacked with record albums. A friend suggested I contact a local record shop that sold collector items. When I reached the owner by telephone, to my surprise, he rushed over to the storage facility. His eyes grew large when he saw my collection of over 3,000 record albums including The Beatles, Rolling Stones, Malcolm X speeches, *Richard Pryor Live* and Motown icons, not to mention an incredible jazz collection from the 1960s and 1970s. He offered me $2,500 and I took it before he changed his mind. Honestly, I didn't know how I would ever get rid of my precious record collection and I couldn't afford to ship it back to California. Finding that record store was an unexpected blessing.

I donated some of the more precious things, like my Paul Robeson 78 RPM collection, to a mobile museum that features African American memorabilia. It made me feel good to know that some young people would be exposed to important historical items at that museum, like the music of Paul Robeson.

It took a week and a half to go through all those boxes of stuff.

I worked it like a day job, arriving at the storage facility at nine in the morning and leaving at five. I couldn't believe how much I had collected over the years. A lot of it wound up in the garbage bin, but anything usable was donated.

My nephew ran across an old jewelry box full of broken pieces of jewelry, most of which was fake. But he showed me a few single earrings without a mate that were obviously gold and some old gold chains I had forgotten about.

"You can make money selling this gold, Auntie," he suggested. "I know a place."

"Okay. Let's go see what we can get for it," I agreed.

> *I looked at the bill for my storage space and a chill ran down my spine.*

One gold chain was broken and three earrings were stuffed in a soft, purple, velvet bag, but there was only one of each. I suppose I'd lost their mates years ago. I doubted I would get much. The next morning, at the gold redemption place, a woman weighed my jewelry and when she told me she could give me $1,500 for the pieces, I nearly fainted. Another blessing!

I took some of that money and paid my nephew and his sons for their help over the past week. I used some of the money to ship home a few precious things, ones I couldn't bear to give away. I discovered that for about fifteen dollars you can ship a large USPS Priority Mail box, regardless of the weight, and it will arrive at its destination in just two days. That saved me a lot versus paying the airline for baggage charges.

When I returned to California, I was ecstatic. I had stopped the storage fees, found new homes for my usable items, and had even made a few thousand dollars, after expenses, by selling the gold and the record albums.

As a senior citizen, living on a fixed income and making extra money by writing features for magazines, it can sometimes be tough making ends meet. When I look back at all those years I was paying storage fees, I think about how I could have used that money to help put some of my grandchildren through college. As I write this, I wonder: what took me so long?

~Dee Dee McNeil

26

Hung Up

*Unless you are prepared to give up something valuable
you will never be able to truly change at all, because
you'll be forever in the control of the thing
you can't give up.*
~Andy Law

Almost every bit of wall space, from the basement to the upstairs bedrooms of our Cape Cod–style house, was covered with artwork and artifacts. Visitors called our home a museum. I took it as a compliment. I like museums and I enjoyed living in one.

After sixty-three years of marriage, and me long retired from my fifth-grade classroom, Arthur and I were moving to a smaller space, a sunny condo apartment nearby. Which pieces of art would we take with us? What would we dispose of? Slowly, we began the process of making decisions and taking everything down.

And then a funny thing happened along the way.

Warren, the younger of my two sons, is an artist. It seems to me that he was doodling and drawing from the time he was old enough to hold a crayon. His orange and black bullfighter painting won first prize in a competition when he was eight years old. Fifty years later, that painting was still hanging in my kitchen. Dozens of others — many of them large canvases — watercolors, acrylics, and oils, created when he was in high school, added color and warmth to a dark basement.

Now a professor of visual art, Warren has worked in a variety of mediums, including "visual literature." His living quarters are small, and my home had become the repository of his work. Beautiful collages made with flax, Earl Grey tea leaves, Chinese spirit paper, fabric, music notation and foreign language symbols were hanging in every room of our house — along with an abundance of other *objets d'art* we acquired along the way.

Friends and relatives, doodlers as well as serious artists, knew where they'd find an appreciative audience — and wall space. We were the delighted recipients of their work: a mother/child photograph, pebble sculpture, wool weaving, paper cutouts and assorted paintings. When traveling, we searched for unusual handcrafted decorative plates. On weekends, Arthur and I sought out arts and crafts fairs. The work we bought from the mostly young artisans competed with our son's for wall space.

I was, and still am, an antique nut, with many collections — clocks, carnival glass, irons, trivets, trays, and trunks. Whether traveling abroad or browsing at a local yard sale, I rarely came home empty-handed. Except for our trunks and glassware, we found a way to mount them all.

We managed to find space for posters, picture postcards, and glossy photographs torn from calendars and magazines. Treasured family snapshots were hung in various places, a visual orgy of nostalgia. For celebratory occasions, Warren sent original poetry and colorfully illustrated handcrafted cards. We hung those too of course — in his old room.

I was forty-four when my kid brother became ill and died — a devastating time. Not long afterwards, while passing an upscale Manhattan art gallery, I spotted a colorful impressionist painting of three young children that could have been a portrait of his two sons and daughter. I couldn't get it out of my head. It far exceeded our budget, so I kept returning — just to visit it. "My Brother's Children," I called it. Eventually, I gifted myself, and squeezed it onto a busy wall.

In retirement, I registered for two adult education courses — collage and decoupage. "You've been doing this for a while," the instructor commented when she glanced at my first attempt, a skyscraper collage. "I've been doing it in my head for years," I whispered. Subsequently,

I mounted my own series in the attic foyer. For my decoupage class, I found a sheet of wrapping paper imprinted with Bruegel's famous "Children's Games" painting, and patiently applied many coats of shellac. It became a "museum" favorite.

I couldn't bring myself to dispose of anything. Most every piece on my walls had a story to tell, all meaningful to me. Our moving date was getting closer, and we needed to get on with it. "Perhaps we could put some of it on the ceilings," I joked.

We began by taking down the smaller and incidental pieces: calendar and magazine art, photographs, posters, prints, and greeting cards. As I emptied the walls, I was overcome with an unexpected sensation. The rooms suddenly felt brighter, cleaner, sunnier, larger. The newly exposed white walls became interesting surfaces of their own, reflecting an ever-changing display of light and shadow. It seemed to me that I felt calmer. Each piece of furniture rose to a position of greater prominence. Guests inquired about our new chairs, trunks, cabinets and tables, items they'd sat on or walked past for years.

> As I emptied the walls, I was overcome with an unexpected sensation. The rooms suddenly felt brighter, cleaner, sunnier, larger.

I envisioned my apartment walls — spare and sparse — a selection of major pieces, each strategically hung: a butterfly tray collection over the living room couch; decorative plates above the dining room server; a friend's weaving capping a large old trunk; my Bruegel decoupage crowning the den sofa, an eight-year-old's prize-winning bullfighter painting in the kitchen. And didn't "My Brother's Children" deserve its very own space? Not exactly spare and sparse, you say? A gallery, rather than a museum.

I didn't trash my prized pieces, now removed from prominent display. I took each from its frame, split the pile into three slim folders, and stored them in an antique file cabinet, where I'd be able to revisit them whenever I wished. The frames were thrown into three large cartons, awaiting an upcoming yard sale.

Warren took some of his smaller paintings, and gave permission to dispose of his large teenage canvases. "They're not very good," he said. I left some for the new homeowner, kept a wild abstract for the apartment, sold the others at our yard sale. Newlyweds, recently relocated from across the country, "to study art" they told us, arrived at the sale toward the end of the day, looking for a chest of drawers. "Artists?" my husband exclaimed, pulling a remaining carton with dozens of frames from the garage. The young couple would have loved to buy them all, but confided they couldn't afford it. Oh good, I thought, I could fill a wall with those things.

Instantly, I stifled the thought, and pushed the carton in their direction. "A wedding gift," I heard myself offer. They were flabbergasted, and delighted. So was I. The wide smiles on their faces matched mine.

~Ruth Lehrer

27

Coffee Corner

I orchestrate my mornings to the tune of coffee.
~Terri Guillemets

I opened my eyes and stared at the green numbers on my bed-side clock — 4:30 a.m. Last time I'd dared to peek, it had been 3:45. Clearly, I wasn't going to be able to talk myself into going back to sleep. Might as well get up. At least I'd have time for some quiet meditation and maybe even a walk around the block before the demands of the day came at me full force.

But first... coffee.

I padded down the hall to the kitchen, flipped on the light and headed to the coffee corner, which occupied every inch of counter space between the sink and refrigerator. When I'd moved into this house more than twenty years ago, the only thing I'd kept in that spot was the electric percolator I'd inherited from my favorite aunt. Though it made good coffee, it had been such a hassle to clean that I'd eventually bought a drip coffeemaker to use instead. I didn't get rid of the percolator, though. Sure, I lived alone and didn't really need two coffee pots. But what if I had a big crowd for breakfast and needed to serve a whole lot of hot coffee all at once?

Not long after I bought the drip machine, I learned about the benefits of fresh ground coffee beans. So I bought a grinder and wedged it between my two coffee pots. Then I bought an espresso machine — which I used twice. I don't even like espresso.

A few years later, I succumbed to advertising pressure that had me convinced I couldn't get along without a single-serve coffee maker. Though such a machine was expensive and took up lots of room, the idea of fixing just one cup of coffee — in less than a minute and whenever I wanted it — was impossible to resist. As was the idea I could have a dozen flavors, in decaf or regular, at my fingertips if I would purchase a handy-dandy forty-eight-pod carousel to keep nearby. Which I did, of course.

Add a sugar bowl, which I never used but which I kept on the counter because it was pretty, and a matching cream pitcher I never used because I poured cream straight into my coffee from its carton in the refrigerator. And a small basket where I kept packets of three different kinds of artificial sweeteners.

Get the picture?

Above the cluttered counter was the cabinet where I stored my mugs. On the top shelf were cups and saucers that matched my dishes. The middle shelf held an assortment of plastic travel mugs in various sizes, along with a hodge-podge of lids, most of which didn't fit any of the mugs but which I couldn't bear to throw away.

I loaded the percolator, espresso maker, single-serve machine and bean grinder into one box. Then I wrapped the sugar bowl, cream pitcher, and every mug except the one I was using and put them in the other box.

The bottom shelf was home to my miscellaneous collection. Mugs that pictured Santa and Rudolph and a family of happy snowmen. Orange and black Halloween mugs. Mugs from seven different national parks. An Atlanta Braves mug. An Elvis-in-a-white-jumpsuit mug. And my favorite — a mug that said "Teachers do it with class." Although it had been decades since I'd taught school, something about that mug made me smile. Maybe it was the sentiment, but just as likely it was the size, shape and handle style that made this the mug I reached for every time it was clean.

Which, much to my delight that morning, it was. One decision I wouldn't have to make, thank goodness.

But I did need to decide which coffee maker to use. The single-cup machine didn't seem like a good choice. At this hour, a whole pot was what I needed. I opened the cabinet to grab a filter for the percolator, but the box was empty. Scrounging around behind an almost-empty bag of hazelnut beans and an almost-empty bag of regular beans, I finally found a filter that fit the drip machine.

I unplugged the single-serve machine, plugged in the grinder and emptied both bags of beans into it. Then I unplugged the percolator and plugged in the drip machine. I debated which kind of artificial sweetener to use, chose the yellow and pulled the cream carton out of the refrigerator. By the time my first coffee was finally ready to drink, I was too out of sorts to meditate.

So I did something else instead.

I chugged my coffee and then went to the basement and found a couple of sturdy cardboard boxes. I loaded the percolator, espresso maker, single-serve machine and bean grinder into one box. Then I wrapped the sugar bowl, cream pitcher, and every mug except the one I was using and put them in the other box. I would keep the cups and saucers (twelve in all!) that matched my dishes and donate everything else to the thrift store. I'd take my leftover single-serve pods and handy-dandy carousel to the coffee bar at church. On the way home after work, I would stop at the store and buy a canister of already-ground coffee and a box of paper filters.

Which is exactly what I did.

I smile every time I walk into my kitchen these days, even if it's four-thirty in the morning. My coffee corner holds everything I need and nothing I don't. In a jiffy, I can set a pot to brewing, pour a steaming mug just a few minutes later and be in exactly the right frame of mind for meditating. And still have time left for a walk around the block before the demands of the day come at me full force.

~Jennie Ivey

28

One Bag Rule

Simplicity is about subtracting the obvious and
adding the meaningful.
~John Maeda

I was the girl with the backpack stuffed full of things that I would never need but lugged around anyway. I always had an extra pack of loose-leaf paper, a box of pencils, various pencil sharpeners, and more. All of the other girls had their trendy shoulder bags or purses and carried around just one binder. They always seem relaxed and happy, never lacking anything. Yet, here I was with a bag big enough to fit a human body and still feeling like I didn't have enough. I got stared at every day as I scuttled through the high school hallways feeling like a freak. I wanted to be one of the cool kids, but I couldn't bear the thought of giving up that box of tissues.

When I started at university, I figured that the same rules would apply. I had a locker on campus, and I jammed it full of all of the extras I could think of. I had a large leather rucksack that I carried from class to class, filled with books and food. After all, I didn't want to be caught off guard if I found myself in one class with free time to work on homework from another, right?

Before long my back started to hurt constantly, and I wasn't enjoying much of anything, because I was too busy and tired from trying to haul that huge bag around. By the time the summer rolled around, I was fed up and ready for a change. There was nothing to be gained by being in physical pain all the time. After all, what was I accomplishing by carrying extra notebooks and pens when everyone else made do with one small bag with the essentials? I was missing out on all sorts of social events because I was in pain and exhausted all the time. Enough was enough. When second year started, I deliberately chose a small blue backpack and told myself that — other than textbooks and food — everything would have to fit in this bag. If not, it didn't get to come with me.

> *The "one bag rule" has been so successful that today I refuse to go anywhere with more than one bag, be it a weeklong trip or a day at the mall.*

I absolutely hated it at first. I was outraged that I couldn't carry half my house in my backpack every day. What if I needed that extra box of staples? What I came to learn, however, was that I could still have everything required, I just had to prioritize: instead of five binders, I had thin folders that were easy to carry and could still fit all of my notes; instead of pencil sharpeners and boxes of pencils, I switched to mechanical ones, and simply kept extra erasers and lead packs in my bag; I had a tiny container full of paper clips and extra staples that fit basically anywhere I needed; I adapted to using a mini stapler that met all of my stapling and de-stapling needs without fail; instead of having an entire box of highlighters, I downsized to carrying one marker of each colour.

That small blue backpack really helped me make the permanent change to carrying less stuff. It had all sorts of compartments and pockets so that I had everything I needed, but still kept the bulk to a minimum. The change from a ten-pound weight to a three-pound one was fantastic, too.

As I got used to my new lifestyle, I realized how much calmer I felt. I was more relaxed in class because I didn't have to worry about digging through my bag and finding that one pen I was looking for. My books and notes were more organized, and there was no worry that I had forgotten something. When it came to heading home, I just had to grab a textbook or two and be on my way. My back no longer felt like it was dying, and I enjoyed heading out with friends after class.

Transforming from the girl who had six or seven bags, to the "one bag lady" really helped make me into a better person overall. I learned that it didn't mean having to give up the necessities that made university life possible. I also learned that the whole world wouldn't fall apart if I didn't have the extra bottle of Whiteout or the box of tissues.

There were times, of course, when I didn't have something that I needed for a fleeting moment. Instead of getting worked up about it, I would be momentarily frustrated and then move on to something else. Having everything in one bag made my life more flexible. I could work on my homework anywhere I wanted and not be inconvenienced by carrying multiple bags. When I felt stifled on campus, I would walk or take the bus downtown and work on assignments in a coffee shop. It became a habit of mine that helped me be much more productive academically and socially, not to mention that I became a coffee expert.

Developing the "one bag rule" really improved my academic experience overall. I was more confident, easier to talk to, and genuinely enjoyed being a student. I got good grades and made lasting friendships, which were as good as they were because I took the stress and physical discomfort out of student life by simplifying my life.

The "one bag rule" has been so successful that today I refuse to go anywhere with more than one bag, be it a weeklong trip or a day at the mall. Teaching myself that I didn't need as much stuff made me stronger, braver, calmer, more adventurous and so much happier. When I compare my miserable high school self with the confident university graduate that I am now, I am incredibly grateful that I finally decided to make the change. That battered blue backpack that I bought in second year is one of my absolute favourite possessions that — even though it's much too worn to be of use anymore — will always mean a lot to me.

Getting rid of all of the extra supplies allowed me to really focus on what was important, both academically and emotionally. Even though that small blue bag was half the size of the old one, it really held so much more — it held the key to the new me.

~Kelti Goudie

29

The Small Simplicity Challenge that Changed My Life

> *The ability to simplify means to eliminate the unnecessary so that the necessary may speak.*
> ~Hans Hofmann

It was only the first week into a sparkling new year, and I was already feeling stuck. My life felt overwhelming and chaotic, rushing by in a flurry of social media and distractions and constant "busyness." I was desperate to slow it down. To savor it. I wanted my days to be made up of beautiful moments, not long to-do lists. I wanted to be more present — to be aware of, and grateful for, every minute of my unique and amazing life.

Serendipitously, I stumbled across a TEDx talk by The Minimalists about authenticity and simplicity: paring down your life in order to make space for what truly matters to you. Something lit up in my soul. Simplicity. Time. Space. Room to breathe, and learn, and grow, and simply be.

I decided to set a challenge for myself. Little by little, over the course of the year, I would simplify my life. I would rid myself of clutter — physical, mental, emotional. I would reflect on what was most important to me, and why, and what I aimed to do with that knowledge. I hoped that by the end of the year, I would be less stressed, more present, and altogether happier in my simpler life.

My first step was to identify a few items that I tended to over-purchase: tea, stationery, and scarves. I pledged to purchase no more of these items for the entire year (or until I used up the embarrassingly large stash that I already possessed). After signing the self-pledge, I was a little surprised at my impulse to continue purchasing these items, even during the first week! Especially tea. I tended to visit the tea aisle whenever I went to the grocery store, just to see if they had any new flavors or good sales. So, I made a conscious choice not to even walk down the tea aisle. Same with stationery. I refrained from browsing greeting card displays. Instead, I used notecards I'd purchased the year before for all my holiday thank-you notes. A little thing, but progress!

In the weeks and months that followed, I slowly sorted through my clothes, shoes, purses — and, yes, scarves — and donated three full bags to charity. In the past, I might have been tempted to go out shopping to refill the empty spaces in my closet with brand new items, but not this time. I actually had space to slide hangers back and forth and didn't have to cram T-shirts into my dresser drawers in order to wedge them shut. I could easily see every item in my closet — and, for the first time in my life, I absolutely loved every single item I owned. Getting dressed each morning became a breeze.

Motivated to continue my momentum, I donated boxes of books and magazines to my local library and ended my subscriptions to a couple of magazines. I cleared out my filing cabinets of old receipts and organized my haphazard piles of papers into neat, labeled folders. Now I could find whatever I needed easily and quickly.

Next, I tackled digital clutter. My e-mail inbox was always over-flowing, distracting me from important tasks I wanted to complete. I began by unsubscribing to the various promotional e-mails that I always deleted without reading. That was the easy part. The harder part was unsubscribing from lists that I was genuinely interested in, but simply had no time to read. I realized that I had subscribed to these e-mails because I hoped that some mystical future version of me would one day find the time to conscientiously read through them. Instead, the build-up of unread e-mails had been stressing me out.

The simple act of unsubscribing from e-mail lists made me feel freer and more at peace.

This may seem obvious, but I also realized how much less stressful tasks are when you do them in advance of deadlines. I started getting tasks and chores done in advance, which made me feel like I was "on top of things" and boosted my self-confidence. I also worked on squashing that impulse to try to squeeze in "one more thing" before I left the house, which was always making me late. Not only did I feel rushed and stressed about being late, I wanted to change this habit for others, too. Being on time shows respect and consideration for other people's time and commitments.

I did figure out one way that I could squeeze in "one more thing" without negative consequences! I started listening to podcasts while driving. I love learning, and had a long list of podcasts I wanted to check out, but I couldn't seem to find the time to listen to them. I realized I had precious pockets of time that I wasn't using as opportunities. Twenty minutes in the car here and fifteen minutes in the car there really add up. Now I actually find myself looking forward to my car/podcast time instead of being annoyed by my commute.

The simple act of unsubscribing from e-mail lists made me feel freer and more at peace.

When I look back at my life before my "simplicity challenge," on the outside it appears much the same as it is today. I have the same job, live in the same house, take part in the same outside activities with their responsibilities and commitments. I did not make any drastic or big changes. And yet, on the inside, my life feels completely different. Small changes added up. I have time and space to pursue what I love most. I feel freer, and calmer, and more energetic. It's funny: only now that I have gotten rid of so much unnecessary stuff, does my life feel truly full.

~Dallas Woodburn

30

Christmas Without Electricity

*There is a force more powerful than steam and
electricity: the will.*
~Fernán Caballero

I was at work the day before my long awaited Christmas vacation, ready to enjoy some quality time with my family. We received a large snowfall the previous night, which was very deep, so I had a fun eight-mile ride to work on an ATV (4-wheeler).

Around lunch my wife called and said, "Honey, we have a problem. The power went off an hour ago, and we are getting cold." She was alone watching our two children. They were four and six years old. There was more snow in the forecast. I called the utility company to inquire when the electricity would be restored. The receptionist informed me that the electricity could potentially be out for several days, maybe a week.

During the long ride home, I wondered what I could do to get my family through a week without electricity. Then it hit me. "Call Dad. He will know what to do. Or, even better, he will ask us to stay with him and Mom." I knew it was a great idea. Arriving home, I called Dad. He lives five miles away, but did not have electricity either. Dad was not sure what they would do. Discouraged, my immediate reaction was, "Well great! Now what? We're on our own."

I located a flashlight, and went to the basement. I was looking for anything to help us during this crisis. I was burrowing through the junk that had collected down there when I remembered some advice from my grandfather: "Boy, don't worry about what you don't have. Do the best you can with what you got."

I keep things around the house, not like a hoarder, but rather a "Collector of Everything," like my grandfather. I located a kerosene heater along with thirty gallons of fuel I had stored for an emergency years ago. I looked at my cordless tools and pondered, "How can these help?" I always have batteries charged and ready for use in those hand tools. I discovered a plastic desk fan. I kept digging and uncovered a box of candles and a box of hurricane lamps that I picked up at a yard sale. The small, rusty wheels in my head were spinning. I was not in panic mode any longer. I was in the "I can do this" mode, and I started to feel pretty good about things. The heater worked and so did the lamps. This wasn't going to be so bad!

After breakfast, we sat and talked about the "good ole days." We did not realize we were reliving them.

I made trips upstairs, like an Olympic sprinter. I carried parts to repair our life. The items were piled on the living room floor. I dug through the mound as a child would on Christmas morning. The kerosene heater started generating a bit of warmth. I placed a lamp in every room. I tore the fan apart and inserted the plastic blade into the cordless drill. I positioned the drill in front of the heater, pointed it down the hallway, and tied the trigger in the on position. Warm air began migrating down the hall into every bedroom. We had a 500-gallon propane tank for the water heater and stove. Neither hot water nor being able to cook was a concern. At least we could use the stovetop. We ate supper, watched the snowfall, and went to bed. Things were slowly getting back to normal.

I called Dad the next morning, Christmas Eve, to see how he and Mom were doing. He still did not know what they would do. He said, "We were cold last night." I asked them to come to our house. We were not at full comfort level, but were able to help. They arrived in his Jeep. It was loaded with food, clothes, and presents. He stopped to get my sister, brother-in-law, and nephew. Dad said, "The drive was slow, but it was better than freezing at home." We sat around reminiscing while the kids played games. We had a candlelit supper of hot soup. Everyone enjoyed a warm shower, hugs, and went to bed. I went to sleep thinking, "It was a pleasant day."

We awoke Christmas morning to wonderful aromas filling the house; my wife was cooking bacon, eggs, sausage, gravy, country ham, fried potatoes, and pancakes. Biscuits were atop the kerosene heater. The smells reminded me of Christmas morning at Grandma's house. The scents of hickory smoked bacon, sage sausage, and country ham were creeping through the house, like a slow, London fog. After breakfast, we sat and talked about the "good ole days." We did not realize we were reliving them. Later that evening, the snow started to melt.

Around six, as we were opening gifts, the electricity came alive. We left everything alone for an hour, making sure the electricity would stay on. We put the house back to normal and finished opening presents. After several hours of holiday enjoyment, everyone loaded up and went home.

As I look back on that Christmas, I realize what a great time it was.

Since then, many changes have occurred. My dad passed away. The children are grown, building their own lives. We have not had much snow during the winter months. Around Christmas season now, I sometimes long for another Christmas without electricity.

~Christopher E. Cantrell

Chapter
4

the joy of less

Joyfully Unplugged

31

Friends Less

A friendship that can end never really began.
~Publilius Syrus

Delete. Delete. Delete... Oops! I'd accidentally deleted my mother. I was going to hear about that one! It had taken me a good six months to work up the courage to delete all but six of the nearly one thousand "friends" I had collected on my social media account.

I was addicted and I didn't even try to hide it. I carried my social media friends with me everywhere I went via my smarter-than-me cell phone. I took them to work with me, we went grocery shopping together, and all one thousand of them were my "plus one" at a friend's wedding. They even tucked me into bed with their "goodnight" posts after each long day. They had become my second family, which at first, didn't seem like such a bad thing. Actually, for a time, it was a very good thing.

In early 2009 my mother began sending me posts from a social media site. They were sweet, and often funny, stories about my daughter Kyley as told by her friends. Kyley died in December 2008, and these memories being shared by her peers were precious to me. I created an online profile so I could join the group and read them for myself.

I began receiving friend requests and even sent out more than a few myself. I felt a tinge of excitement whenever someone accepted my invitation to connect. I'd always been a pretty private person, but I found myself pouring out my heart to this new body of friends. I shared my heartache over the loss of my child. I shared amazing stories of signs from Heaven. I shared the humor I sometimes used as a way to cope with my pain. I shared the joy that crept back into my heart as I began to heal. I shared it all in very raw, often very long posts on my social media page. I received incredible feedback in the form of "likes" and encouraging comments. I even created an "author" page after eight of those very long posts were converted to story form and published in seven different *Chicken Soup for the Soul* books.

For several years my social media page, with all of those "friends," was a lifeline. It provided a sense of community and kept me connected to the outside world during a period of time when my grief kept me confined to my home. The interaction it allowed was therapeutic and I believe it was instrumental in my healing. That's why it's difficult to admit that what had once given me the freedom to connect with others was now the very thing keeping me from feeling truly connected.

> *What had once given me the freedom to connect with others was now the very thing keeping me from feeling truly connected.*

It was a gradual process. I'm quite sure I didn't even realize it was happening... that I was becoming addicted to social media. There were signs, though, plenty of them. My phone was never more than an arm's length away. I checked my social media accounts several times throughout the day, even at work. I didn't want to miss an important status update like how one of my friends ordered a hamburger for lunch and she received mustard instead of the requested mayonnaise. And then there was the grocery cart incident.... I'd been checking my social media account for more important breaking "news" when my cart collided with another. I apologized profusely and tried to pretend I hadn't been looking at my phone. I felt a little better when I noticed the lady I'd crashed into had been doing the same.

When I missed the toast at my friend's wedding because I was "checking in" with my social media friends, I had to trust the eyewitness accounts of others that it was absolutely "perfect." And I had been social media guests were invited. I even became more mature in my spiritual life in the absence of those one thousand voices, and I used this new quiet to draw closer to God.

It's been a year since I first hit the delete button and while I may be "friend poor" on the Internet, my relationships with those who really matter are richer than they've been in ages. And that, my friends, is pure joy.

~Melissa Wootan

sitting right there in the same banquet hall!

One evening as I sat on the couch, phone in hand, I looked up from the small screen to my husband and I was suddenly nostalgic. He sat there engrossed in something on his laptop monitor as a television program neither of us was watching played in the background. I found myself longing for the nights when we'd lie on the floor of our living room and play a mean game of checkers, laughing and sharing the events of our day after tucking our children into bed. We had a good marriage but it seemed like we were missing out on more and more opportunities to be truly present with one another because of time spent on the Internet. And I missed my friends, too. Not the thousand online friends, some of whom I didn't even know, but the flesh-and-blood ones, the ones I used to share long phone calls with just to catch up on life.

It seemed the majority of our interactions now consisted of "liking" each other's pictures on various social media accounts. When I did manage to get in a lunch date with a girlfriend, it was painfully obvious by the numerous glances at her phone that she, too, had brought along all five hundred of her online "friends."

My self imposed social media blackout was met with gasps of disbelief but those gasps were almost always followed by wistful confessions that my friends, too, longed for the days of less social media and more heart-to-heart interaction with family and friends. "You know you don't have to actually delete all of your friends, don't you? You can just 'hide' them and then you won't be able to see their posts," a relative offered. I knew. And I also knew that desperate times called for desperate measures. With each click of the delete button I became one social media friend lighter. I was so light that I nearly floated into my friend's home when she invited me over for coffee one day. I left my phone in the car and something surprising happened — I didn't even miss it!

I'd be lying if I said it was easy at first but as time went on I came to realize I was benefiting in ways I had never even considered. My adult ADD improved significantly without the 24/7 bombardment information. I reconnected with my husband over dinners where

Goodbye TV

If it weren't for the fact that the TV set and the
refrigerator are so far apart, some of us wouldn't get
any exercise at all.
~Joey Adams

I am addicted to TV, mind-numbing, time-sucking, waste-of-a-good-day TV. I know some will say I should just be able to turn it off and ignore it, but it calls to me: Cindy... just come and spend a little time with me to wake up... watch the morning news... you have to know what's going on in the world. An hour later, when I should be doing dishes or laundry or a million other things, I am intrigued by the promos and I have to watch the next show. Just a little, I tell myself, and another hour goes by.

Finally, I make myself turn it off and get busy with the chores of life. I make lists and check off items as I get them done: make beds, clean bathrooms, unload/load dishwasher, file papers, pay bills, etc. I work for an hour or two, and lo and behold, it's time for lunch. Who wants to eat lunch alone? I turn on the TV for a little "company." I watch some reruns of one of my favorites and enjoy my hour-long lunch break with my "friends."

Then I decide to keep the TV on, "just for noise," while I continue with my list of chores. I bring in laundry to fold, but end up watching TV and folding laundry only during commercials. I bring things into the living room so I can "listen" while I work, but once again, TV is too enticing and work is relegated to the commercials.

Suddenly, it's time to make dinner. I still keep the TV on while I cook, because the five o'clock news has come on and I need to "stay informed." My husband and I eat dinner while watching TV, because he, too, wants to "stay informed." After a long day at work, he wants to watch a little TV and relax. Who am I to deny him this privilege? Naturally, I keep him company, because I haven't seen him all day. The evening disappears in a few sitcoms and a "made-for-TV" movie. I even force myself to stay up and watch the last show, although I am clearly tired from such a strenuous day of TV watching. Being enlightened is so much work!

I calculate that the TV is on in our house for about fifteen hours a day! That's 105 hours a week, 450 hours a month, 5,400 a year!

> *It's time to take my life back. I'm taking the plunge and disconnecting from TV.*

Gone are the days of reading, sewing, painting, taking walks, or sitting on the swing in the garden talking to old friends on the phone. All are put off until the next commercial or the end of the show.

It's time to take my life back. I'm taking the plunge and disconnecting from TV. Fortunately, my husband has agreed to this drastic measure. I have unhooked the cables, packed the equipment in the box, including the three remotes, and taped it up ready for shipping. No going back now.

Goodbye TV, I will miss you and all the good times we had together. A little tear comes to my eye. There will certainly be a big void in my life now that you are gone. Whatever will I do to fill it?

I think about the friends I have ignored and the things I loved to do and "never seemed to have time...." Well, now I've got the time. Where to start? I think I'll dig out my scrapbooking materials, turn on the radio, and put my time to a little better use. Where's that book I've been meaning to read and when was the last time I spoke to my sister? Hmmm, so much to do, and so much time. I'd better get to it.

~Cindy O'Leary

The Freedom of Shabbat

*A being is free only when it can determine and
limit its activity.*
~Karl Barth

They had Shabbat at the sleep-away camp I went to when I was ten, and I wanted to take it home with me. I made a pretty challah cover in arts and crafts, and carefully packed it in my suitcase to try to take Shabbat home, but it didn't work. The challah cover just stayed on a shelf in the linen closet after I unpacked it.

Years later, I found the lavender and white carefully needlepointed cover neatly folded in the back of the closet, after I returned from a trip to Israel one summer. I pulled it out and tried to bring the Shabbat I had experienced in Israel into our home. This time it lasted for two sweet Friday night dinners. Then I must have forgotten about the challah cover again. Other stuff seemed more important.

It wasn't until I lived within a community of people who observed Shabbat that I finally got to experience it on a weekly basis. For a person who is very driven, it is a healing oasis. I don't think there is anything but a higher spiritual purpose that could get me to stop wanting to accomplish more things.

When I finally began to welcome Shabbat on a weekly basis, I heard the expression that Shabbat is the "pause that refreshes," and that just fit so perfectly. It fits even more now than ever before. Now, it's a chance to unplug from all the ways in which we are wired. This past Shabbat I was pondering how Shabbat becomes even more noticeably distinguishable from every other day of the week as we progress technologically. Shabbat moves in, and we lay down all the gadgets that accompany us all week long. We are left with just ourselves — and the people right around us. It feels so gloriously natural and old-fashioned — but there is no way I would free myself up in this way without a strong spiritual incentive motivating me.

It's ironic, because from the outside it may look like those of us who are observing Shabbat are curtailing our freedom, but I know there is no other way we would release ourselves from all our gadgets. We are actually choosing to "disconnect" in order to more fully reconnect spiritually one day each week.

> *Shabbat moves in, and we lay down all the gadgets that accompany us all week long.*

It's fitting that we use the expression, "observing Shabbat." Shabbat becomes the only chance we give ourselves each week to slow down and observe the people and places that are beside us. It provides us with time to more fully appreciate and savor all the blessings we can see (like candles shining) and feel (like welcoming hugs) and taste (like warm challah) and smell (like chicken soup simmering) and hear (like singing together, and even conversing with a real live person next to us).

We're all here on our unique spiritual journeys — searching for different missing parts. Shabbat gives us the time and space to be mindful and observe where we are on our journeys. When we slow down to a Shabbat pace, we can pause to reflect upon the week that has passed, what its highlights were, and hopefully, reconnect with our purpose.

That challah cover I once made in camp got used so many times after I got married and was blessed with children that it became irreparably stained — with lots of spilled cups of wine and grape juice. We eventually replaced it, and for a while our little ones played pretend "Shabbat" with my old stained challah cover — on regular weekdays.

We get lost from our purpose again and again in our lives. It's coming back to it that is miraculous.

~Bracha Goetz

Why I Gave My Smartphone a Lobotomy

Your cell phone has already replaced your camera,
your calendar and your alarm clock. Don't let it
replace your family.
~Author Unknown

I prided myself on being unattached to any device. Then, I got a smartphone.

It's not a very fancy smartphone. My son figures it is the last iPhone 4S that Apple ever made. I bought it for ninety-nine cents at a Verizon store. It has eight gigabytes of memory, two-thirds of which the operating software needs to run. I figured there wasn't enough memory left to make this phone all that important to me.

I was wrong.

An early warning sign was the water-resistant, rubber-coated, shock-absorbing, plastic case I bought for the phone. Clearly, I intended to carry it with me, not leave it in the glove box.

That first night, I logged into our family's Apple ID and ferreted out my favorite apps: Gmail, Google, MLB at Bat, the Enquirer, the Free Press, NPR, Michigan Radio, Audible, Kindle…

These apps used hardly any memory. A few downloads, a few passwords, and ta-da! All my self-control issues with the Internet were now in a portable box.

Getting lost online wasn't just for procrastination anymore. It was for commercial breaks, the line at the bank, the three minutes it takes for popcorn to pop. I even checked my phone while on the phone with someone else.

I broke the most sacred technology rule I have with my kids — no devices in the bedroom. I didn't just take the thing in the bedroom. It charged there.

Soon that device was the first thing I grabbed after waking — checking the weather, the news, my e-mail, my messages, all before going to the bathroom or letting out the dog.

Eventually, it moved from my purse to my pocket. I knew its weight and I knew when it was missing.

There is a lot of sporadic downtime as a parent. I used to keep a book with me for these times; now I kept the smartphone. Some apps I opened without conscious thought — swipe, tap, tap, refresh, refresh. Remembering to move up in the pickup line or look up on a sports field became a challenge.

> *I broke the most sacred technology rule I have with my kids — no devices in the bedroom.*

Recently, I was waiting for my youngest child's soccer game to start, trying to answer e-mails, text my husband, and update a website. The phone lost its signal, but not before I made a mistake updating the website.

I couldn't correct it until I had a real keyboard and reliable Internet. Knowing that didn't stop me from refreshing the screen throughout the game.

I drove home and made a beeline for the laptop. Coat still on, I started troubleshooting. My oldest sat across from me.

It was the first time we had been together since breakfast. I asked the standard Mom-questions half-heartedly, half-listening as she responded. She was talking about some music opportunity, something she was excited about....

I glanced up from my screen and saw her looking right at me. My fingers froze. An awful feeling crept over me. I realized it was the first time I had looked at her.

I started apologizing, but she just laughed.

"My friends are much better at multitasking online."

Ouch.

The next morning, I did something that was more painful than I'd like to admit. I deleted my apps. When I finished, my smartphone was just a phone again — something I could forget in the car.

Hopefully, I remember how to do that.

~Nicole L.V. Mullis

35

Trading Bandwidth for Bonding

A family is a place where minds come in contact
with one another.
~Buddha

At our house, we can watch TV shows and movies on four television sets, two tablets, two computers and five cell phones. We can play games on all thirteen of these "smart" devices too.

But when I walk into the room and see my children, who are six, twelve, and fourteen, with their heads bent over screens, faces awash in artificial blue light, it doesn't feel "smart" to me. It feels unnatural.

I've read the blog posts by "experts" wagging their fingers at parents who allow their children hours of butt-sitting, game-playing, social media-scouring and television-watching time on screens large and small. "It's unhealthy," they say. "It promotes sedentary lifestyles. There's no brain enrichment."

I've read the other blog posts by "experts" claiming time on electronics is time well spent. It can be a time for learning, a time for socializing with friends or expanding creativity and imagination. My six-year-old would gladly testify in a court to defend Minecraft as more than just a game. My older girls would swear social media is the best way to get to know their friends, "No different than you, Mom," referring to when I spent hours talking on the phone with the cord stretched all the way into the closet.

I'm no judge and jury. I find myself guilty of too much time on social media and news websites. What I do know is that a time came when I felt disconnected from my children. Perhaps this is where the unnatural feeling originated. Buried in their online worlds, my children were not poking their heads out to breathe. Or say hello. Or say anything to me other than, "I'm hungry." They were growing, changing and making new friends, deciding on a new favorite color or maybe even developing a new skill. They were finding a new online celebrity to follow. I'd ask questions, but get no answers. "Fine," doesn't really describe how one has been doing lately.

> *Our family had become more connected to the online world than to each other.*

The hours of screen time had to be cut. Our family had become more connected to the online world than to each other. My motherly instincts screamed at me to fix this.

One afternoon, I walked into the living room to find the kids with their heads bent over their various screens like plants in need of water. "Listen up, family," I said. "I think it would do us some good to have time when all electronics are turned off. We will call it a blackout night, and instead of our noses in screens, we will make art and play games. We will talk about whatever you want. We can plan our summer vacation or be silly. I don't care what we do and I'm open to suggestions, but absolutely no electronics, including cell phones, during this time."

I braced for the whining.

"Cool! Can we paint bottles? I've seen some designs online I'd like to try," Mackenzie, the middle child, responded.

"I have an idea too. Let's do a fire in our fire pit with outdoor games," said Madison, the oldest.

The youngest chimed in, "Can we color together? I'd like that."

I was stunned. This was not the reaction I expected. Instead, my children agreed, and we made a list of several fun ideas for our blackout days. We decided Friday evenings would be a good start since we rarely had plans.

For our first blackout Friday we built a fire in our fire pit, roasted all beef hot dogs on sticks and made ice cream s'more sundaes, played football, and talked about space travel, stars and planets as the sky began to darken and sparkle. No cell phones or other electronic devices were allowed.

The second blackout Friday we colored in coloring books, but not just any coloring books. I purchased a nice set of colored pencils and "adult" coloring books, which are full of small details to shadow and take a long while to complete. We ate homemade pizza and talked about our favorite colors, our favorite seasons and our favorite classes. I taught them about the color wheel.

By the third blackout Friday, my children were turning off their tablets and cell phones ahead of time. I found them, dark and abandoned, tossed about the house.

It hit me. They were enjoying this as much as I was. They needed time to connect as a family as much as I did.

Spending less time in virtual reality strengthened our family bonds. Now we spend more time updating the status of our relationship with each other than any of our social media accounts. Who knew unplugging could lead to feeling so plugged in?

~Mary Anglin-Coulter

36

Keeping the Lens Cap On

Happiness, not in another place but this place... not
for another hour, but this hour.
~Walt Whitman

The waiter carefully placed two gold-rimmed plates, filled with linguine and panko-crusted chicken, on the table. "Enjoy your meal. Let me know if you need anything," he said with a courteous smile as he scurried off to serve the other guests in the restaurant.

Raul lifted his fork to begin eating before I interrupted him, "Wait, can I take a picture for Instagram?"

He sighed, "Go ahead." I took out my cell phone and took the picture for Instagram. Then, I spent the next thirty seconds deciding on which filter would bring out the best in my food and which clever hash tags to include in my post.

By the time our chocolate-drizzled ice cream dessert came around, I was getting ready to take my fifth picture of the night. Raul rolled his eyes. I quickly snuck in a shot of the dessert before asking him, "Sorry, am I bothering you by taking pictures?"

"I'm not gonna lie, it's a little annoying," he said hesitantly. "But it's okay. I want you to do what makes you happy."

I put away the phone, a little bit embarrassed, and decided to just enjoy our date. While we conversed over dessert, his statement lingered in the back of my mind. It wasn't until I reached home that I really contemplated the issue. Did taking pictures of my life, to show

500 followers whom I barely spoke to, make me happy? Well, there was definitely that indescribable feeling I felt when my post amassed over twenty likes. It felt good; it felt like I won. But, what was the prize? I looked through the stream of photos that I had posted of Raul and me throughout our two-year relationship. Most were of our time spent at fine restaurants or the latest attractions near our city, and the brand name gifts we bought each other on holidays. I clicked on the profiles of other people I knew (or rather, was acquainted with) and noticed a similar trend.

It seemed like social media platforms were akin to the stages upon which spectacular plays are showcased. Everything grand is put on the stage as part of one big competition to see who has the best life. People are always trying to validate themselves and their relationships by posting pictures of their fancy vacations, their romantic dinners and the many lavish things that their paycheques can buy. Unfortunately, it's easy to get caught up in the competition, even when you don't realize it or intend to do so. It's funny, the pictures are always so perfect but we're all well aware that life isn't. I wondered how many of these seemingly perfect pictures that flashed before my eyes coincided with an argument, or an annoyed bystander.

I called Raul that night, "I'm sorry about the pictures tonight. I had a good time but I think it could have been better if I just didn't take any pictures," I admitted to him.

"Don't worry about it, it's honestly okay," he replied.

"No, it's not. I've been thinking about it all night. I actually came up with a good idea."

"Really? What's this big idea?"

"How about for at least the next year, we ditch the fancy restaurants and going out to expensive places and just go on free dates? And I promise I'll stop taking so many pictures. I'll limit myself to just one for each date."

"Wow, you're really okay with doing that?"

"Yeah, I'm serious. I mean, who are we trying to impress? We should be having fun, not worrying about what others think, right?"

"You're absolutely right. I think it's a great idea. It's not about where we go or what we do; it's about being together and being happy. We'll save a ton of money, too."

"Yeah, I know! I can start making a list of date ideas if that's okay and if I miss anything, we can add it in later."

"Sounds good. I'm sure you'll think of some exciting things." He was right. As I put my pen to paper, I thought back to our previous conversations about his childhood, things he dreamt of doing and things we did before we were together.

I recalled him telling me that back in the Caribbean, where he grew up, they would fly handmade kites on Easter. This was meant to symbolize the Risen Lord. They would also tie prayers to their kites, hoping that the message would reach God. He told me about the different types of kites he made with his friends and how odd he found it when he moved to Canada that no one flew kites on Easter. Fly a kite, I wrote at the top of the page.

> *Did taking pictures of my life, to show 500 followers whom I barely spoke to, make me happy?*

Another special memory was the day we first kissed. It was on a trail behind our high school football field. I stumbled to get past the boulders and twigs that were lying on the ground. He had held my waist gently to make sure that I didn't fall. We finally made it to a log that was stable enough to sit on. I saw him staring at me out of the corner of my eye but I was too nervous to look back so I stared at the clouds slowly drifting across the sky.

"It's so pretty here," I said.

"I really like you," he said, completely ignoring my attempt at small talk, "You're so different from all the other girls here. It sounds lame, but it's true. Your face isn't caked with make-up, you care about your future and you walk around like you don't care what people think of you. More girls need to be like you."

I looked at him and smiled. "Thank you," and it just happened. There were no fireworks but there was the sound of nature all around us. Everything about that moment felt natural.

I added "go hiking" to the list. By the end of the night, I had everything from playing board games to building a blanket fort on the list. After he approved every item on the list and added a few more, we began scheduling our first new-style date.

"The first time I saw you, you were looking at the paintings in the showcase near the art classes. So, I think we should do something artistic. How about painting a picture together?" he asked.

"Sure, that sounds great. I'll come to your house on Friday."

When I entered his garage that Friday, there were paintbrushes, bottles of paint and a large canvas laid out on one of those white, fold-up picnic tables.

"Ready?" he smiled.

"Of course, this looks amazing!"

We sat down and began painting a beautiful landscape together. Not only was it liberating to release our emotions on a canvas through our brushstrokes and choice of colours, but there was something special about allowing our creativity to flow, having fun together and being far from the world's eyes.

~Selena Singh

Itching for a Change

*Becoming acquainted with yourself is a price well
worth paying for the love that will really address
your needs.*
~Daphne Rose Kingma

I wanted to be a receptionist in a doctor's office when I grew up. As a kid, I played with a blue plastic phone and a calendar, answering the phone with a smile and filling in time slots for patient appointments. Fifty years later I am still filling in my calendar, but my plastic phone has been replaced by an iPhone and as a clinical psychologist I serve as my own receptionist. A vanilla candle on the corner of my desk perfumes the air with a subtle scent as I listen to life stories in forty-five minute intervals—sound bites of love, loss, dreams, and tragedy. Worn green leather chairs cushion our time together. I have a photographic memory for only two things: my patients' lives from one week to the next, and baking recipes.

One Christmas holiday a few years ago, my work stress was intensifying due to the difficulty of cases and the number of clients I chose to see in a day. It was a cold Thursday evening that I sat listening to a young woman recount a horrific car accident she had witnessed the previous night: "She flew through the air as the car careened around the curve and slid off the embankment. I knew it was my neighbor when I saw her red and green socks through my headlights as she hit the pavement. She always wore funny socks with her snow boots."

I drove home holding tight to the steering wheel, snow beginning to fall. As I opened our front door to the smell of baked potatoes, my neck suddenly became hot and itchy.

My daughter asked, "What are all those red spots, Mom?" A warm bath seemed to help but the next week it happened two more times after a long day of work. I realized I was itching for a change. I had to figure out how to simplify and live my next fifty years more peacefully.

Shortening my workweek and seeing fewer patients was only the beginning. More importantly my mid-day is now reserved for someone special whose self-care trumps all others. My blue yoga mat sits regally in the corner of my office, always a reminder of the importance of my own physical, emotional, and spiritual alignment. I steal away to a small yoga studio around the corner. It is my sanctuary where I connect to myself. I need to do that — it's at the core of my ability to help heal and connect with others.

> *Yoga is like putting on my reading glasses, allowing me to see what is closest to me, which can get blurred when caring for others.*

Yoga is like putting on my reading glasses, allowing me to see what is closest to me, which can get blurred when caring for others. When I am centered and balanced, I can better read my patients' stories. A therapist's work is all about change and transition — both our personal growth and that of our clients. The inevitable pain and challenge of our journey is softened in yoga class as we experience a sweet calm in the transition between our in breath and our out breath and from one pose to the next. Standing poses challenge my balance, reminding me of the importance of finding that equanimity in our busy lives. I try to wear clothes that easily travel from one practice to the other, from mat to office, my seams holding the healing energy.

Like the soothing bath on a cold night just a few years ago, I now bathe in the light of daily yoga and meditation to sooth the inevitable rough spots in life. As I meet my true self on the mat I am better able to meet the truth in others. What an honor to hold on to the simplicity of that receptionist job I dreamed of as a child.

~Priscilla Dann-Courtney

38

Why I (Mostly) Quit Facebook

One day I hope to have as good a life as everyone
on Facebook.
~Author Unknown

I have a love-hate relationship with Facebook. I'd heard how addictive it could be so I never signed up. But a few years ago, after my sister begged me, I reluctantly became a Facebook user.

I decided to treat my venture into Facebook as a lark. I would use it once, just to see what the buzz was about, and never visit the site again. I created a bare-bones account using my work ID photo. For about ten minutes, my sister was my only friend. As I looked at her page and her friends' pages, learning new things about them, a dear high school friend "friended" me. Once I accepted that request things snowballed. In the next thirty minutes, I had sixty-three friend requests — all former high school classmates, many of whom I'd hardly spoken with since graduation. It was intoxicating. And interesting too — to read their profiles and see what they were up to and what we had in common. My life suddenly seemed richer. Why had I avoided Facebook so long?

After a pleasant lunch hour, I logged off, intending not to visit Facebook much in the future. However, the next day, a colleague sent me a friend request. After I accepted, I noticed that this colleague was

Facebook friends with other colleagues. It seemed only polite for me to make these friendships official and public too. So I "friended" my colleagues. And while I was on, I "friended" all my college friends as well. I'd definitely stop there though.

I'd only been on Facebook a week when I felt an almost rabid need to collect friends. I had to have everyone I ever went to school with, worked with, the parents of my kids' friends, and seemingly everyone I'd ever met. I made it my goal to collect 1,000 Facebook friends, and imagined how great it would feel to be so connected.

> *Time is the most precious commodity. It's the only thing we really can't make more of.*

By now, if I had no lunches with friends scheduled, I'd check Facebook, laughing and sympathizing with the updates of my new online community.

I wasn't sure about the etiquette involved with responding to posts. Did I have a responsibility to read all the headlines that Facebook generated for me and to respond to all my friends' updates and photos with a personal comment or "like"? Need I acknowledge every Facebook friend's birthday? Did my friends compare what I posted on other friends' walls? If I liked someone's new baby pictures, was I unintentionally hurting another friend's feelings by not reading on to learn about and like his job promotion? Could I ever take a day off from Facebook? As fun and exciting as Facebook could be, it was also very stressful.

I updated my status rarely, crafting a breezy, but hopefully pithy, comment on life, or announcing something monumental like my wedding anniversary. Then I'd wait with bated breath to see who would respond.

I updated my photographs even more rarely, deliberating endlessly about my choices. What was I saying by only including myself in my profile picture, or choosing one with myself and only one of my three kids? Was I dissing my husband and other kids?

With my Facebook e-mail synced to my work e-mail, I'd get constant Facebook updates and e-mails all day long. It took tremendous discipline not to respond immediately. I could easily be lured into checking out someone's status change, then sucked in deeper, marveling over shared experiences with people I was hardly friends with in real life. People sometimes shared the most ridiculous things, like how they ate a burrito at lunch, and yet receive 100 responses from fellow burrito eaters. They'd rave about the inherent deliciousness of burritos and debate the best and worst places to buy them. These threads would continue for days. People would post that their cat or kids threw up, drawing sympathy from forty-two of their friends. I hated devoting time to thinking about such things, yet was unable to stop reading. More than once I found myself looking at engagement or vacation pictures of friends of friends, people I'd never met.

I also found myself thinking a lot about people I hadn't thought about for years, measuring their home and work situations, their kids' activities, against mine, drawing conclusions about their lives based on their posts. I have severe motion sickness, and don't particularly like sailing, yet felt intense jealousy when one friend bought a boat and posted a dozen photographs of her beautiful, happy family's boating adventures. It seemed to follow that this friend probably also had children who did everything the first time they were asked, an easy commute, a self-cleaning home, and laundry that spontaneously washed, folded, and put itself away. I considered buying a boat.

Posts like these affected my in-person interactions. I got grumpy with my family for no reason other than I'd been feeling bad about things I'd read on Facebook. Everyone on Facebook seemed to be having more fun than me.

Despite my best intentions, I, too, could let Facebook eat up hours of my time on any given day. In addition to scheduling fewer lunches with friends, I was now devoting an increasing amount of family time to it. I resented when I had to log off to cook dinner, read to my kids, or watch a movie with my husband. As my online connections grew, my real social life stagnated. My husband complained, but I ignored him. I felt happier, and yet also unhappier, but completely addicted.

It was only when my four-year-old hit his two-year-old brother with an Etch a Sketch, saying he ruined his Facebook picture, that I knew I had a problem.

The same day, I lunched with an old friend. In the course of our conversation she said she'd realized lately that "time is the most precious commodity. It's the only thing we really can't make more of." Her words hit me hard. Why was I wishing I didn't have to read to my children or watch movies with my husband, activities I'd always loved? Why had I been devoting so much time to relationships that meant relatively less to me?

That night I changed my personal Facebook policy. Though I kept my page up, I now limit myself to fifteen minutes a week. If anyone has anything important to say, they can tell me personally. I'll probably never quit Facebook completely; it's helped me connect with old friends I might never have reunited with otherwise. But these days, I regularly meet friends in person for lunch again. I read more books, watch more movies, and take joy in spending time with my family. To paraphrase the great humorist Erma Bombeck, I now cry and laugh less on Facebook — and more while living life. It feels like time well spent.

~Kate Lemery

39

Cutting the Cord

*If you want your children to turn out well, spend twice
as much time with them and half as much money.*
~Abigail Van Buren

The blare of the television drowned out my voice as I told the kids to work on their homework. I tried to talk to my husband about an important issue, but he was so engrossed in the show he was watching that he didn't hear a word I said. I had the opening song of a number of shows memorized, and I dreaded hearing them. I knew that when those songs came on, I would lose my family, each of them in a different part of the house, caught up in a world created by Hollywood. My youngest daughter's sassy attitude mirrored those of the girls in the television show — girls whose parents are irresponsible, not present, or the butt of a lot of jokes.

And then everything changed.

We'd dreamed of living in the mountains ever since we were dating. And then, in one bold, "I can't believe we're doing this" moment, we did. We sold our beautiful house in the suburbs and moved to the mountains. A thousand square feet smaller than our old house, the new house lacked a lot of other things we once took for granted. The biggest being the lack of access to television. Too far from the city to get any antenna reception, we also could not get the cable company to come out. Satellite television was too expensive, way more than what people in the city paid, and with fewer options. Which meant we could only use our television to stream movies from the Internet (with limited selection, since most services charged more than we were willing to pay) or watch movies.

I'd tried for years to cut the cable cord that had been slowly strangling my family, but it took geography to make my dream a reality. In the new house, we didn't have room to have more than one television. Instead of everyone retreating to a different room to catch their favorite shows, we stay in the same room and watch something together. When someone wants to watch something the rest of the family isn't interested in, rather than that person going to another room to watch it alone, we talk about it. We compromise. We work things out. Instead of being individuals who get to do whatever they want, when they want, we are a family unit, and we work together to make good choices about what we watch on television.

> *I'd tried for years to cut the cable cord that had been slowly strangling my family, but it took geography to make my dream a reality.*

We've dusted off the board games, puzzles, and books, and when the weather is nice, the kids go outside to hike or play. But the real proof of making the decision to cut the cord came when my youngest daughter, Princess, had her birthday party. I had a house full of preteen girls and where they once would spend the whole time watching their favorite shows, they had to find something else to do.

Princess decided to take her friends for a hike around our property. I went with them to make sure they were safe, and as we hiked the property, I could hear them chatter.

"Pretend my name is Julianna, but you can call me Jules."

"Pretend my name is Angelique, and you can call me Angie."

"Pretend my name is Constance, and you can call me Constance."

They went on and on, building a story world for themselves. The girls were explorers, having discovered a new land on a new planet. We came upon a group of boulders, which the girls decided was the perfect place to establish their new colony. Immediately, they divided up the work, such as foraging for food, finding shelter, and everything you would think necessary to colonize a new planet.

They spent the entire morning playing on the boulders. This group of girls turned a clump of boulders into a thriving colony on another planet. I didn't hear any complaints of boredom or fighting over which show to watch next. Every single girl had a good time. As I watched them laugh and play, I realized that I hadn't just bought a new house, I'd bought a better childhood for my kids. Instead of spending their childhood in front of the television, my kids are outside, using their imaginations and playing.

Sometimes not having as easy access to television is a challenge. Our family no longer watches the latest shows. We sometimes don't agree on what to watch. But what we watch, we watch together. We watch less television. We go on more hikes. We work on projects together. Notice the word: "together." Because that's the difference cutting the cord has made. My family is closer. When I talk, they hear me. I don't get the sassy answers.

A year ago, while we were still in our old house, my husband thought I was crazy when I said we should cancel our cable service. He didn't see how our family could be happy without the constant blare of television. But as I sit on my couch, looking out the window, watching the changing leaves, the television off, I wish I'd been able to convince him sooner. It took moving to this place without cable service to make my dream come true. We've been in the new house for almost six months now, and our family is closer than it's ever been. Less television has given our family so much more!

~Danica Favorite

40

The Power of Play

Creative people are curious, flexible, persistent, and
independent with a tremendous spirit of adventure
and a love of play.
~Henri Matisse

I t was a dark and stormy night. Really. The rain had stopped but the wind kicked up and was ferocious. It howled and the rattling windows sounded like someone was outside beating on the glass trying to get in. It was also New Year's Eve. We were having our annual party and had a house full of people just starting to celebrate. We really didn't think that much about the wind because we were inside, safe and warm, and had no plans to go out. Our family and friends were all staying overnight and we had our delicious and extravagant dinner to look forward to as well as our champagne brunch for the morning.

And then things started to happen. We heard explosions. Loud explosions. We looked outside and up into the hills near our house and saw sparks flying from electrical transformers. We saw one area after another go dark up in those hills. Then there was the loudest explosion of them all and our house went dark too.

I groped around and found every candle we had and we lit them. If you could forget that we had no power, the candles actually made everything look very lovely. Kind of soft and glowing. But we had problems. Big problems. We had fifteen people standing around and we still had to cook dinner. How would we do that? We had electric ovens and an electric cooktop. They worked great but not without electricity! We needed to improvise.

The barbecue! We would cook on the barbecue. Our New Year's Eve menus were always extravagant and the gourmet menu this year included Beef Wellington, lobster tails, twice baked potatoes and asparagus—not really your usual barbecued items. But barbecue them we did! The men went outside, some holding flashlights and others cooking. They did a wonderful job cooking our feast. The women stayed inside, out of the wind, and got the salads and desserts ready.

Everything was delicious. I don't think we have ever had a better meal and I don't think we have ever laughed as much as we did while preparing it. But what would we do for the rest of the evening? We still had a few hours to go before the beginning of the new year so we all sat around the dining room table and sang. And harmonized. We started with the letter "A" and chose a song title that started with that letter. Then on to "B" and so on. We had problems with "Q" and "Z" but we made up song titles that started with those letters and the lyrics to go with them.

And then it was just a few minutes before midnight. We couldn't gather around the television and watch the ball drop in Times Square but that wouldn't stop us from celebrating. 10, 9, 8, 7, 6, 5, 4, 3, 2, 1… bounce! Bounce? What was that? Why it was a tennis ball hitting the hardwood floor. Instead of watching the Waterford crystal ball drop at the stroke of midnight I stood on a chair in our dining room and, with the help of someone's watch to tell us the time, we all counted down and I dropped a tennis ball! We all screamed Happy New Year and popped the champagne open. We didn't need electricity for that!

The next morning was beautiful and sunny but we were still without power. Now that it was daylight we could see the extent of the damage from the wind. A big tree had blown down in our front yard and there were trees down all over the neighborhood. We could see the neighbors out walking, surveying the damage… in their PJs. We decided to join them so we all went outside, also in our PJs, and walked around. We all wished each other a Happy New Year. The damage to the trees was terrible, the streets were littered with debris, but thank goodness no people were hurt and no houses were damaged.

After our morning stroll, we went back in and started making breakfast together. We cooked omelets, bacon, sticky buns and more… all on the barbecue. We boiled water for coffee… on the barbecue. And we popped the champagne open to wash everything down.

Now it was time to watch the Rose Parade, but that wasn't happening without electricity. If we couldn't "watch" the parade, we decided we would "be" the parade. Maybe our floats would not be as beautiful and artistic as the ones in Pasadena but ours were certainly creative. We took turns — two people at a time — making up the themes for our "floats" and parading down the hall and past the dining room door for the rest of us to see. We had the dish-drying float — our son and his wife each took a plate and a dishtowel and marched by the door, pretending to dry, as we sang marching songs. Then there was the dog-walking float. Yes, even our dogs participated! We put their leashes on and paraded back and forth past the dining room door. A pot-lid-banging float, a kazoo playing float, and a tennis ball bouncing float were only a few of our concoctions.

> *I don't think we have ever laughed so much or had so much fun as we did the New Year's Eve when we lost power.*

Our friends and family left in the afternoon. No one showered because we didn't have any hot water. The power didn't come back on until the next day and we were very thankful when it finally did. We still get together with the same group to celebrate New Year's and we still talk about that special night. I don't think we have ever laughed so much or had so much fun as we did the New Year's Eve when we lost power.

~Barbara LoMonaco

Chapter
5

the joy of less

The Joy of Sharing

41

Pass on the Party

This is the power of gathering: it inspires us,
delightfully, to be more hopeful, more joyful, more
thoughtful: in a word, more alive.
~Alice Waters

I used to love those "home parties" where a friend would invite the gals over to pitch cookware or jewelry or designer baskets. We "guests" would chat and sip Sangria while the "hostess" demonstrated the latest make-up trend or showed us a great new gadget for chopping cucumbers into fifteen distinct shapes. Then she'd pass around the order forms as we nibbled tiny pastries and decided what to buy — because we always felt like we had to buy something.

"Just come for a girl's night out, it will be fun!" the party-thrower would insist beforehand, but those evenings rarely ended without all attendees opening their checkbooks.

Somewhere along the line, these purchasing parties began to lose their appeal. It seemed suddenly everyone I had ever come in contact with had me on their invite list, peddling a dizzying array of consumer products. There were events pushing charm bracelets, designer stationery, wine, nutritional supplements, children's books, T-shirt appliqués, lingerie, gourmet chocolates, even "fashions for the well dressed pet." And thanks to the Internet, declining an invitation due to schedule conflicts or family illness was not even an option.

"You can attend electronically!" the hostess would gush whenever I hesitated about my participation. "I'll e-mail you a link, just click on it and you can see what we're offering and order directly online."

Of course, this meant no munchies, no social interaction, just fork over the money and we'll drop your merchandise in the mail. Even so, I kept on going, often begrudgingly, enjoying the food and fellowship less and resenting the pressure to purchase more.

The worst part about being on the home party circuit was the stuff I was steadily amassing. Stuff I did not need. Stuff I did not really want. Stuff I bought out of a sense of obligation, then tossed onto a back shelf or stacked in the garage.

So when the mailman delivered a little cream-colored "you're invited!" postcard from my neighbor Marlene, I was dreading having to either make up an excuse or write another check. But to my delight, this invitation was very different from the other get-together requests I was used to receiving from family and friends. Her card read:

It's a Pass It On Party!
Bring something you bought and never used
Share the story of when, where and why you got it
Enjoy refreshments while telling your tale and listening to others
All items will be donated to our local elementary school's silent auction

I actually laughed out loud reading this incredible proposal! After years of acquiring unnecessary things, I now had the opportunity to hand merchandise off to people who could really benefit from it. All while enjoying the best part of these events — gathering with friends and trying something new. I immediately sent Marlene my acceptance, then spent a good part of the afternoon going through my "home party inventory" to find a suitable contribution to the cause.

The Pass It On Party was the best girl's night out I've ever had. We sat in Marlene's comfy family room sampling veggie trays and tea sandwiches as each woman took a turn showing off her treasure and describing the circumstances under which it was obtained.

"I really thought I needed a 30-piece cake decorating set," my friend Patty laughed, pointing to the large box beside her. "When I ordered it I had visions of birthday parties with cakes that looked like some prize-winning project from The Food Channel. Of course that never happened, and the kids have been perfectly happy with plain old cupcakes and frosting from a jar."

Sarah held up a collection of still-shrink-wrapped make-up brushes, fanning them out so we could see all eight. The smallest was about the size of a toothpick, and the big one looked like it was designed to put bronzer on an elephant. "Why did I ever think I had to have these?" she said, rolling her eyes. "They're supposed to be made of Angora rabbit fur or mink or something; I don't remember. Maybe I thought I could use them to clean around the house?"

The worst part about being on the home party circuit was the stuff I was steadily amassing. Stuff I did not need. Stuff I did not really want.

And so we made our way around the sofa, simultaneously admiring and deriding the assortment of superfluous stuff. Our assembled lot included my canvas handbag with a dozen interchangeable covers to complement any outfit, a gold necklace and matching earrings sporting an Egyptian pharaoh motif, two gallon jugs of "miracle cleaner" guaranteed to get ANY stain off carpeting, a nested set of blue plastic serving bowls with matching lids, and four different configurations of scented candles in various decorative jars. The night was fun and funny and therapeutic. Everyone had a great time, and no one had to write a check.

About a month later, I got another postcard from Marlene. This one said:

Thanks to everyone who contributed to the Pass It On Party! Through your generosity and the contributions of others, our school earned over $3,200 from the silent auction. The money will be used toward new play equipment. You've made a lot of children very happy with your donation!

And if you enjoyed our get together and think this type of party would work for your event, be sure to pass it on!

~Miriam Van Scott

42

Birth of the Rototiller Club

*Coming together is a beginning. Keeping together is
progress. Working together is success.*
~Henry Ford

After many months of fruitlessly searching for our perfect
first home, we decided to build in a small development
in a rural area of New Jersey. The houses were great
starter ranch-style homes that attracted other young
cash-strapped couples. Because we were all new to the area, it was
easy to make friends and the neighborhood quickly bonded.

The first spring in our new home we decided to try our hand at
planting a vegetable garden. Other neighbors shared our enthusiasm
and planned to do the same. Unfortunately, the ground in our development was hard and filled with rocks. Our attempts at turning over the
soil with a pitchfork didn't last long. We needed a rototiller but it was
too expensive for any of us to purchase on our own. So we decided
to share! Five families chipped in and we even put aside some extra
cash for future maintenance.

It was early spring 1976 when the rototiller arrived. The five families
gathered for a celebratory backyard barbecue. Thus the Rototiller Club
was born and we dubbed our barbecue the First Annual Rototiller Picnic.

Over the years, the tiller was well used, well maintained and
celebrated at our yearly picnic. Our gardens grew and so did our

families. One family was transferred and one departed for a larger house in a nearby town. Rights to the rototiller went along with the sale of the houses.

On July 4, 1991 the three remaining families hosted a fifteen-year reunion of the original members of the Rototiller Club. All five of the original families attended along with the new members who had inherited rights when they bought their houses. The tiller was ceremoniously rolled out looking like new, all decorated in red, white, and blue streamers. It was started up to the sound of cheers and clicking cameras.

Through the pooling of our resources in those early cash-poor days we saved money, had one less material possession, freed up garage space, and shared maintenance costs. Best of all, sharing that rototiller with our neighbors produced not only successful gardens but beautiful lasting friendships as well.

> *Best of all, sharing that rototiller with our neighbors produced not only successful gardens but beautiful lasting friendships as well.*

~Mary Grant Dempsey

The Rain Jacket

No one has ever become poor by giving.
~Anne Frank

I was not a shopaholic. Yet, duplication abounded in my tiny one-bedroom apartment and somehow I never got around to purging the excess. One night, I remember Patrick, my then fiancé, pointed this out while I poked through the closet, coming up empty handed. "I have nothing to wear tonight," I claimed.

"Really?" he returned. His playful look of disbelief sent me back to look again. He was right. "Nothing to wear" doesn't make a lot of sense coming from someone with so much to choose from.

Months later, after we married, the subject of clutter clearly needed to be addressed. Our abundant shower and wedding gifts needed places to call home. The purging process was really necessary, yet still I fought it.

I remember one day Patrick questioned why I had two rain jackets. They were very alike and both did the job effectively. One was red and the other green. "I know," I said sheepishly. "I can't decide. I love them both and I just can't decide."

Months later, on a rainy afternoon, my indecision was defeated in the blink of an eye. It was the same day I was wallowing in self-defeat. I had just been "downsized" at a job where I had worked incredibly hard for four years. I had given my heart and soul to that job in a way that had pushed out other important things in my life. In the end, the crushing weight of the way I was dismissed wounded me. Instead of accepting a demoralizing three-month descent into part-time work, I handed my boss my resignation in the most polite language I could muster.

I drove like a zombie from work to home that day in the rain. The irony was not lost on me that I was living a life that was full of "stuff," yet feeling so empty. Just then, as I pulled off the exit ramp to my street, I saw a man cowering in the rain, drenched in a T-shirt and grungy muddied jeans. He held a sign made from a pizza box that said "HELP ME."

> *I had never been so thankful for something I gave up.*

Had I seen this man many other times and been preoccupied? Other drivers had surely passed him by today without a second look. My heart hurt for him. Glancing over at my passenger seat, I saw both of my rain jackets. The universe was on the loudspeaker and I understood.

Without a second to lose before the light turned green, I rolled down my window and handed the man my beloved hooded green rain jacket. I just barely caught the look of gratitude in his eyes before the cars beeping behind me forced me to move on. But I saw him mouth the words "thank you" before wriggling into the weatherproof garment and pulling up the hood.

As I drove away I thought about how that jacket had kept me warm and dry in the mountains of Colorado, on family vacations, canoe trips, and once when I stood in a long winding line at a concert. Now I prayed that my jacket would shelter him from not only that day's rain, but also perhaps many more days to come. I knew without question that he would value the jacket far more than I had.

I had never been so thankful for something I gave up. Seeing that man made me feel ashamed at my own self-pity. I had a roof over my head, clothes to wear and many ways to rebound from my current misfortune. I knew when my last paycheck arrived from my job that I had savings to fall back on, and my husband was poised to help me figure out the rest.

We sometimes count our blessings in things. The truth is one of the greatest blessings we have is our own ability to look beyond ourselves.

~Leah Shearer Noonan

44

The Joy of Freecycling

*I only feel angry when I see waste — when I see people
throwing away things we could use.*
~Mother Teresa

When my wife and I moved our family to the North Carolina mountains to simplify our lives, we were thrilled to find a home with plenty of storage space: a full garage, six closets and two walk-in storage areas in the loft. It brought home to us what a prosperous country we live in, one where we have so much room to store so much stuff. The downside is that it's been a real challenge to maintain our simple approach to life when our home is constantly filling up with stuff.

Maybe it's that my wife and I have recessive hoarding genes. After all, when Ann drives the forty-five miles down the mountain to visit her mother, she usually returns with the car full of stuff her mother no longer wants. Then there's all the stuff we've acquired from the two rental properties we own when the tenants move out and leave behind their own stuff.

And it's not that some of this stuff isn't good, usable stuff. It often is very good stuff: toys, clothes, furniture, household appliances, dishes, pots and pans, even a five-burner stainless steel grill. But for whatever reason these items didn't make the grade when it was time for the tenants to move on. So we were left to figure out what to do with it all.

Lucky for us we discovered freecycling shortly after one of our tenants vacated a three-bedroom house, leaving behind a massive amount of stuff, not all of which was trash. The concept of freecycling is simple, as explained on their website: Freecycle is "a grassroots and entirely nonprofit movement of people who are giving (and getting) stuff for free in their own towns. It's all about reuse and keeping good stuff out of landfills."

After that tenant moved out, my wife washed ten laundry loads of children's clothing, then folded and organized them according to size. We offered the clothes on Freecycle. They were scooped up by several families who expressed their gratitude with notes and e-mails back to us. The same was true for the many different toys, kitchenware, and several pieces of still usable furniture. We have given away TVs, couches, clothes, tables, shoes, make-up, shampoo, and luggage — all perfectly usable stuff that stayed out of the landfill. All of it found new homes through Freecycle.

One of the best things about freecycling is that by pulling together in their local communities, people have kept tons of perfectly good, usable stuff out of landfills.

We started recycling so much stuff through Freecycle that we had to set up a special "Freecycle table" next to our garage so people who'd requested the items we posted on our local Freecycle e-mail list could pick them up at their convenience. Suddenly, we became very popular in our small mountain community.

But freecycling works both ways. We have often posted requests on Freecycle before purchasing something to see if anyone had what we were looking for. Often, within a day or two, we have someone offering to help us out. My daughter found a great pair of rhinestone shoes that she needed for her upcoming prom. Then when it was time for her to start setting up her own household, she received her first set of dishes, a bed frame, and a headboard, all through Freecycle. Some of the other items we've received were plants for our garden, microwave dishes, curtain rods and brand new pillow stuffing my wife made into pillows for our sofa. We even received carpeting left over from a new installation that we cut up and used for entryway mats and a rug in our guest bedroom.

One of the best things about freecycling is that by pulling together in their local communities, people have kept tons of perfectly good, usable stuff out of landfills while at the same time helping their neighbors. Now that's what I call a win-win-win scenario.

~W. Bradford Swift

45

Nun the Worse for Wear

*Objects really do acquire a life of their own, when
they've been held and loved for years.*
~Vito Giallo

I was dusting the furniture in the living room and I realized we never used this room anymore. I had long bemoaned not having enough space for our dining room table and here was an entire area adjacent to the kitchen that would be perfect! It was filled with living room furniture that was as good as new because we never sat in there. Surely, someone else could put this beautifully upholstered, three-piece sectional with two cherry tables to good use.

My husband, the keeper of all things, would need a solid explanation. I had one. He would need justification. I had that too.

When George came home from work that night, I poured him a cold beer and he sat down to read the newspaper while I put the finishing touches on dinner. When he was sufficiently relaxed, I announced we were ready to eat. We sat down at the table. The stage was set and I was on.

"I'd like to sell our living room furniture," I announced.

"Which living room?" he asked. "And why?"

"The one upstairs, in the next room. We never use that furniture anymore. We always gravitate to the family room downstairs. I'd like to convert this larger room to a dining area so I can put the leaves in the table when we entertain. We have the breakfast bar in the kitchen for the four of us in the morning."

He pondered those thoughts and surprised me by saying, "You're right. What's your plan?"

I shared my idea of putting an ad in the *PennySaver* and on craigslist. George was happy to give me free rein, leaving the planning and execution entirely up to me. So I placed the ad.

I didn't realize how emotionally attached I was to this living room set until the first prospective buyer came to take a look. They talked about reupholstering and taking it apart and weren't sure they liked the wood. I felt my stomach churn. I wanted to yell, "That's solid cherry!" and I was outrageously glad when they left, saying they needed to think about it. I also needed time to think because something was telling me to hold off selling this furniture.

> *It was filled with living room furniture that was as good as new because we never sat in there.*

Several nights later, I had a vivid dream. Of nuns. They were the nuns in the convent across town who worked at the Catholic elementary school our son attended. In my dream, they urgently needed a new couch. We delivered our furniture to them with our pickup truck and a few strong men placed it in their living room. I saw the sisters run their hands over the unblemished upholstery while they marveled at the lovely cherry tables. I remember being happy to know the set was going to a good home.

Over breakfast, I shared my dream with George. He looked at me, smiled, and gently patted my cheek. He said, "It'll be okay." I'm sure he thought I would need counseling after letting the furniture go.

As soon as he left for work, I called the convent. I spoke with one of the nuns and asked if I could drop by that afternoon. She said they would have the teapot on and looked forward to seeing me.

When I arrived on the doorstep of the convent and rang the bell, I was greeted by the principal of the school. "Come in, come in, we've been waiting for your visit."

She ushered me into their living room. "Please have a seat," she said. "But be careful on that old sofa; it has a spring poking through it and can hurt if you sit on the wrong spot." Sure enough, when I sat down, I felt the offending spring prodding me to move to the right.

The sisters and I talked over tea and I addressed the reason for my visit, the living room suite for which I was trying to find a home. I described the design, size and color and asked if they thought they could use it.

The principal put her hand up to her mouth. "We've been praying for a way to replace the old sofa, but I'm afraid we can't afford to buy anything for the house at this time."

"I don't want to sell it to you, I want to give it to you."

The sisters clapped their hands with unabashed glee as they praised the Lord for an answer to their prayers. It was just like my dream. Now I knew why I wasn't supposed to sell that furniture!

The deal was done and we set a date for delivery. I reassured the sisters that we would arrange to have the manpower to unload the set, place it in their living room and remove the old sofa.

Later that week, our living room sectional was taken to its new home in the convent. The nuns were immensely delighted and I was relieved. I had explained to them how badly I wanted a good home for our very first furniture on which as newlyweds, we had cuddled while watching TV and later had held our children as we read stories aloud.

As George and I were leaving the convent, the wise and kind sisters called out from the doorway, "You have visiting rights for as long as you need!"

~Nancy Emmick Panko

46

Getting It Gone

Go into the world and do well. But more importantly,
go into the world and do good.
~Minor Myers

I was planning another garage sale. I was looking around the basement deciding which objects were to be liberated when I had an awful recollection. The last garage sale I had taken part in a few years earlier had taken days of planning, sorting, setting up and pricing. I had been sure I was going to make a killing. The only thing that came close to being "a killing" that time was my narrowly escaping death due to heat stroke. I don't think I cleared enough to even pay for the paper price tags I bought.

It occurred to me it might be crazy to try that again. The items I planned on selling this time were usable but not big ticket. There was too much to schlep to Goodwill and not the right kind of thing for the places that pick up clothing and household items, and with shipping costs it would not have made sense to put them on eBay.

I had once cherished some of these things and I had already gotten good use from them. Maybe they could be cherished and useful for someone else now. Did I really care if I didn't get a few dollars for the lovely Christmas tablecloths that I had used when the family Christmas gatherings were bigger? That's when it hit me. I could just give these good, but unneeded things away—joyfully, with no haggling, no worrying about donation receipts for taxes.

That Saturday morning I spray painted FREE STUFF on a piece of plywood and dragged it and half my unwanted things out to the driveway. I went back up to my office and started doing some client work. Two hours later, I noticed people poking around starting to take things. Encouraged by this, I started dragging the rest of the stuff out.

That's when the fun began. When people saw me they started asking questions: Is it really all free? Can I take as much as I want? I offered empty boxes and told them to fill them up. One woman walked up to me, shook my hand and said, "You are the smartest person I ever met. I sat out in my driveway for two days last weekend and only made forty dollars. This is much more fun." And indeed it felt like a party!

That's when it hit me. I could just give these good, but unneeded things away — joyfully, with no haggling, no worrying about donation receipts for taxes.

People were so happy. One elderly woman approached me with my beloved Christmas tablecloths in her hand. She actually had tears in her eyes and told me that she always wanted tablecloths like these for her family holiday gatherings but could never afford them. A teacher was thrilled to find a box full of craft supplies she could bring to her students. It was such a display of gratitude and an atmosphere of fun that soon I was going into the house to find more things to put out!

One guy hauled away two lamps and someone asked me if I was worried he was going to profit from them by selling them on eBay or something. I said more power to him — if it meant someone else would enjoy them and they wouldn't end up in a Dumpster. But that did cause me to make another sign that suggested that if anyone sold my stuff, they should consider giving part of the money to a charity.

By the end of the day I had one lonely box of old LP records left over — poor Dionne Warwick, Barry Manilow and Neil Diamond. Everything else was gone.

Looking back, no amount of money I could have made from those things would have been worth as much as the joy I felt that day. I was able to simplify my life by giving stuff away, and instead of losing part of my history, I got to add new memories related to all those former possessions.

~Geri Moran

Little Free Libraries

I think of life as a good book. The further you get into
it, the more it begins to make sense.
~Harold Kushner

As a professional writer, I can't afford a lot of stuff, so I don't buy a lot of stuff. Anyway, where would I put it? I live in a one-bedroom apartment. I acquire only what is necessary and keep only what I use. There's no space for more.

However, I started my career submitting fiction to short story anthologies, and every time my work was published I received contributor copies of those books. After years of prolific authorship, I amassed boxes of books.

Then I read Stephen King's *On Writing* and it got me thinking. He suggests editing out ten percent of whatever you write — your novel, short story, whatever it may be. Ten percent of what you've written is unnecessary. This may not be true for everyone, but I'd always been a wordy writer. Cuts improve content.

I started looking around my apartment and wondering if the same might be true for books themselves. It's hard to see books as stuff — they're so much more. There are whole other worlds inside their pages.

Even so, my bookshelf was overrun with fiction I'd purchased at library fundraisers or picked out of people's garbage. I kept books I had read. I kept books I hadn't read. I kept books I'd gotten bored with after the first few chapters. I'd kept every book I bought in university, some of which I'd never cracked because the professor changed the course syllabus—and some of which I'd never cracked because, let's face it, I wasn't the world's greatest student.

So, in addition to multiple copies of anthologies that featured my writing, I owned shelves of books I didn't "need," in the strictest sense of the word. Though I'd managed to pare the rest of my life down to just the essentials, I had this ever-growing mountain of books around me.

But that made sense… because I was a writer. Right?

I knew I could donate books to the local library and they would sell them to people like me, so I put together a big bag. I felt pretty darn good about myself because proceeds would help fund the library's important programming. Although, at a dollar a pop, my books were barely a drop in the ocean.

At Christmas, I gave my books as gifts. Friends and family always asked to read my writing, so it seemed like a good idea. Turns out most people consider a book you wrote yourself to be a bit of a cop-out, as a gift—somewhere between self-promotion and free shampoo samples. My grandmother's always happy to receive a book I contributed to, but everyone else seems to prefer homemade jam.

Books kept rolling in—wonderful for my writing career, not so wonderful for my tiny apartment.

And then one day, while walking home from my local community centre, I spotted a tiny house on someone's front lawn. It was propped up on wooden post, which made it look somewhat like a birdhouse, but right at eye level and right next to the sidewalk.

Instead of birdseed, the tiny house contained books.

It was a Little Free Library: an adorable structure with flowers painted on both sides and a Plexiglas front door that swung open to reveal a world of reading. "Take a book. Return a book." That's what the sign said. No library card necessary. No late fees.

It was for anyone. It was for everyone.

Just a sweet little home for books, continuously stocked by members of the community.

"Hey," I thought. "I'm a member of the community. Why don't I contribute?"

As soon as I got home, I opened my big boxes of books and selected a few I thought the neighbours might like. The next day, I walked back to the Little Free Library. I'd only gone there to contribute content, but I spotted a novel by an author I'd been meaning to read for years. I came away with a book to devour and return — one that wouldn't add to the clutter of my overstuffed bookshelf.

As the months went by, Little Free Libraries sprang up like flowers across the city. Everywhere I went, I seemed to stumble across one. I started carrying books with me so I'd always have something to contribute.

My collection of short story collections dwindled, and I felt great about getting them out into the world. What good were they doing boxed up in my living room? Books are meant to be read.

After donating books I've read and books I've written to Little Free Libraries, I feel like I'm part of something.

Every time I walked by a Little Free Library I'd contributed to, the last book I'd put in there was already snapped up by another eager reader. The libraries seemed to enjoy complete and frequent changeovers. Shelves didn't stagnate. There was always something new.

Little Free Libraries became my go-to spot for book browsing. I still purchase new books by authors I cherish, but now I get the added pleasure of thinking, "When I'm finished, I get to share this with the entire neighbourhood!"

Last summer, I met the owner of that very first Little Free Library I came across. She was sitting on her porch, reading a book, of course. I thanked her for providing this wonderful resource to the community. She asked me if I'd read anything good lately.

At the end of our book chat, to my surprise, my neighbour thanked ME — not for contributing books to her library (I hadn't disclosed that I'd done so), but for borrowing from it. She seemed genuinely overjoyed that the neighbours were using it.

People who live in big cities — and especially people like me, who live in huge apartment buildings — often don't feel a special sense of community. We think that's reserved for small towns. But after donating books I've read and books I've written to Little Free Libraries, I feel like I'm part of something. I felt a sense of belonging. And, unlike boxes of books, a feeling of community is something you can't keep a lid on.

~Tanya Janke

Editors' note: You can learn more at littlefreelibrary.org.

48

Real-Time Inheritance

*What you leave behind is not what is engraved in stone
but what is woven into the lives of others.*
~Pericles

"We're inviting you to claim any of our family possessions you want," I e-mailed to our three adult children. My husband and I had recently completed our living wills and our attorney urged us to let the kids choose their favorite items now to avoid future squabbles. He had witnessed siblings who battled for years over a dish shaped like a chicken once their parents were gone.

Purging raised questions. Were we ready to part with our belongings when we would probably still be around for decades? Would our kids want antiques and collectibles that had been passed down through the generations?

Our children rose to the challenge and got to work.

Lori disliked "old junk" but selected the mahogany bookcase her dad had made, the chair where I rocked her and her siblings, the heavy Norwegian Bible, and for her five children, the tents and sleeping bags.

Steven wanted the grandfather clock and the butter churn so his son could crank it like he did as a boy. He also reserved the orange, 1969 Camaro Rally Sport convertible when his dad stopped driving it in the future.

Betsy appreciated antiques and wanted to pass them down to her three girls. "I feel an obligation to preserve the family heirlooms," she said. "We have space in our home and the cabin, and our girls are into "olden day things" after reading the *Little House on the Prairie* books." She flew in from her home in Maryland and visited us in Florida.

She brought the layout of her floor space on graph paper and wandered through our rooms measuring the furniture. She chose the heavy pie safe, a small oak table for her desk, the four-poster bed for pre-teen Amy, a cane-seated rocker for third-grader Anna, and the coffee grinder to fascinate first-grader Ava. The list grew to include crystal goblets, cut glass bowls, and china. Her family would return during Christmas week, load everything into a commercial container, and ship it to Maryland.

Now, when we visit our children and grandchildren, we take a trip down Memory Lane as we view our treasures in the homes of the next two generations.

Purging was liberating and we discovered that we still had a houseful of things to enjoy. Now, when we visit our children and grandchildren, we take a trip down Memory Lane as we view our treasures in the homes of the next two generations.

~Miriam Hill

49

The Ugly Socks

The test of our progress is whether we provide enough
for those who have too little.
~Franklin D. Roosevelt

A couple of years ago, just as I do every winter, I bagged up all the items in my closet that I no longer wore, along with the clothing my sons had outgrown. I issued a call to action to all of my family and friends, asking them to do the same. It is always my hope to re-purpose those things that do nothing more than take up space in our homes, things other people might make better use of. Nothing bothers me more than selfishly squirreling things away, things that we know we will never use or wear, while people in our community go without.

I found an ugly pair of hand-knitted socks in one of the bags donated by a friend. Not to be mean, but they were a dreadful mixture of colored yarn: orange, purple, yellow and blue. I had to decide — garbage or donation? It wasn't like they were unusable. They were simply unpleasant to look at, surely not something anyone would choose to wear. I imagine they were a homemade gift gone bad.

I put the ugly socks in the garbage, but ten minutes later, I took them back and put them in the donation pile. Later that afternoon, my mother and I drove down to Madison Avenue in downtown Phoenix. Every winter she and I load up my Jeep with our own cast-offs and the donations from friends, and we take them downtown, along with food and water, to distribute to the men and women living on the street. Sometimes I even get my boys involved.

On this particular afternoon, as Mom and I distributed warm clothing and hot food to a small crowd of people outside a local homeless shelter, I reached into the bag and pulled out the last of the donations — the ugly socks. Surreptitiously, I held them in my hand as the crowd of homeless quietly dispersed, each with a grateful smile, a fistful of food and an armload of clothing. Just as I was about to drop the socks back into the empty bag, laughing at myself for even bringing them along for the ride, a teenage boy ambled up to me.

"Can I please have those socks?" he asked, his blue eyes sparkling in the sun.

My eyebrows lifted. I'm ashamed to say it, but I was still a little embarrassed by the donation and disappointed that we hadn't anything left to give him except for those socks.

It's proof that there is happiness in life's simplest things, and we'll never know how much until we've shared those things with others.

"Of course," I replied, handing him the thick, ugly, hand-knitted socks. As a mother of two strong, healthy boys, I couldn't help but feel for this kid. He was the youngest I'd seen that day. He could have been my son, no more than nineteen years old or so. He looked as though he had lived a hard life. His clothes were dingy. Clearly, he hadn't showered in days, but he had the best smile.

"Thank you so much, Ma'am!" he grinned. "These socks remind me of my grandmother. She used to knit stuff like this for me!"

I watched in awe as that young man raced to the sidewalk. You'd think I had given him a brand new car or a million bucks. He sat down on the curb and slipped out of an old, tattered pair of tennis shoes. It was an unusually cold day and I was saddened to see that he had no socks on his feet. My heart broke and my eyes filled with tears as he slipped into those chunky, hand-knitted socks and then back into what was left of his tennis shoes. He stood up, stomped his feet and smiled at me. Bits of the brightly colored yarn poked through the holes in his shoes. It was quite a sight!

"They're perfect!" he smiled.

And to think that I was going to throw those silly socks away.

Not only were his feet warmed that day, but so was his heart—and mine. Of all the more handsome clothes we distributed that afternoon it was those darn socks that were the biggest hit! They had rekindled the memory of that young man's grandmother, a woman who must have loved him dearly. How could I have ever been so thoughtless as to think that those socks, as pitiful as they appeared on the surface, didn't still have a purpose? To this day I think about that young man. I wonder where he is. I even think about those silly socks. As unassuming as they were, they continue to bring me joy. It's proof that there is happiness in life's simplest things, and we'll never know how much until we've shared those things with others.

~Natalie June Reilly

An Empty Garage

The miracle is this: The more we share
the more we have.
~Leonard Nimoy

After we moved from our large four-bedroom house to a smaller one in a retirement community, we vowed to remain minimalists, keeping only the things we really used. Many of our new neighbors shared our commitment to minimizing our belongings; thus was born the Marigold Drive Sharing Co-Op. Our motto was Don't Buy It — Borrow It!

We and our neighbors signed up, listing the things we owned that we would be willing to loan. Categories included items for entertaining, medical needs, sports/exercise, household items, tools, and miscellaneous. A list of available items was e-mailed to everyone.

> *Many of our new neighbors shared our commitment to minimizing our belongings; thus was born the Marigold Drive Sharing Co-Op.*

When I hosted a gathering for new neighbors, I needed a 32-cup coffee maker and a punch bowl. They could both be found at #21 Marigold Drive. Company was coming and I needed two inflatable beds. Sure enough there was one on the loan list at #14 and another at #9.

It was amazing how many infrequently used items were instantly available just doors away. Up for loan were over 100 items including a wheelbarrow, post hole digger, hedge trimmer, chainsaw, travel iron, card tables, knife sharpener, corn hole game, croquet set, crutches, shower stool, wheelchair, walker, paper shredder, fax machine, jumper cables and even a portable sewing machine.

We have a list at our fingertips now. It saves us money, time, and space. And amazingly, we can all park our cars in our garages!

~Mary Grant Dempsey

Chapter 6

the joy of less

Less Is So Much More

51

The Summer of Their Discontent

Things are only impossible until they're not.
~Jean-Luc Picard, Star Trek: The Next Generation

It started out as the summer that I officially became the worst mother in the world. Don't believe me? Just ask my four children who were left home alone together over a long summer vacation. They already knew that there'd be no excursions to a pool and no trip to an amusement park. I had to work all summer so they were staying home. And the story gets even worse.

As a single parent, money was always an issue. So, when the June cable bill arrived reflecting yet another rate increase there was only one solution. I cancelled our cable service. Okay, it seemed like a good idea at the time. After all, I could just hook up the antenna, right? Wrong. Apparently, hooking up the antenna was well beyond my technical abilities. Now, I had no television combined with four cranky children at home during the heat of the summer. Even the air conditioner was temperamental.

The first few days were beyond agonizing. At work my phone rang constantly with reports of "he's doing this" or "she's doing that." Most of the calls were to repeat their mantra: " there's nothing to do." Everyone in the office frowned each time my phone rang. They knew who it was before I even answered. I tried desperately to whisper my responses but it was useless. Everyone knew it was my kids calling.

Again. Oh, how I missed the television — I might have missed it more than the kids. At least when they could watch television they'd sit quietly together and I could work in peace.

Thankfully, the phone calls eventually slowed down from one every ten minutes to only one per hour. At home the phone calls were replaced with a different kind of parental torment. Every evening I battled bumper-to-bumper traffic to get home. There, four scowling faces and four pairs of accusatory eyes greeted me. And silence. The words hung unspoken in the air. "It's all your fault that we have no television." The grimacing faces and sour dispositions were an improvement of sorts. I still felt bad about their summer but I didn't know how to fix it. It seemed hopeless. Short of robbing a bank I had no idea where to get the money to turn the cable back on.

> *They had found creative ways to fill their days — all because they couldn't watch television.*

Then one day it happened. Do you remember the first time your baby slept through the night? That was exactly what it felt like when the phone calls from home stopped. I looked at the clock and realized that it was lunchtime already. Lunchtime and the kids hadn't called! My hands shook as I dialed our home number. One ring. Two rings. Three rings. My heart was pounding. A million scenarios ran through my head. Something was wrong.

On the fourth ring the oldest casually answered. I tried to sound casual too, but my words shot out, sounding like an accusation: "Nobody's called me. What's wrong?"

"Nothing," was her one word reply.

"Is everything okay?"

"Yeah."

We weren't getting anywhere. I knew that she was okay, but what about her sisters and brother? Were her siblings tied up and tossed in a closet somewhere?

"Are you sure everything's okay?"

"Yeah."

And then silence.

"Can we call you later, Mom? We're busy."

I knew it! Every mom knows that "busy" is the code word for "trouble."

"Busy?"

"Yeah, we made up our own board game and we're playing."

I didn't know whether to laugh or cry tears of joy. They'd found a solution to entertain themselves. Their summer of discontent had turned into a summer of creativity. They made up board games and card games. They wrote stories and one-act plays. Their imaginations had sprung into action, blossoming and growing. They had found creative ways to fill their days — all because they couldn't watch television.

It's funny; they still remember that summer as "the good old days." I might have even lost the title of World's Worst Mom. They have carried their love for board games and card games into their adulthood. They still get together to play and enjoy each other's company. Sometimes, you just have to have less to realize how much you really have. Oh yeah, and turn off the television.

~Debby Johnson

52

Priorities

Spend the afternoon. You can't take it with you.
~Annie Dillard

When my husband got a sales job
and could do his work from home,
it sounded like a pretty sweet deal:
no commute
and more time with our son
and me.

Until
his work phone rang
in the middle of dinner
and he had to answer it
or lose a commission.

Or he stressed about his quota,
and worked 'til one a.m.
in our own living room.

Until he worked longer hours at our house
than he ever did
in an office.

We thought things
would never change.

Then through the gossip grapevine
at the high school where I taught,
I heard about a job
my husband would be perfect for
and I knew he would enjoy.

Most important were
the magic words:
school hours
and the summers off.

My husband was reluctant though.
He worried that we'd have less:
money,
stuff,
and fun.

And in some ways,
he was right.
He took a giant pay cut.
We cut down on buying stuff.

But we didn't have less fun.
We had
MORE.

More sun-drenched summer days
splashing
in a sparkling swimming pool.

More Christmas movie marathons
with Rudolph and the Grinch.

More time to teach our son to golf,
to plant a tree and hunt.

More time to cook
his gourmet meals
instead of frozen pizza
(which I always burned).

More time for trips
and baseball games
and staring at the stars.

More time, as well, for cleaning house
and sorting socks and paying bills.
But even sorting socks
is fun
when you do it together.

Life is all about the stories
and the time we share with loved ones.
The joy of working less
is having more
of both.

~April Serock

53

The Joy of Simpler Gift-Giving

The manner of giving is worth more than the gift.
~Pierre Corneille, Le Menteur

Several weeks before Christmas, inspired by articles on "alternative gift-giving" as a way to take the stress out of holidays, I decided to include my entire extended family in an e-mail discussion about how we might make Christmas easier on everyone. I ticked off the reasons in my head: (a) we all had plenty of "stuff" without adding more; (b) some of us were on limited or fixed incomes; (c) most of us led busy lives and might enjoy skipping crowded shopping malls and post offices.

Nevertheless, I approached the task with trepidation. My sister, after all, had six — that's right, six — artificial Christmas trees she decorated every year, each with a special theme. I didn't know how it would strike her that I wanted to simplify gift-giving. Other family members all seemed to be fine with the traditional way of buying gifts. Would they think I was trying to ruin Christmas?

My first e-mail went out in September: "I'm starting a dialogue early this year. I know that we all have our own ideas about gift-giving but maybe we could try something different this year. Please share your thoughts." I attached copies of the articles I'd read.

As the weeks went by, e-mails flew back and forth. My son, who had recently discovered the joys of working with clay, wrote, "I think we should all give pottery!" I replied that I would welcome homemade gifts.

My mother-in-law sent a lengthy e-mail about what she didn't want to receive as a gift, including charitable donations given in her name. It didn't seem personal enough, she felt. I affirmed her willingness to speak her truth.

All of us chimed in with gift ideas that were both meaningful and simple. The declared winners were: (1) a family photograph from the past that came with a special memory, perhaps with a written explanation of that memory; (2) a used book that somehow expressed an attribute of the person receiving it; or (3) a special card. The only "ground rules" were that we could each choose any of the three ideas, and that no "store-bought" gifts would be exchanged or expected.

> *I relaxed into the season in a new way, free from the gift-buying anxiety that had plagued me in past years.*

As the days between Thanksgiving and Christmas passed, I experienced a new spaciousness to the holiday season. Instead of making endless lists of gifts and trooping through malls looking for things my family might like, I roamed through my own bookshelves. Suitable books for various family members almost leaped off the shelves. I relaxed into the season in a new way, free from the gift-buying anxiety that had plagued me in past years.

Three weeks before Christmas, all my "shopping" had been done and I had a wonderful time wrapping my selections in beautiful pictures saved from old calendars — just the right size for books.

Inspired by my newfound freedom, I also decided to create a special booklet of favorite quotations for each family member, to go along with their books — something I had wanted to do in previous years but never found the time to accomplish.

Finally the day came. Our gift exchanges were joyous and peaceful. Each book was a treasured gift. My mother-in-law gave each of us a handmade card and asked us to write in them a wish for ourselves for the coming year. She collected the cards and said she would give them back to us at the end of the year to see if our wishes came true. From my sister I received a beautiful framed childhood photo of the two of us that brought back special memories; from my daughter-in-law came a humorous book that recalled my Southern heritage.

And my son... He gave us his best pottery creations to date — "memory bowls," he called them, each uniquely created to hold whatever family treasure or written memory we wanted to place in it.

Freedom from the tyranny of gift-buying — the tyranny of living up to cultural expectations of what Christmas "should" be like — also gave me freedom to experience the joy and diversity of who we are as a family. I can hardly wait to see what we'll do next year!

~Maril Crabtree

54

Downsizing to Our "Yacht"

Have nothing in your houses that you do not know to be useful or believe to be beautiful.
~William Morris

"What is all this stuff anyway?" we'd ask ourselves as we weaved in and out of the labyrinth of accumulated junk. After thirty years of marriage, with three sons raised and out of the house, did we really need all this "space" now, particularly since we tended to fill it up with things of questionable value?

One day, as a pile of bills dropped through the mail slot, we realized we were paying separately for cooking gas, heating oil, electricity, water, sewage, and garbage removal, while our friends who lived in apartments or condominiums paid one single (and modest) fee for all of those. We started investigating apartments in our area, and found that we could live at a little over half our present housing costs if we switched lifestyles.

But moving from a house, with basement, garage, and several bedrooms, to a smaller apartment would mean we'd have to cull through an entire adult lifetime of stuff. Did I really need to keep those college term papers on how Shakespeare influenced the poetry of Lord Byron? The answer was pretty clear.

Much of what we had kept — and boxed up and moved with

us several times from place to place — had no present purpose and no imaginable future use. Our guiding principle became a ruthless utilitarian assessment: will we ever use this again? If no, out to the curb with it!

Week after week, for a month, the curb in front of our house on garbage collection day was lined with stuff. It was astonishing, like the parade of clowns emerging from a car parked in the middle of a circus ring. Why did we keep that stuff and how did it all fit in our house?

Moving day came, and I had very carefully measured the apartment into which we were moving and planned every inch of book shelving and furniture placement. Bookshelves or tall wooden closets lined nearly every wall in the apartment, but one wall in each room was left "clean" and empty, a concession to our need not to feel "trapped."

> *If we were living in a space this size, and this well-organized, on a yacht, we'd think ourselves very fortunate.*

Now here is where we discovered the serendipity of our new home: the long living/dining area led up to an east wall that was almost entirely waist-to-ceiling-high windows. Thus, the place was flooded with light from dawn until mid afternoon. That was already a plus. Every other room in the place also had large windows facing either east or south, so despite the floor to ceiling bookshelves on most walls, we don't feel imprisoned in our space.

We also had brought with us our huge fresh-water aquarium, which further "opened up" the place so that we didn't feel boxed in. There is nothing like a micro environment full of plants and moving, brightly-colored fish to avoid the closed-in feeling that an apartment can impose upon someone more used to larger spaces.

Now that long narrow living/dining area that is the central space of our home feels like the carefully apportioned spaces of a yacht!

We're not wealthy, but had enjoyed the good fortune of others who were, and when we began to see ourselves as living "on a yacht," instead of merely a small apartment, we had to laugh. We may not be sailing around, island-hopping the Caribbean, and the view out

Less Is So Much More |

the windows only changes with the seasons, but still, we often tell ourselves: if we were living in a space this size, and this well-organized, on a yacht, we'd think ourselves very fortunate. So, why not enjoy it? (The fish, by the way, and their little world inside ours, contribute to the effect.) Sometimes how you feel about where you live comes from how you see it.

~Gene R. Smillie

55

When Less Truly Is More

Owning fewer keys opens more doors.
~Alex Morritt

We stood in the middle of our living room, overwhelmed by the task of sifting through our charred belongings. The evening before, we'd returned from dinner and a show with friends to find two fire trucks and an ambulance in front of our house. The firefighter said he wasn't sure how the fire started, but luckily our neighbor called 911. We had left the windows open and the fans running to help with the scorched smell, and we spent the night in a hotel.

"Where do we even start?" Ed asked.

"I guess we should start throwing stuff in these trash bags," I ventured. "If there is anything that looks like it might be salvageable, let's put it on the front porch."

I ripped open a box of trash bags and handed one to Ed. I put on a pair of disposable gloves and picked up what had been a photo of the two of us on vacation in Hawaii. How could I throw it away? Ed barely looked at an item before throwing it in the trash bag.

"Maybe we should go through things together," I said.

"Honey, that's going to take twice as long." He gave me the "are-you-going-to-control-this" look that I'd gotten from him several times throughout our twenty-two-year marriage. It was usually followed by a comment about me acting like my mother.

"Okay, you're right." I went back to working on my own corner of the room while trying not to cringe every time he threw something away. He didn't understand. Our house had been a great source of pride for me over the years. It was almost as if creating the perfect home was a way of creating the perfect life, even though real life had never quite matched the life I tried to create. We owned china and silverware for elaborate dinner parties that we never threw. There were extra bedrooms for children that we never had. Suddenly I realized how much of my life had been spent preparing for my life. I began to cry.

"Honey, it's okay." Ed tried to console me. "We're just lucky we weren't here when it happened. They're just things. They can be replaced."

He kissed me on the forehead and then looked at me tentatively. He was always visibly uncomfortable when I cried. I calmed myself and we continued to work well into the night and then headed back to our temporary home.

> *Suddenly I realized how much of my life had been spent preparing for my life.*

The efficiency we rented was 500 square feet. Our house was more than four times that size and I couldn't image how Ed and I could live here while the house was being repaired. For the first time in years, we'd have to share a bathroom. I looked at the tiny table that was so close to the stove; it would be impossible for both of us to share a meal there.

"Do you want to go out for dinner tonight?" I asked.

"Sure. I saw an Indian restaurant about six blocks away. We could walk there."

That night was the beginning of the end of our routine lives. In our home, Ed had his man cave and I had — well, I had the rest of the house. Often, after work and on the weekends, we would spend time in our house completely separate from each other, only meeting up at the end of the night when it was time for bed.

In a four-bedroom house, it was easy to grow apart, but living in one tiny room changed that. We went to outdoor concerts, museums and new restaurants together. I no longer spent an entire Saturday doing housework because it took only fifteen minutes to tidy up the apartment. Getting dressed also became a breeze because I only had a fraction of the clothes I'd previously owned so I didn't spend hours trying on clothes or looking for matching accessories.

We spent almost three months living in what was essentially an oversized hotel room, but we enjoyed our time there. Learning to live without the items that we thought were essential helped us to realize that they weren't essential at all.

When the renovations were done, the house no longer looked like our home. The new paint colors, hardwood floors and appliances that I'd selected were beautiful, but they weren't for us. I had no desire to begin filling the rooms again with stuff that we rarely used and didn't need. It occurred to me that I had bought so many things that were supposed to make life easier and better, but they'd done just the opposite.

Five months later we sold our house to a lovely young couple with two kids. Spending time outdoors was something that Ed and I discovered we loved, but brutal Chicago winters kept us indoors a lot, so we moved to Florida. The proceeds from selling our house were more than enough to buy a two-bedroom condo. The best part is that it's within walking distance of the beach, which is where we now spend most of our time. I never thought I would be grateful for a fire, but I feel freer and lighter than I've felt in years.

~K.D. King

56

Warming Up to Less

*What seems to us bitter trials are often
blessings in disguise.*
~Oscar Wilde

Our nine-year-old refrigerator broke earlier this year — the second breakdown in two years — and we decided to buy a new one instead of paying to repair it again. Over the course of the next month, we ordered five different refrigerators from various companies, even an old refurbished model, and each one arrived shiny and spacious and ready to be filled.

There was only one problem. Each time the deliveryman plugged one of the refrigerators into the kitchen wall socket, my wife had to retreat to our bedroom covering her ears, and I had to ask the delivery crew to take the new refrigerator away.

Until then we had thought my wife's hearing was as normal as any other fifty-five-year-old woman's, just a little more sensitive to noise than most other people. As it turned out, she had developed in middle age an extreme sensitivity to high-pitched sounds — the kind made by the new, energy-efficient compressors that most new refrigerators are equipped with these days. (It's a condition known as hyperacusis, and our attempts to replace the refrigerator were our first clue to this new stage in her life.)

After failing to find a regular sized fridge to replace our old one — and not wanting to continue filling our picnic cooler with twenty-pound bags of ice from the grocery store every other day — we thought a smaller refrigerator might make less noise. So, we bought a mini-fridge, a 3.2 cubic foot model the size you might install in a dorm room, and put it in the garage. It's now sitting plugged into the socket as far from the living area as possible, and my wife doesn't hear its high-pitched sound in the house.

At first we worried about how many times we'd have to go out to the garage every time we wanted something. But after installing the mini-fridge in the garage, we discovered something unexpected: we didn't really need a large fridge, after all.

Many of the items that we thought needed to be kept cold, such as onions, potatoes, tomatoes, mustard, jelly, ketchup, and salad dressing, didn't need to be refrigerated at all.

After installing the mini-fridge in the garage, we discovered something unexpected: we didn't really need a large fridge, after all.

And now that our freezer, which is barely the size of a shoebox, can no longer hold a gallon of mint chip ice cream, we don't keep ice cream in the house. If we want any ice cream, we go out to the local ice cream or frozen yogurt store.

But that's okay. Not only are we eating less ice cream, we're exercising more since each time we need to get something from the fridge, we have to walk an extra ten yards into the garage and another ten yards back to the kitchen again.

The only real challenge to keeping a refrigerator in our garage, aside from having to walk the extra yards, is that my wife has to use noise-reducing earplugs or noise-muffling earphones each time she goes out to the garage to retrieve food from the fridge or to get in her car.

It's taken a few months, but we've fallen into a routine, and, much to our surprise, we've found that we're eating less and fewer times a day, and what we're eating is healthier, which means we're making more nutritious meals. That's because every week we buy fresh fruit and produce, and we plan our dinner menu depending on what is available at the store.

Fresh fruit and vegetables — apples, grapefruit, peaches, peppers, tomatoes, carrots, and such — ripen on our kitchen counter and taste as if we had just picked the fruit off the trees or bushes, or pulled the vegetables straight out of the earth.

Even better, from an environmentalist's point of view, our energy footprint has shrunken since installing the small fridge. Each month I check my electric bill, pleased to find that we are using significantly less electricity than we used in the past to power the larger fridge (though it's not always true that smaller fridges use less energy than larger fridges).

Of course, there are some downsides. If I want a beer or hard cider or just a glass of tomato juice, I've learned to enjoy drinking it at room temperature, or else I need to plan ahead and put my beverage in the mini-fridge to chill.

Warm cider, I have to admit, is an acquired taste. But I've discovered that I actually enjoy its rich, bold flavor at room temperature almost as much as I enjoy it cold.

It turns out that my wife likes sipping it warm, too, especially now that she can remove her noise-cancelling earphones in the kitchen and enjoy her drink in silence.

~Bruce Black

57

The Family Farm

Where thou art — that — is Home.
~Emily Dickinson

A few years ago, my in-laws made a big announcement. After forty years in their farmhouse, they were selling the house and moving to a retirement community. This came as quite a shock to us, not just because the house had become a family "heirloom," but also because of my father-in-law's packrat tendencies — none of us thought he could ever let go of the stuff he'd collected over the years. My in-laws' farmhouse sat on five acres of land that had numerous structures, including two barns and a large workshop. And these buildings were stuffed to the rafters with the many tools, spare parts, old furniture, and other treasures my father-in-law had accumulated over the years. In order to get the apartment they wanted, my in-laws had needed to act quickly, and they left themselves only three months to sort through and pack up forty years worth of stuff.

Over the years, I've found my mother-in-law to be unflappable, a strong and calming presence when life throws its curveballs. But the sudden rush of this move had even her rattled, as she wrestled with her emotions and worried about my father-in-law's reluctance to part with anything.

We were heartbroken to see the old house go, but despite this we put on smiles, wanting to make the transition smooth for the two people who had done so much for us over the years. Privately, my husband and

I worried. This house had been a labor of love for my in-laws for most of their adult lives. They had taken it from a dilapidated eyesore to a magnificent dwelling, raising three boys (as well as one dog, two goats, and twenty-five chickens—but that's another story) and holding down multiple jobs along the way. In addition, through their generosity and hospitality, my in-laws had turned the home into a sweet haven for the extended family, giving us many wonderful memories of Christmases around the fire, summer solstice celebrations, and explorations in the property's woods and pond. So much of their life was tied up in that house, not to mention my father-in-law's collections. Could they truly leave it all behind? And what would their life be like once they did?

When we arrived the first day to help, we realized how valid our concerns were. Although my mother-in-law was making good progress in the house, she was on edge, and the two barns and workshop were huge messes. My father-in-law insisted on facing these beasts alone, but we doubted that he could actually sort through it all and part with most of it in just three months. We joined my mother-in-law in the house, and she and I talked about everything that was happening. "I love this house, and I've loved our time in it," she said. "But we're getting older, and we're tired. We want to be able to relax and enjoy the years we have left. It's time to move on."

> *I realized that the tremendous experiences we had enjoyed in this house had come at a high cost.*

As I listened to her, I realized that the tremendous experiences we had enjoyed in this house had come at a high cost. While we took for granted this place that provided us with so many joyous memories, my in-laws were working harder and harder each year to make sure the experiences could continue. And they were doing so with a 200-year-old house that required large-scale maintenance each year and with bodies that, although healthy, were suffering the natural aches and weaknesses that come with age. And when I really thought about my father-in-law's "hoarding tendencies," I realized that the things he had amassed over the years were not silly collectibles, but things he and my mother-in-law needed to restore and maintain their "labor-of-love" house.

At that moment, I knew. It was not the house that had given us our memories… it was my in-laws. Without their loving presence, their amazing hospitality, and their incredibly hard work, the house was nothing more than a house. And in honor of all they had given us through the years, it was now time for us to give back. We needed to embrace this change and their readiness for it. As I listened to my mother-in-law talk eagerly about the new direction in which their lives were heading, I resolved that we would give these amazing people our best and enthusiastically support them every step of the way.

As we trekked over to the house each week for the next several weeks, we began to notice the changes. First the garden decorations were gone. Then the curtains were down and most of the furniture packed up. But most astonishing were the barns and workshop… little by little, the accumulations disappeared, and with them much of the weight that had sat on my father-in-law's shoulders for so many years. He seemed to realize that his possessions had served him well but were no longer needed, and it was time to send them to new homes (ours one of them!) and jump into the wonderful new phase of life he and my mother-in-law so richly deserved.

Finally, the time came for the big move. As we pulled into the driveway of the farmhouse for the last time, everything felt different. The house was becoming just a house, and it would soon be a house that belonged to someone else. As we approached the front door, we saw my in-laws standing on their porch for the last time. And the looks on their faces said it all — their expressions showed not sadness, but beaming pride for all they had accomplished with this house for so many years and excitement for the new adventure they were about to embark on.

Two years have now passed since my in-laws' move. They have settled into their retirement community, and by all accounts it seems that the move has given them a new lease on life. Wonderful new friends, daily activities, and adventurous trips now fill their schedule, and we find that they are busier now than they have been in a long time! But at the same time, they are also more relaxed and at peace than they have been in a long time. And most importantly, they are enjoying the reward for the hard work they put in for so many years, providing a wonderful haven for their family. And, with renewed vigor, they are creating fantastic new memories to add to the special ones we will always have of the old farmhouse and what they made it into for us.

~Maggie Hofstaedter

58

A Second Chance at Love

A bargain is something you can't use at a price
you can't resist.
~Franklin P. Jones

My mother's home has a revolving door. Not really, but she loves to shop and then she needs to give things away since her house gets too full. It's a constant battle for her. She needs to get rid of stuff but she's not able to resist buying things. Fortunately, she likes to shop at tag sales, thrift stores, and Goodwill, since she doesn't like to spend a lot of money—and every day there are new things to buy!

Although her house is jammed with stuff, she is diligent about getting rid of it—since she has also acquired all the books about organizing, throwing out, and the joy of living with less! We've tried to help her rein in her shopping habits over the years, but the bottom line is that she can afford it, it gives her enormous pleasure, and it keeps her busy. The rest of us just shake our heads when she comes in excited about her new purchase.

One day when I was at her house she showed me a small, beautiful bone china pitcher that she had just bought at one of her favorite haunts. Although it was mostly white, the bone china had a delicate pattern, and it was hand painted with a green decorative line, small tulips and other flowers.

I looked more closely at the pitcher. It actually looked very similar to one that I had seen before at her house.

"Mom, don't you already have one just like it?" I asked.

She stopped and looked at it. She thought for a moment. "Huh, yes, I guess you're right," she replied. "But I gave it away."

> *"I might have bought back the pitcher I gave away!"*

I looked at her wondering if what I thought had happened, had in fact happened.

She burst out laughing. "You know, I think I might have bought back the pitcher I gave away!"

"Yes, Mom, I think you did," I said, incredulous.

I waited a beat before I continued, "So much for that bargain. You bought it twice!"

"Don't look at it that way," she replied, happily. "I just fell in love with it all over again!"

~Gwen Daye

59

Helping More Animals by Having Less

We can judge the heart of a man by his treatment
of animals.
~Immanuel Kant

When my cousin and I were about ten, both our moms had babies. A few weeks later, my aunt told Mom, "Gordie keeps wanting to hold his new brother and give him his bottle. Is Susie excited about the baby?"

Mom rolled her eyes. "Maybe if he was a baby horse — or a dog — she'd want to hold him. But a human baby? Not a chance!" My dream was to grow up and have lots and lots of animals.

Eventually, I grew up and had babies of my own, but animals were still my passion. By the time my kids were grown, we still had a houseful. Of animals.

At the peak, we had four dogs, four cats, a rabbit, and two guinea pigs. When my youngest daughter needed to move home for a while, she also brought in her pets: a dog, three cats, and a tank of fish. We have a big old farmhouse, and my daughter took care of her own pets, but I still knew we'd exceeded our limit.

Every morning, I did what I called my "barn work." I grew up in farm country and had a horse for many years. Cleaning out guinea pig cages and tossing them hay felt like a familiar, though tiresome, routine.

Unfortunately, between the cages and the litter boxes alone, an hour or more quickly passed. One of my cats, Chester, was pre-diabetic, and tended to "think outside the box." That meant picking up soaked papers, washing the utility room floor around the litter area, disinfecting, and replacing fresh paper. Then, I had to go outside and scoop the yard, where the dogs did their thing. This was a little bit like hunting for Easter eggs, but a lot less fun.

The dogs all had different needs. Fourteen-year-old Sofi was a big, shaggy mixed breed with a tendency to itchy hot spots she bit and scratched till they were raw. She developed dementia in her last year of life, and it made her paranoid and mean-tempered. She growled at all of us — as well as the walls — and started attacking one of the other dogs at every opportunity. She still loved going for short walks, but became more and more arthritic and needed help with steps.

Most of my pets were senior citizens at this point, so I made a tough decision. As they passed away, I would not replace them.

I was doing cattle dog rescue, and it's a notoriously high-energy breed. My Elvis needed at least an hour walk every day or things got eaten. Things like my grandmother's Bible, my mother's childhood cradle, and the arms and legs of an antique doll.

Red was another cattle dog, but he was blind and needed eye drops three times a day. Spike, the tiny abused foster dog we'd ended up adopting after his recovery, wouldn't stop yapping and also wasn't house trained.

The cost of food and routine vet bills was staggering. And there were always emergencies on top of that. Emergency testing and hospitalization, insulin, syringes, and blood-glucose testing for Chester. Emergency testing and medications for Elvis, who contracted Lyme disease. Regular specialist appointments and high-priced eye drops for Red. Blood work and surgery to remove two massive tumors from my guinea pig, Tyrone.

My best friend called me an animal hoarder. "But I take care of them!" I protested.

She just smiled and shook her head. "I know you do, but…"

Despite my protests, I knew I'd exceeded my capacity to cope. Most of my pets were senior citizens at this point, so I made a tough decision. As they passed away, I would not replace them. No more taking in every abandoned dog or cat that melted my heart.

My oldest cat, Paw Paw, passed first. Then, one by one, all my guinea pigs but Tyrone passed on. Sofi could no longer struggle to her feet, so we made the trip to the vet's office and I held her as she left us. My eleven-year-old rabbit, Henry, went next, and the vet was amazed at his extreme old age.

My daughter had moved out some time before, so her animals were already gone. My other daughter moved away and took little Spike. Red, who was not so old, passed suddenly of cancer.

At this point, I am down to my one cattle dog, three cats, and one guinea pig — from eleven animals to five in a matter of months.

I love my animals. More than one person has told me they wish they could come back as one of my pets, because they're so well loved and cared for. They are a joy and a challenge to me, and the fulfillment of my childhood dream "to have lots and lots of animals."

But there's a new peace in the house, more time in my day and more money in my checking account. I have more time to focus on each of my animal companions and appreciate them.

And — ironically — having fewer animals of my own has freed me to help more animals. When the house was full, and I was struggling to keep up, my goal was survival.

Now I can provide temporary homes for animals. In the last three months, I've been able to foster and re-home two cattle dogs, and I have another on the way. The first was an active six-month-old boy, who stayed with us for just a few days. Then for a month, we had an eleven-year-old blind dog, Dingo, relinquished by his family to a high-kill shelter. My husband, daughter and her fiancé and I — and little Spike — drove him nine and a half hours to his new home, and got a road trip in the process.

My experience with old and special needs animals has perfectly equipped me to foster dogs like Dingo, who need a little something extra. My heart always went out to these critters, and I'd end up adopting them. Now, I realize I can help so many more, just by keeping my own home a lot more streamlined, and getting the neediest of creatures into someone else's loving home instead!

~Susan Kimmel Wright

De-cluttering a Brain

As you simplify your life, the laws of the universe
will be simpler.
~Henry David Thoreau

"My brain is too full! Don't tell me anything else to do," I yelled. Even I was surprised by my overreaction to Ken's helpful suggestion. I burst into tears and hurried upstairs to get away from him, overwhelmed by yet another thing to think about.

It was just an idea Ken shared with me about redoing my pothole-filled driveway. I took a few deep breaths as I hid in my room. Ken was retired and had been living in a private apartment in my home for the past year in exchange for help around the house. After calming myself down I sat on my bed and tried to figure out what had happened.

I went back down to Ken's apartment to apologize. He was watching a football game. Ken muted the television as I walked in. "I'm sorry. I didn't mean to yell at you."

"Julie, I didn't mean to upset you. I was just trying to be helpful."

"I know. It's just that I am so frustrated by everything I have to do. Since my brain injury I've tried to stay on top of everything but I get tired. You know how people say that their plate is full, that they have too much on their plate to do anything else? My mental plate is so full right now that even adding an unexpected thought or idea is completely overwhelming."

Ken was so gentle with me, so patient as I tried to explain.

Chores and tasks fall into the urgent category and need daily attention. Spending time with family and friends is important and needs to be a priority. I try to be there to celebrate their special moments and share their painful ones.

I have responsibilities and projects at work that demand energy, time, and effort so I can be effective. The children and people I help at work need my attention and patience as I support their efforts to work through their own traumas and struggles. All of these are important and all are priorities. All of these wear me down and overload my brain.

> *My mental plate is so full right now that even adding an unexpected thought or idea is completely overwhelming.*

Decisions are much harder for me now. Spending time with people drains me more than before. I have to filter my thoughts and words as I interact so I don't accidentally say or do something that is inappropriate. I don't have the stamina I had before the car accident that caused my brain injury.

Ken sat back in his recliner and looked at me with tenderness in his eyes. "Julie, you can't do everything. You need to take care of yourself, not let yourself get overloaded. Let people help; let me help. Figure out what is most important and let go of the rest."

As I returned to the kitchen to wash the dishes that had piled up I thought about what had happened with Ken, and his comments. Sitting down at the table, I opened a notebook to a fresh page and made a list of the parts of my life that only I can do.

Important:
Spend time with family and friends
Spend time with my boyfriend Bill
Work as a probation surveillance officer and private investigator
Spend time with my black Lab Brady
Strengthen my relationship with God
Take care of myself by working out and eating right
Work with foster kids and traumatized children

Tasks to do:
Daily chores
Errands and groceries
Split and stack wood for the winter
Maintain the yard and gardens
Clean the house
Projects on the house

Relaxing activities:
Read
Do jigsaw puzzles
Hike or snowshoe
Sail or kayak
Go to the beach with Brady

I continued to add things to my lists throughout the week. One evening I reviewed the six pages I had filled with everything on my lists. No wonder I was so overwhelmed. I spent the next few days planning how to better balance everything. And I asked for help.

My mom offered to cook extra meals that I could microwave during the workweek. I asked my cleaning lady to stay an extra hour each week. She began to use this time washing windows, tidying the garage, and doing whatever she felt needed attention to keep my house looking fresh. I hired some neighborhood kids to help with some of the yard work and to stack wood. My boyfriend came over each week and did one project from my list.

As the weeks went by, I began to relax. I focused on spending my time more productively, using my planner to schedule downtime between my other commitments. I gave myself permission to not finish every craft project I had ever started and began to de-clutter my cabinets and drawers of half-started ideas. I removed extra clutter from my brain by deciding not to put every item I thought might have value on Ebay or craigslist. Instead, I delivered my unwanted things to the mission store.

I began feeling more in control. My house became more organized.

Time and activities with family and friends became easier. I rediscovered my love for my work and the people I work with. My family and friends understood my requests for the additional time needed to make decisions and think about invitations. I made room in my brain for new ideas that might come up.

The next spring Ken approached me as I was outside playing ball with Brady. "I'd like to talk to you about how I can help fix your driveway if you are ready to talk about it."

"That would be great," I was able to say with a smile.

~Julie Sanderson

Chapter 7

the joy of less

Joy on the Road

61

Life in a Rolling Cardboard Box

*Where we love is home — home that our feet may
leave, but not our hearts.*
~Oliver Wendell Holmes

Sunlight is now my alarm as I rise to light the gas stove for my coffee. I peer out into our living area where all four of my children sleep — girls on the couch, and boys on the floor. We told them it would only be for a year. I smile, as in January it will be five. The traveling life has woven our family together from separate pieces of cloth into a quilted piece of art.

I think back to our old life with a new house I designed and built on my great-grandfather's farmland. Jon worked more than forty hours a week — on-call weekends and vacations as the only IT person for the bank and its eleven branches. I stayed home with the kids, found volunteer opportunities, and kept up with the demands of their public schooling. I look back now and see how as a couple we lived parallel lives — Jon had his work bubble, I had the home bubble, and on weekends Jon could visit my circus show.

In 2008 our marriage shattered like a mirror. Jon and I decided to pick up the pieces and eventually, after therapy, decided that the best way to reclaim the relationship we began as eleven-year-old kids was to hit the road with our children.

Now our life fits into 200 square feet of living space in this motorhome and a 5x7 storage unit. With such limited storage space something new comes in only if something old goes out — or so I keep telling my children. This lifestyle holds me accountable, especially when I walk through a store.

Today, I sit to write in the quiet of the morning. I begin a new travel blog as Jon sets up his TV tray next to me in the corner of the bedroom. Jon eventually found work on the road after a year and a half dry spell. With no money, times were desperate until he found a fellow traveler, now friend, who also lives with his family on the road. A gracious man who offered to mentor Jon from the back of his camper in the art of warehouse software development. Our friendship has now morphed into being more like relatives. That's how it is on the road. Your crazy traveling friends become your crazy traveling family. After living literally next door to each other one can only hide personality quirks for so long. Or maybe that is just me with the quirks?

> *Now our life fits into 200 square feet of living space in this motorhome and a 5x7 storage unit.*

With the Internet the only requirement for his work, Jon clicks away in a T-shirt and shorts. Interesting how productive one can be when out of the sterile environment of a cubby or basement. I work on editing my latest YouTube show as I step out to share my life with the world. A life I am finally happy with living where we are not just surviving, but thriving.

The motorhome feels cozy. It's a space that has brought loving things into our lives, from beautiful places to accepting people. A space where busyness has been removed and in its place we have practiced connection. I have permission to find myself, to spend time with my husband, and to know the passions and struggles of my children. I was unable to find this depth in my old life.

Today, I will rub elbows with my kids quite literally as we pass through the hallway we call a kitchen. I will talk to them as I make brunch, be asked to look at their newest interests, and laugh at their latest funny video find. Traveling friends will soon cram into empty spaces on the floor and couch as they pass around the popcorn and play another round of *Clue*. There is nothing better than listening to the kids' laughter pulse through the cardboard walls as they chatter until the moon gleams its light.

Later in the week we will find a hiking trail to breathe in the gift of nature. Hiking has become a family activity that requires little equipment and provides an array of adventure. It spreads us out and gives us an opportunity to talk one-on-one with each kid as we walk. It has been an activity we continue even as they morph into their teen years — a time when society has warned us we will be at odds with each other. We don't think that has to happen to us.

I never knew we could be more content with so much less stuff and less space. Our ancestors may have lived with less stuff and in one-room homes from necessity, but today we are choosing this life every day because it allows us to focus on each other. Sure there are moments where I feel like I might explode from the intensity of sound and proximity. Yes, there are times I fire up the van and squeal away to a coffee shop to just hear my own thoughts! Yet, I now feel such depth of joy and connection in my life.

In letting go of the busyness of schedule and stuff, my arms are now free to embrace today. And so I embrace the essence of today — the people with whom I share this adventure of life in a rolling cardboard box.

~Jema Anderson

62

Mental Selfie

*Slow down and enjoy life. It's not only the scenery you
miss by going too fast — you also miss the sense of
where you are going and why.*
~Eddie Cantor

I picked up my phone to take a picture of the beautiful scenery we were passing through while the tour guide spoke. We were heading to our hotel where we would be spending the night before traveling to the next country on our tour.

I swiped my iPhone lock screen to get to my camera and got a message that was one of my worst nightmares during a vacation: "Cannot take photo: There is not enough available storage to take a photo. You can manage your storage in Settings." I panicked and quickly went to my camera roll to see what pictures I could delete. No candidates. I needed to keep all 1,456 of the photos I already had. So I tried the next best thing: to delete some apps: Yelp — need it! Facebook — nope! Need to stay in touch with friends and family and the same thing for Instagram and Twitter and GroupMe and Viber and Whatsapp.

My dread turned into anger — anger at myself for not remembering to transfer my photos the night before; anger at Apple for having apps that I couldn't delete that took up valuable space that I needed at this moment; and anger at technology in general for failing me when I really needed its cooperation.

Then, I accepted defeat. I would just have to ask my newly made friends in the tour group to share their photos with me.

In the minutes that I spent working through my storage issue, I missed many breathtaking views that the tour guide was pointing out. I would probably never get to see them again, and wasn't I on this trip to see them? I thought back to the conversation I had with my brother a couple months before planning this trip.

I had wanted to visit Switzerland, Italy, France and many other European countries for as long as I could remember. As I started to book the trip, my brother said, "What is the point of actually going there? You're spending pretty much all of your savings to buy tickets, then you'll have to sit on the long flight there and then once you reach your destination you'll have to deal with countless more obstacles and crowds in order to experience these countries for just a few hours or if you're lucky maybe for a day. Instead you can sit here in the comfort of your own home and look at thousands of pictures and videos of Switzerland and all the other countries you want to visit and much more. You will probably also be able to get a much better and complete view of it than if you were to actually visit it." I knew what my brother was saying was all just crazy talk! How could photos and videos compare to actually going to Switzerland and experiencing it?

I was forced to take mental pictures and to experience Switzerland without a camera coming between us.

But wasn't that exactly what I was planning on doing? I was planning on looking at Switzerland through a screen in order to take pictures and that is exactly what I had been doing since the beginning of this tour. Sure I got to see some things when I gave myself a chance to look up every once in a while between taking pictures, but I was robbing myself of the experience that I had been looking forward to for so long. So while at first I was annoyed at myself and heartbroken that I wouldn't have pictures of my own, it was actually a blessing in disguise. I was forced to take mental pictures and to experience Switzerland without a camera coming between us. Throughout the last couple days of the tour, I reminded myself of this and forced myself to experience the other countries the way that I had with Switzerland.

Now, a year later, as I continue to share my travel experiences with my friends, I no longer use countless pictures that they could see on Google to tell my story. Instead I use my memory and my unique experiences to create an image in their minds that no picture could ever match, because this experience was mine: the mental pictures that I took, the beautiful and sometimes horrible smells, the taste of different cuisines, and the first time I ever touched a snowflake. These were all things that I touched and felt without a screen getting in the way.

Is my first instinct still to reach for my phone to take a picture? Yes! But over time I have trained myself to limit it to a couple of photos rather than 1,456.

~Shehfina Mamdani

Finding Mount Fuji

I like to walk about among the beautiful things that
adorn the world; but private wealth I should decline, or
any sort of personal possessions, because they would
take away my liberty.
~George Santayana

"Where's the rest of it?" I peered in the doorway of what was to be our home for the next twelve months, convinced that the nineteen-hour flight to Japan had adversely affected my vision. There was no way our apartment could be this small.

"This is all of it," my husband Pete responded.

"The rental agent said our apartment was a mansion — this place can't be more than three hundred square feet."

"It's a mansion by Japanese standards," Pete reminded me.

"It's a mansion if you're a Polly Pocket doll," I retorted.

I surveyed my surroundings. Ever since Pete and I were notified that his company was transferring us overseas, I had envisioned what life immersed in the Japanese culture would look like. Nothing I saw before me came close to what I had anticipated. With dismay I realized that the tiny space I was standing in was both the family room and the bedroom — the setup of the futon would determine what role the room played. Stepping forward a few feet, I slid the rice-paper door that divided our sleeping/living area from the kitchen/dining area.

If I wanted to cook, it would be in a contraption that looked like an Easy-Bake Oven — if I figured out how to use the controls, which were all labeled in kanji. The dorm room-sized refrigerator meant daily trips to the grocery store. And while the kitchen was stocked with dishes and cookware, there was no garbage disposal or dishwasher; apparently KP duty was also on my list of expatriate chores. Then there was the bathroom — not much larger than an airplane lavatory, yet somehow the washer/dryer was crammed in there next to a tiny bathtub and single sink. The heated toilet seat, while novel, was hardly a consolation. I wanted my soaking tub, massage jets, and steam shower.

"This place is claustrophobic," I told Pete.

"Maybe it'll look better in the morning after we've gotten some sleep," he answered.

"Maybe it'll look better in twelve months — when we're moving back to the U.S.," I replied.

The apartment didn't look any better, or bigger, in the morning. If anything, daylight illuminated how cramped and unsophisticated our quarters really were. A bulky contraption haphazardly attached to the wall functioned as both heater and air-conditioner. We had a television, but no access to American programming. We had a bike for transportation, but no car. And as for clothes — I now understood why we were told to bring only one suitcase each. We would be sharing a closet that was one-fourth the size of the space we had at home.

For the next several weeks, I hid in our apartment and moped. I came to Japan picturing sprawling landscapes, lush cherry blossom trees, glamorous ladies wearing kimonos, and awe-inspiring shrines. I expected dinners at expensive Japanese restaurants, overnight weekends in Tokyo, invitations to tea ceremonies, and abundant opportunities to be the token "American friend" to my Japanese neighbors. Instead, I was stuck, alone, in a studio-sized apartment overlooking an active construction site and congested city street. The homeless lady who spent her days sitting on the bench outside our doorway was a constant reminder of how displaced I felt. I missed my spacious house, my friends at the gym, my lively social life, and my stocked freezer. I craved Diet Pepsi, peanut butter, and candy corn. I wanted my car, my TV shows, and my cleaning lady.

And then one afternoon, bored and depressed, I saw it — Mount Fuji — right outside our kitchen window and, until now, hidden by the summer smog which had finally lifted. I was awestruck and incredulous that we had been living within eyesight of this iconic and majestic landmark yet hadn't seen it until today. I suddenly realized how insignificant everything I missed from the U.S. really was compared to the once-in-a-lifetime opportunity I had before me. I had been letting all I longed for back in America cloud my experience here in Japan. I needed to stop dwelling on what I had left in the U.S. and start focusing on what I could find in Japan.

Finally inspired by Mount Fuji, I began to explore our little town of Tokorozawa. The grocery store, the convenience store, and the post office were all easily accessible on my one-speed-bike-with-a-basket — who needed a car? Emboldened, I ventured farther from home, taking the train to Harajuku, Roppongi, and Tokyo. And while I loved the bustle and vibe of those progressive and energetic cities, I realized that I was comforted upon returning to what was becoming my welcome-home place — my small, cozy apartment that was simple, clutter-free, and "home."

When our assignment in Japan ended, I re-entered the U.S. with a new appreciation for all the conveniences life in America offered but very little desire to take advantage of them.

I learned to appreciate the simplicity of my lifestyle in Japan. It was liberating not to sort through an overstuffed closet deciding what to wear; I fell into a predictable rotation of jeans, sweaters, shorts, and tops. Surprisingly, I didn't feel the urge to update my wardrobe — what I had on hand was good enough. I began to look forward to my daily trips to the grocery store. Unable to fall back on frozen food or pre-packaged meals, I challenged my culinary skills and exercised my creativity in the kitchen — something I found I actually enjoyed.

I resumed journaling and writing letters to friends and family and discovered a renewed appreciation for something as simple as a reply sent via airmail. And, when one of my afternoon excursions led me to a vending machine that dispensed Diet Pepsi, I was thrilled by this small luxury. I realized that I didn't need or even care about all the luxuries afforded to me back home. The size of my house, the labels on my wardrobe, inclusion in a social scene — what did that really matter? What did that prove about my worth? Absolutely nothing. And that knowledge was absolutely freeing.

When our assignment in Japan ended, I re-entered the U.S. with a new appreciation for all the conveniences life in America offered but very little desire to take advantage of them. I was overwhelmed by the size of homes we were bidding on — why did I need all this space? And TV — how could anyone focus on one particular show with so many choices? Much of what we had left in storage, I donated to Goodwill — it no longer had a hold on me. And when we finally moved into our new home, the one item I held most dear was a print of Mount Fuji — artwork I hung in our foyer as a daily reminder of how much abundance can come from having less.

~Stacy Thibodeaux

64

Trading Houses

You don't have to be rich to travel well.
~Eugene Fodor

When I tell people that my husband and I are able to travel so much by trading houses with strangers, I usually get one of two reactions: "Wow! I want to try that!" or "Ew! You let people you don't know sleep in your bed?" House trading is not for everyone; it takes a certain adventurous spirit, flexibility, and a bit of faith in humanity, but we've found that taking that leap of faith has been well worth it, both in expanding our travel options and opening us to new experiences.

My husband retired early, and I work part-time as a freelance editor. This gives us lots of time and flexibility but not a lot of funds. And while we have happily chosen free time over money, we do love to travel, and travel is usually expensive. Still, we've managed to take a lot of affordable trips, and the best way we've found to keep the cost down is by house trading.

House trading is not the same as Airbnb or renting out a room in someone's home; house trading involves no exchange of money. We connect with people in cities we want to visit who are looking to visit our area — and then we trade! While there are businesses that facilitate house trading, such as Homeexchange.com, made popular by the 2006 film *The Holiday*, and HomeLink, which has been in operation since 1953, we've found all our trades through craigslist's "housing swap" category or through friends of friends.

There are, of course, commonsense precautions you should take before handing over your house keys (and sometimes car keys) to virtual strangers, but we've had more than fifteen successful trades so far. After the initial contact through craigslist (we post an ad both in our area and in the area we want to visit, and we also browse those areas to look at other people's ads), we exchange photos and e-mails with our potential trade partners. If both parties feel comfortable (a lot of it is just gut feelings for me), and we come up with dates that work for both, we'll move on to a phone call or two to work out the details, such as how we'll exchange keys.

House trading is not for everyone; it takes a certain adventurous spirit, flexibility, and a bit of faith in humanity.

We've found a whole range of trade partner styles — from the young couple who left the keys to their San Francisco apartment in their mailbox for us along with a note that said "Enjoy!" to the family who provided us with a three-ring binder full of information. I admit that I fall more into the "binder" category. Along with where to find things in the house, I include maps, tourist brochures, and menus from nearby restaurants. While it's fun to stumble onto new places on your own, it is even more fun to have an "insider" tip about the little taco place around the corner or the pop-up ice cream vendor who shows up at the park on weekend afternoons.

With no money involved, house traders feel more like guests in each other's homes. My husband and I are generally relaxed about people using our things, and we just assume our trade partners will treat our belongings as well as we'll treat theirs. Staying in someone else's home creates a certain intimacy. I always enjoy looking at our trade partners' artwork and décor, the books on their bookshelves, and the pictures on the fridge. By the end of our visit, I feel as if I know these former strangers pretty well. We've been lucky enough to find some trade partners to do multiple trades with, and they have truly become new friends. On our very first trade, our trade partner welcomed us with a bottle of wine and a cheese platter in the fridge We've continued that gracious tradition with our own "guests."

The best part of trading houses, besides the savings, is being able to experience a new city more like a resident than a tourist. Having a kitchen means we can do a lot of our own cooking, shopping at a local market for groceries. We often find a favorite coffee shop nearby, and it quickly becomes "ours" with repeat visits. We find that when we slow down and enjoy the new atmosphere, we begin to feel the unique rhythm of the city or town we're visiting. We are happy to spend a lazy morning on the patio reading the paper, not feeling that we have to rush to see the major attractions.

Yes, house trading did begin with our desire to travel on the cheap, but it's become so much more than just a way to save money. It's thrown us smack dab in the middle of the true sharing economy, reinforced our faith in the goodness of people, let us get glimpses of places we might never have explored otherwise, and confirmed our decision to choose a lifestyle that values time over money. We all learned to share by the time we were in kindergarten, right? It's not too late to rediscover that basic lesson on a whole new level.

~Marjorie Woodall

65

Trusting Serendipity

Don't be a tourist. Plan less. Go slowly. I traveled in
the most inefficient way possible and it took me exactly
where I wanted to go.
~Andrew Evans

"Ladies and gentlemen, we have just landed in Helsinki," said the flight attendant as our airplane rolled to the gate.

I looked at my boyfriend, Robin, who responded with a cheeky smile. He knew that I was nervous.

I was not nervous because of the trip. I was not nervous because we were about to spend a few days in Finland where I could not even pronounce the street names. I was nervous for a much darker, scarier reason.

I had not made any plans.

Over the years, I had developed and refined a routine that I used whenever I travelled to a new city. For weeks before the trip, I would obsessively read everything I could find on the Internet. What were the most important attractions? Which regional delicacies did I have to try? Which operator gave the best tour of the city? Whenever possible, I would order maps of the city from the destination's travel office. I would watch promotional videos of the city. Then, I would start making lists: a list of things that I absolutely needed to see; a list of "nice to see, but not need to see" places; and a list of foods and drinks I would taste.

Once I arrived in the city I had been wildly fantasizing about for weeks — or even months — I would start squeezing these lists into a schedule based on the weather and other factors. Go to Museum X on Monday morning and then eat at Restaurant Y that is in its vicinity, and so on and so forth. After all, my short time in a foreign city had to be optimized. There was no way I was going to leave it with regrets. That only made sense, right?

Robin thought otherwise and had suggested that we make absolutely no plans for our trip to Helsinki. In a moment of weakness, I had agreed.

So here we were, in the Finnish capital, with no plans, but armed with a map, which I had insisted on bringing but had not been allowed to open before our arrival. Compromises are an important part of a healthy relationship. A kind airport employee explained to us the bus connection to downtown Helsinki, and off we went on a public bus.

As we rode from the airport to the central train station and from the central train station to our host's apartment, I was glued to the bus window, taking in the atmosphere of the Scandinavian metropolis. I tried to look at some street names but the bus drove by too fast, and anyway they contained far too many vowels for me to remember, let alone pronounce them correctly.

The sun had set by the time we got off the bus in a residential area. We found our apartment relatively easily and were greeted by our host, Taras. Taras was a twenty-something Ukrainian expat with a friendly smile and warm brown eyes. He showed us the room we would be staying in and invited us to have tea with him in his small but cozy kitchen.

Robin, Taras and I spent the rest of the evening chatting in the kitchen. I opened my map of Helsinki, spread it on the table and eagerly asked Taras if he had any recommendations for our stay. This obviously did not count as planning, since we were already in Helsinki. Taras gladly gave us tips, marking our maps with dots and crosses. He looked like he had already done this with dozens of other guests but did not seem to mind.

I slowly sipped my tea while he told us where to find a traditional sauna and where we could get the best view of the city. I automatically started constructing mini-itineraries for the next few days in my head. When Robin and I excused ourselves and went to sleep, I carefully took our precious annotated map and put it in my purse for the next day. I fell asleep dreaming of saunas and elks.

The next morning, Robin and I had breakfast and headed out towards the city center. Our first stop: a café with one of the best views of the city. Unfortunately, the café was closed. I was disappointed but Robin said we could certainly get nice views of the city elsewhere. We headed east on foot. The next target on my list was *Helsingin tuomio-kirkko*, Helsinki's famous white cathedral and perhaps its most well-known landmark. A must for our photo album.

> *Why was I so set on cramming our vacation time with commitments until it did not feel like a vacation anymore?*

Suddenly, Robin started pulling me to the left, when we were supposed to go right.

"Let's check out that building; it looks cool!"

He was pointing at a tall, funny-looking wooden building. I quickly checked the map.

"Taras didn't mention anything there."

"Come on, what's the rush?"

I could not answer that question. I was on vacation, but somehow still felt like the slave of my precisely scheduled itinerary.

"Fine."

We ventured into a large square that was bustling with busy-looking people in suits and approached the mysterious construction. It was a massive and asymmetrical wooden cylinder, which looked swollen in the middle. Its facade was made of smooth, wooden planks.

We entered the building and found ourselves in a small lobby. Some pamphlets indicated that we were in *Kampin kappeli*, the Chapel of Silence. Intrigued, we entered the main room of the chapel.

It was empty and breathtaking. The ceiling was as high as the building and the walls were made of the same beautiful curved wood as the exterior of the chapel. The furnishings were minimal: a dozen pews and a plain pulpit. The most striking feature in the chapel was the complete absence of noise: the buzz of the city, the cacophony of traffic and the chatter of pedestrians were all completely blocked by the soundproof walls.

We sat on the floor for a while, in awe. I grabbed Robin's hand and smiled at him.

We left the chapel a few minutes later, and I felt a wave of pure excitement overcome me, as if our trip was starting anew.

During our quiet meditation, I thought of how we had stumbled upon this wonderful chapel and realized that there would be plenty of other amazing surprises awaiting us around every corner. Why was I so set on cramming our vacation time with commitments until it did not feel like a vacation anymore? My pet phobia, the fear of missing out, suddenly seemed less scary than the prospect of spending my vacation marching from one popular attraction to another like a zombie. Fewer plans meant more room for pleasant discoveries.

I considered ripping my beloved annotated map as a symbol of my newfound sense of adventure, but quickly decided that it was not necessary and that it could still come in useful if we got lost or kidnapped.

We spent the next few days wandering through the city. We ate cinnamon rolls, we got lost, we explored an abandoned fortress on an island, we biked through the city, and we were attacked by seagulls. And, most importantly, we had fun.

~Terri Kafyeke

Birthday Blast

*Teaching kids to count is fine, but teaching them
what counts is best.*
~Bob Talber

"I want a superhero birthday party," my nephew Eli
announced one evening when I was at my sister's house.
We were all aware that his tenth birthday was approaching. He had been reminding us daily, and his parents
planned to invite a few of his friends from school and serve pizza,
with some cake and ice cream for dessert.

"Okay," replied my sister. "What exactly is a superhero birthday
party?"

"I want Batman to come to the party," Eli explained enthusiastically.
"And The Flash, Spiderman and Wolverine. I want all the kids from my
class to come and I want chicken tenders with ranch dipping sauce to
eat. Oh, and chocolate cake with chocolate marshmallow ice cream."

"That seems like a lot," my brother-in-law said.

Eli smiled. "C'mon, you guys, I want a good party like everybody
else." He carried his empty plate and cup to the sink and then headed
to his bedroom to finish his homework.

"What's that supposed to mean?" asked my sister, rolling her eyes.
"Where did these extravagant ideas come from?"

"Unfortunately, he gets those ideas from his friends," I said. My
sister and brother-in-law both worked weekends, so I was the one
who took Eli to his friends' birthday parties.

One boy had a party with three of those giant inflatable bouncy houses and a magician that walked around on stilts.

Another boy had a drone party for his birthday. His parents hired guys to come and help the kids fly actual drones around the backyard obstacle course. Even I thought it was cool.

A girl in Eli's class had a princess party. Her parents put up a huge tent behind the house, decorated it with balloons and twinkle lights and had teenage girls dressed in gowns and tiaras, carrying scepters, who introduced themselves as Princess Anna and Princess Elsa.

"Wow," replied my brother-in-law, as he got up to pour himself another mug of decaf. "When I was a kid, one of my friends from school had a piñata at his party and we talked about it for months afterward."

"I remember my favorite birthday party," said my sister. "It was when my cousins came over for pizza and we had a sleepover."

"My best birthday was when my dad took me camping for a weekend," I said.

"Birthdays are supposed to be fun," complained my sister. "It seems like these social extravaganzas are turning into competitions."

Then I had an idea.

I shared it with my sister and brother-in-law; they agreed whole-heartedly. Then I told my nephew.

"Going camping for my birthday?" A horrified look came over Eli's face. "That doesn't sound like any birthday party I've ever been to."

"That's the idea," I told him.

Three weeks later, on the evening of his tenth birthday, Eli and I were sitting on the shore of Hidden Lake. The setting sun was turning the sky over the surrounding forest pinkish-orange. The breeze was lightly rippling the water.

I had taken a few days off from work and, though Eli complained the whole time that this wasn't the birthday party he wanted, I had enthusiastically insisted we pack the car and head out on a camping trip. This was going to be fun! Eli did not share my enthusiasm.

However, his mood improved after we started hiking and we found the trail to the lake blocked by a fallen tree. We had to climb over it; Eli commented it was just like the cyborg army guys in his video game.

We came to a wide, shallow stream that intersected the trail and, not wanting to get our shoes wet, we decided to attempt to cross it by using the steppingstones. Unfortunately, the mossy stones were slicker than I expected; I slipped, fell to my knees in the water and soaked my pants. For the first time since the trip began Eli and I shared a laugh.

When we reached Hidden Lake the afternoon sun was high in the clear blue sky, so we pitched our tent in a shady clearing in the pine trees, I changed into dry pants, and we spent the rest of the afternoon fishing.

Now, surrounded by the stillness of approaching twilight, Eli was anticipating starting his first campfire to cook our dinner. We hadn't actually caught any fish, just lots of snags, but luckily my practical-thinking sister had packed some hot dogs in a small cooler we had brought along.

> *"It seems like these social extravaganzas are turning into competitions."*

"Look." Eli pointed. "Those ducks are all in a line."

A procession of mallard ducks, a mother and six ducklings, paddled in the water in front of us; their wake split the calm surface into an ever-widening V-shape.

"Yeah," I replied. "They're having a parade for your birthday."

Eli laughed and waved at the passing ducks.

We were quiet for a while more; then Eli said, "This is an awesome birthday, Uncle David."

"There's no inflatable bouncy house," I said. "There are no drones. There are no superheroes. We don't even have any chocolate marshmallow ice cream. Are you really sure it's awesome?"

"Yep, I'm sure." He nodded.

A slight melancholy tugged at me. I knew that in a few years my nephew would be grown and celebrating his birthdays in his own way; I might not even be involved in the festivities, other than to send a card or call him on the phone. I felt satisfied that at least for this one birthday, I was able to make it something meaningful for him.

I guess what my father had taught me many years ago was still true — you don't need entertainment, a fancy cake or even a piñata to make a birthday memorable. You just need to share it with someone special.

~David Hull

Letting Go and Moving On

It always seems impossible until it's done.
~Nelson Mandela

ach time I paced around my sizable home and realized how much work was ahead of me, I became overwhelmed. My heart would race, my head would hurt and I didn't know where to begin—and so I didn't. It had been just a few weeks since my youngest child left home to join the Air Force and in only three more weeks I was to make a significant move. Before that could happen, I had to dispose of at least half of my household goods.

After twenty years of single-parenting three children and equal time as a hard working pastor, I was about to embark on a new chapter in my life. The one thing I was determined to get was very simple: a good rest. It was time to simplify my life and begin anew with ample time for me to take care of me. I had arranged to take a sabbatical leave of one year, which I would spend at a spiritual retreat center in another state. I would live in a tiny cottage on the grounds and work a small number of hours to assist the retreat center in their work. My plan was to refocus and prepare for the next phase of my life—one that I hoped would still be full of meaningful purpose but at a slower pace.

Before I could accomplish that move I still had to deal with all that stuff. In the three weeks that remained, I had to be out of town for one. It was crunch time! There was no time to have a sale, so I began to give things away, even things I was reluctant to part with. Friends generously helped me and encouraged me when I found it difficult to wade through yet another closet. Day by day, it became easier to part with possessions while focusing on what I felt was most important to keep. Because I lived on a very busy street, I could easily put items on the curb and they were gone within an hour. Often a person would check with me as I carried more items out to be sure I wanted to give such good items away. As I saw their delight, I began to take vicarious joy in their discovery of a new treasure.

The time was rapidly slipping by and on one particularly hot day, I faced the challenge of giving away several items of furniture that I truly loved but knew I must part with. My family room was full of wonderful, if somewhat battered, mid-century furniture: a curving three-section sofa, blond wood end tables, a dining room table and chairs, and a favorite contour recliner. I knew someone would love them as much as I did and so we began to move them to the curb. A car with three twenty-somethings pulled into the driveway, and the friends began to talk about who would get which pieces. "Are you sure you don't want any money for this?"

I continued to give away possessions until I only owned what would be useful in my 700-square-foot cottage.

"Yes." I was sure. This was starting to be fun.

As I moved the dining room set to the driveway, an older woman stopped by. She was so elated that she positively bubbled over. "I have dreamed of having a set like this since I was very young." She thanked me over and over. She promised to return quickly with her husband and their pickup truck. As I waited for them to return, I had a flash of what felt like divine inspiration as I thought about this tall, beautiful woman who had so touched me with her sweet gratitude. When she returned, we loaded the furniture on the truck and I asked her to wait for a moment. "I have something for you." As I carried the special gift to her and put it in her arms, tears began to flow down her cheeks.

"No, you can't mean it!" she said. It was a long, like-new fake fur coat that I'd had for years—one that had never flattered me but I had loved nonetheless. She ran her hand over the soft coat and slipped it on over her stately figure. She was stunning! We both wept as she proclaimed over and over, "You're such a blessing, such a blessing."

In that moment, I knew that my real "letting go" had truly begun. My one-year sabbatical turned into a three-year stay in a beautiful place that helped to restore my depleted self in every way. Although I still moved far too many things in my initial move, I continued to give away possessions until I only owned what would be useful in my 700-square-foot cottage. I kept the things I most loved and became very creative with how I used them. Several years later, I still live fairly simply and far more thoughtfully. Do I have a use for it and a place for it? And do I really love it, or would someone else love it even more?

~Kimberly Ross

68

Fire Drills

You know you have reached perfection of design not
when you have nothing more to add, but when you
have nothing more to take away.
~Antoine de Saint-Exupéry

"What are we going to do with all this stuff?" I asked my husband while I sniffled and wiped away tears.

Mark came up with a solution, "Why don't we have a fire drill?"

I gave him a blank stare and then it came to me, "Of course, let's do it!"

We had moved thirty-two times in thirty-five years, so we were accustomed to the moving part, but we weren't so good at getting rid of stuff. Our "baggage" kept following us around the world. This was our last international move and we were only taking six suitcases with us to Ecuador. After the garage sale, we still had books, photo albums, the boys' baby things, all their schoolwork and awards, dishes, and clothes. The boxes filled the entire living room and we had exactly one week before we had to vacate our home so the new owners could move in.

Mark suggested that we set the kitchen timer for ten-minute "fire drills" and take everything of importance and place it on the dining room table.

I actually felt like I was in a race for my life and carefully scoped out the living room and its contents; I already knew what box I would salvage first.

"Ready, set, go!" Mark shouted. I could hear the timer ticking in the background as I ran to the baby and family photo albums first. There were four heavy boxes and I had to scoot them across the living room into the dining room. Whatever I placed on the table would eventually have to fit into six suitcases, so I had to be selective.

I heard the timer go off just as I dragged the last box into the dining room. As I glanced at the cardboard boxes, I realized there was already too much stuff and we had just started. I picked up our younger son's baby album and opened it to the first page. Tears trickled down my cheeks and then an envelope dropped out of the album. Mark grabbed it up off the floor and opened its contents. "What's this?" he asked in pure disbelief.

We had pared thirty-five years down to six suitcases.

"That's Jon's umbilical cord clamp," I whimpered, and snatched it from his hand. "It's coming with me and that's final."

I had spent untold hours on each album. How was I ever going to let go of all those memories and the boxes of photos that had followed us around for thirty-five years? There was absolutely no way I could part with those photos and the family heritage album that took me a year to complete. I lingered on each page of the boys' albums — recalling all their "firsts": first smile, first tooth, first words, and the first day of school. Jeremy — our older son — didn't want his picture taken the first day of kindergarten, but after some coaxing he proudly posed with his Ninja Turtles lunchbox by the juniper trees in the front yard. I could almost smell the peanut butter and jelly sandwich with the crust cut off — just the way he liked it!

While I held on tightly to Jon's umbilical cord clamp, Mark suggested an alternative. "Let's put all the albums in these sealable blue tubs and give them to the boys for safekeeping."

What a great idea, I thought. Why didn't I think of that?

That was round one of the fire drills and it took approximately six more to whittle the living room down to three medium-sized boxes — none of which was going in our suitcases, but to the boys. The boxes now contained family heirlooms, including Mark's grandfather's mandolin from Sicily. We labeled each bin with all of its contents on the side and on the top of the lid, so if I ever felt like I absolutely needed something it would be easy to locate.

The other boxes labeled "Goodwill" and "incinerator" were easy to take care of and we did that the following day. Our home was empty except for six suitcases, which mostly contained clothes. The blue tubs were stacked by the front door to be distributed to our sons — ages twenty-three and twenty-eight. Since our younger son was getting married, my future daughter-in-law, Kim, had already requested Jon's baby albums and I lovingly handed them over to her.

At age fifty-five, we had done something we never thought was possible. The stuff that had been following us around was finally gone. We had pared thirty-five years down to six suitcases.

It's been five years since we "cleaned" house and gave up or gave away all of our worldly possessions. We've never looked back. We've spared our children the trauma of having to go through all of our stuff when we pass away. And now that there's just the two of us in our small two-bedroom, two-bath sparsely furnished condo, we have a new lease on life. Letting go of our possessions gave us the freedom to do the things we've always wanted to do — like traveling the world, learning new languages, and teaching ESL (English as a Second Language). There's nothing tying us down or holding us back. We've never been happier. And we don't need to have any more "fire drills."

~Connie K. Pombo

69

A Heart Full of Memories

I am not the same, having seen the moon shine on
the other side of the world.
~Mary Anne Radmacher

"There is no way I can live out of a suitcase!" I thought as we packed up our home in Venice, Italy. At fourteen years old, I couldn't imagine leaving my friends, school, and all my "stuff" behind to travel the world full-time with my family.

At the time, we were all going in different directions — my sister and I were stressed and focused on school and were rarely home and my parents were focused on work. I was focused on my friends, the latest gadget, and the current fashions — always wanting to buy new clothes that "fit in." Between doing my homework, texting, seeing my friends, and going to my activities, I rarely had time to spend with my family. It felt like we never saw each other even though we lived under the same roof.

That was when my mom had the idea of dropping everything to travel the world and reconnect as a family. One day she sat us down at the kitchen table and proposed the idea, which at the time seemed so crazy. Although I absolutely loved the idea of traveling the world freely, I couldn't imagine leaving my life behind. After several months of planning, packing, and saying goodbye to our old lives, off we went to explore the world with no end date in sight!

That was over two years, thirty-eight countries, and four continents ago! During that time, we have realized how little we really need to be happy. We have learned how the most important moments in life aren't when we get new gifts or things, but when we live happy moments with our family and friends. We know now that experiences are the best treasures.

As we travel, we barely carry anything with us except the essential things like clothes, a laptop, notebooks, and toiletries. We each carry a backpack and all five of us share two suitcases for clothes. After buying new trinkets or new clothes, we give some of our old outfits away to people in need and it makes us so happy to be able to give back wherever we can.

The small amount of baggage we have makes it easy to travel from country to country on planes, trains, buses, ferries, tuk tuks, etc. By traveling so light, we get to do more with less. We are free to explore countries easily and move around as much as we like. Many times we even make spontaneous travel plans and it is so easy to pack up our stuff and go!

At the beginning, it was difficult for us to get used to never having a closet, constantly changing hotel rooms, and never fully unpacking before we were back on the road. But

> *I can honestly say that travel is the best way for a family to become close again, since it takes away all the distractions and reminds us of what is really important.*

over time we have learned to appreciate the value of having less — the freedom to live for experiences and the joy of traveling "light" in mind, body, and spirit.

Meeting new people and getting to know their cultures has been the best part of traveling for me. Instead of focusing on things, we love to focus on the people and connect with them. Wherever we go, we try to make as many friends as we can and feel like we have "family" in countries all over the world!

Many of the wonderful new friends we have made on our journey have opened our eyes to how lucky we are. We have met families in many parts of the world who live in small homes with no running water or on the streets escaping war and violence, yet they always have huge smiles and are willing to share with us.

Without all the distractions that we used to have, we have become connected as a family! I can honestly say that travel is the best way for a family to become close again, since it takes away all the distractions and reminds us of what is really important. We now know that experiences and memories are the most valuable things in life and that they can only be acquired when we let go of our need for possessions and focus on what really matters in life — enjoying our lives each day with the people we love.

So I would now say to my fourteen-year-old self, "I will gladly give up a home full of stuff to live out of a suitcase with a heart full of memories!"

~Kaitlin Murray, age 17

70

Release the Stuff, Unleash the Magic

*All our dreams can come true — if we have the
courage to pursue them.*
~Walt Disney

"How would you feel about selling most of our stuff, packing up the Prius and hitting the road on a cross-country adventure?" We were sitting in our rented duplex in Richmond, Virginia, surrounded by books, furniture, antiques and paintings. It felt heavy, suffocating even.

We had just returned from a three-week adventure in Tunisia and France, my husband's birthplace and childhood home, respectively. Living life from two suitcases each had been surprisingly easy, not to mention freeing. About every three days we were someplace new, experiencing everything from budget living to five-star luxury. One night, while staying with family members whose home had no heat, we huddled underneath seven layers of blankets to keep warm. Having just put on our winter hats to sleep in for the first time, our eyes met in the dark and we both broke into huge grins. "This is fantastic!" we exclaimed. While some travelers might have yearned to be back at the five-star resort, we loved all the diverse experiences. The food, the people, and the places were all new and exciting adventures.

Now we were back in the comfort of our own home, surrounded

by all our stuff, and feeling… stuck.

My first book had just been published and most of my days were spent at home writing and working out how to market the book effectively to its target audience. I was buried under marketing materials, formulas for success and books that claimed to teach me everything I needed to know. But what I really yearned for was to connect with people in person. To have face-to-face conversations rather than deciphering emotions behind e-mails and exhausting myself keeping up with social media's many likes, shares and comments.

> *Life feels like freedom now. Not stuck under stuff and feeling overwhelmed.*

That's when the idea came to me. Thanks to this technology I could technically work from anywhere. And our recent trip proved living out of a few suitcases was not only possible, it was fun.

"Yes!" It took my husband a split second to answer in the affirmative.

And so the challenge of living with less "stuff" began.

The decision took a split second but letting go of our possessions and getting our affairs in order took four months.

We put in our notice to leave our rented home, had yard sales, listed items on craigslist, consigned clothing and donated to local charities. With the release of each piece we were relieved as greater peace of mind washed over us. I was feeling lighter, freer, and more excited at the possibilities that opened up with each passing day.

We arranged to have our mail forwarded and changed as many accounts as we could to online statements. We rented a small storage unit for the few things that we wanted to keep.

With each item, we asked ourselves: Do we love it? Do we use it? If the answer was no to both it was thrown out or sent to a new home.

One day I was looking through a pile of business cards. I came across a person I had met at a conference for aspiring book authors. She was a lovely woman who I wished I had kept in touch with. I probably hadn't because her card got lost in the pile of cards I had stored. There was no website or e-mail address, just a phone number. I felt weird calling, wondering what I could say and if she would remember me. So, I said out loud in the empty room, "If I'm meant to meet this woman again, may you bring her to cross my path once again." Speaking to God, angels, the universe, or whatever higher power handled that kind of stuff, I hoped they would hear me.

Then I let go of the card and forgot all about it.

I began booking events for my book launch, and friends and family offered their homes for us to stay for short periods when we were in town. It seemed the more we released the more magic happened. Out of the blue, a woman I went to grade school with had seen my book come up as recommended reading on her Amazon list and contacted me. She was living in Illinois with her husband and five kids and invited us to stay and even got me local events and my book featured in a local book club!

In April 2014, we set off, our Prius packed, Pittsburgh-bound for the night as we made our way to my hometown in Michigan. As we drove out of Virginia, my husband and I looked at each other in awe. We did it! We really did it!

A few hours later we booked a last-minute hotel through an app on my phone. Later that night, we arrived in the wet and windy city. We went to the front desk to check in only to discover they had no record of our reservation.

I started to freak out inside. Had we made a huge mistake? Should we have just stayed safe, at home with all our stuff?

Seeing the look of terror in my eyes, or just sensing my fear, the receptionist said kindly. "Don't worry, it all works out in the end." Then he repeated it. Twice. It all works out in the end. Message received, angels.

And it did work out. Only ten minutes later we were entering our room, which turned out to be a two-bedroom suite with full kitchen, sitting and dining room, along with a wrap-around balcony. Bliss.

We dubbed our adventure the JOYride and met so many amazing people along the way. We cooked together, ate out together, explored cities and connected with heart-to-heart conversations. Many of the people we met we now consider family.

So many magical moments occurred, including reconnecting with the woman whose card I threw away. She happened to be speaking after me at one of the events! Our books had only been thoughts in our heads when we first met and now we reconnected as authors. That higher power had heard me after all.

What initially began as a book tour has now become a new way of life. Instead of staying with friends and family, we house-sit across the country, and continue to connect with new people and enjoy pet-sitting and exploring new cities.

Releasing stuff wasn't always easy, but it was worth it. When we came back through Richmond a year later, we even released more from our storage unit, knowing we were happy to live with less and share the joy of some of those items with others.

Life feels like freedom now. Not stuck under stuff and feeling overwhelmed. Now our lives are filled with more joy and magic than we ever could have imagined.

Here's my mantra: Release the stuff, unleash the magic.

~Aimee DuFresne

Chapter
8

the joy of less

Count Your Blessings

71

Someone Else's Blessing

Help one another; there's no time like the present and
no present like the time.
~James Durst

I clenched the phone in my hand, blew out a deep breath, and muttered, "Okay Lord, here goes nothing."

My friend answered on the first ring. I closed my eyes and said, "Hi, it's Jeanie. I need your advice."

"Sure," she answered cheerfully. "What's up?"

"What should I do if a good friend offers to help me with something, but I'm too embarrassed to accept?"

My friend thought for a moment. "Is it someone you trust?"

"Definitely," I replied.

"And this person has the skills to help you?"

"Yes," I said, "But I'd be mortified if she saw how bad my problem is."

My friend poured out her gentle wisdom. "Jeanie, if a trusted friend wants to help you, accept it graciously."

"Is that really how you feel?" I asked.

"Absolutely," she said. "Don't let pride stand in your way."

I swallowed hard and said, "In that case, I'm coming over to help you get organized."

There was a long silence before my friend finally said, "That was an unfair set-up."

"True," I agreed, "but you wouldn't have let me in otherwise. I'm hopping in the car now. See you in a few minutes."

When I arrived, empty boxes in hand, she opened the door and said, "How many times have I told you I don't have friends over because of this mess? It's embarrassing."

I glanced at her gleaming hardwood floor and set the boxes beside her pristine sofa, glad I'd left my hazmat suit in the car.

Every time I helped friends get organized I always asked my trademark question: "Are you holding on to someone else's blessing?"

Glancing at the tidy, sun-swept living room, I suspected this wouldn't be the case.

From what she'd described over the years, I'd come prepared for the worst. Maybe her hoard lurked in the hidden depths of her basement.

> *Every time I helped friends get organized I always asked my trademark question: "Are you holding on to someone else's blessing?"*

"Let's walk through your house and you can show me the problem areas," I suggested.

She gloomily pointed out a remodeling project in one room, a figurine-jammed display hutch, and an overly full bedroom. In her airy finished basement a few scattered items sat along one wall.

This is what worried her? What kept her friends locked out for years? I'd expected Mount Mess. This didn't even qualify as a foothill.

"Level with me. How bad is it?" she asked, worry clouding her beautiful eyes.

"Your biggest problem is thinking you have a horrible mess. You don't. You have some things out of order. Nothing major. Definitely no hoard."

Her shoulders sagged in relief. "So this is fixable?"

I bit back a laugh, picturing the household disaster areas I regularly helped organize. "Piece of cake," I said. "Look around and ask yourself, 'Am I holding on to someone else's blessing?'"

Her eyes widened as she got it.

I gestured to the items against the wall. "You can store those things in an armoire."

But she shook her head, eyes gleaming. "I'm not holding on to someone else's blessing. That can all go to Goodwill."

She hurried upstairs, grabbed one of the boxes I'd brought, and disappeared into her bedroom. Her muffled voice came from inside the closet: "I'm not about to hold onto someone else's blessing."

I ducked the jet-propelled stream of clothing flying from her hangers into the donation box.

She emerged and went over her dresser like a magician performing slight-of-hand tricks. Presto chango! One second in the drawer, the next in a donation box. I marveled at her speed.

After the de-clutter, we tucked crisp sheets on the bed and polished the lovely vintage furniture. I scanned the lemon-scented bedtime oasis and said, "You did a great job."

But she grinned. "I'm not stopping yet. I refuse to hold onto someone else's blessing ever again."

She worked with feverish glee, banishing unused items from every area of her home. Everything from purses to exercise equipment to bedding disappeared into donation boxes. My friend dove into the organizing process with the same gusto I displayed when attacking a box of Godiva chocolates.

I'd never seen anyone part so willingly with so many useful goods.

"Um, are you sure you want to donate all that?" I asked.

"Absolutely." She smiled and gestured to the boxes. "Remember, I'm not holding onto someone else's blessing."

She resumed her gleefully ruthless purge, stopping only when every box overflowed. I asked, "Shall I call a thrift store to pick this up?"

She shook her head emphatically. "I'm not waiting. This is going now."

We shoved the boxes into her SUV and waved goodbye. She drove toward the Goodwill store and I headed home.

I pulled into my garage and squeezed past a pile of old lumber. Several bags of charcoal blocked my path and I wondered, "When did this place get so messy?"

I looked around the crowded area and turned "The Question" on myself. "Jeanie, are you holding on to someone else's blessing?"

I inspected our home with clutter-demolition in mind. What I saw was dust covered exercise equipment, packed closets and laundry hampers, and stuffed animals staring at me with accusing button eyes from their lonely exile to toy boxes.

My trademark question, "Are you holding on to someone else's blessing?" mocked me. Why did I have all this lying around when there were so many people in need?

I grabbed the phone and called my favorite secondhand shop.

A bubbly voice answered, "Good afternoon. New Life Thrift Store."

"Hi, I'd like to schedule a donation pick-up."

The jovial woman asked, "What will you be donating?"

I closed my eyes as "The Question" echoed in my brain.

"Blessings," I answered. "A whole bunch of blessings."

~Jeanie Jacobson

72

The Best Choice

We must be willing to let go of the life we've planned,
so as to have the life that is waiting for us.
~Joseph Campbell

I n May 2015 my family was featured on the cover of the finance section in *The Globe and Mail*, a national Canadian newspaper. The title of the article, "One family's downsizing strategy to live within their means," captured the essence of our family and our recent move to a much smaller home.

The article struck a chord with Canadian readers, as comments poured in commending our family and our choice to choose a smaller house in favour of financial security and peace of mind. I have never thought that our choice was radical, or our family's story was special. I've always thought that we were just a regular family doing the best that we could with what we had. For us, that meant living in a smaller home, forgoing luxury possessions, and paring down possessions like toys, furniture, and clothes.

Daniel and I married in May 2011 and spent our first year of marriage in a cozy 400-square-foot apartment. We had to minimize our possessions, take stock of all that we had, and constantly purge the unnecessary.

By our first wedding anniversary our family had grown to three. We welcomed our baby girl into the world and found a larger home to suit our needs. By the time we found out we were expecting our second child, we had moved once again, to an even bigger and better home.

Before our third wedding anniversary we realized that we were in over our heads. We were living a lifestyle that we could not maintain, in a home that we could not afford. At this point our credit card debt was mounting, and we knew that we needed to make a change.

I remember looking around at our large living room and shaking my head in disbelief. When we had moved into this home I'd felt as though I had somehow "made it." Having a home with multiple bedrooms and bathrooms made me feel like I'd matched my competition. I had become sucked into the western ideals of success and allowed my possessions to define me. In the end, my possessions only caused me anxiety and stress, as they became unmanageable both in expense and time.

> *In the end, my possessions only caused me anxiety and stress, as they became unmanageable both in expense and time.*

Daniel and I finally decided that we would take the leap. We would move out of our big house, the home that made us feel like we'd made it. We started our search for a smaller home, and found an above ground basement rental that suited our family's needs perfectly. We also really felt connected to our landlords, a Sri Lankan family who would live above us.

Within a few months we had moved into our new rental, and were ready to welcome our second daughter to our family. Georgia was born in May 2014, and we spent the summer making our new house a home for a family of four. We scrolled through Pinterest and dreamed up ways to frugally decorate. Our older daughter, Penny, even tried her hand at painting with Daniel. Penny and Georgia enjoyed the large back yard that we shared with our landlords and their two children.

Downsizing has allowed us to pay off all our debt. Our expenses are minimal, which allows us freedom to live within our means and not feel suffocated by a budget. When we have an emergency we don't need to pull out our credit cards, because our lifestyle has allowed us to save.

Some people still think that we are at a crossroads, just waiting until we can move on to something bigger and better. But, I don't see our home as a way station. Our home has been a place for us to heal from past mistakes, and to change our definition of what success truly means.

Yesterday, after a long day at work, I heard a "tap, tap" at my door. Penny and Georgia ran to see who it was.

"Hi Brianna, I had some leftovers from dinner, so I thought I'd bring some over to you."

My landlord Udaya passed me a big plate, heaping with mouth-watering Sri Lankan food.

It's moments like these that illustrate why downsizing to a basement apartment was the best choice for my family. Because of our choices, my daughters have experienced true community, and I, an unlikely friendship. Some nights when my husband is at work late and I begin to feel lonely, I just listen to the familiar sound of scraping chairs upstairs. Running water and dishes clanking together fuse with my own kitchen clean-up. It's a comfort, knowing my friend is only one floor up, washing her own dishes, wiping down her own family's kitchen table.

Did we get second best when we moved to a smaller house beneath the feet of another family? No, I would argue, we chose community, friendship, and peace of mind. We chose best. Now we've really made it.

~Brianna Bell

River Flows in You

*Life is available only in the present moment. If you
abandon the present moment you cannot live the
moments of your daily life deeply.*
~Thich Nhat Hanh

I looked around the tiny quaint chapel. It seemed like the perfect venue for the music school's spring recital. The high ceiling with a beautiful glass painting, the gigantic columns that arched gracefully, the dim lights, the magnificent altar and the grand piano that stood on the platform in front of the altar all added a touch of surreal ambience to the recital. It was as if the music to be played by the students was to be an offering to the gods.

I brimmed with excitement that was laced with a touch of pride, and yet as a mother only could, also experienced the butterflies that flitted in my daughter's tummy. She was to perform an exquisite composition called "River Flows in You" on the piano. How I loved that melodious piece. I eagerly looked forward to her performance.

I quickly updated the status on my iPhone: "At a church waiting for my talented kid to perform," switched it to the vibrate mode and looked through its camera to make sure we could get a good angle and a clear view. After all, I would have to post a video of the performance on Facebook for my family and friends.

I was glad we had arrived a few minutes early. At least we had the time to choose our seats and soak in the serene atmosphere. I voiced my opinion on the excellent location to my husband. He mumbled in agreement while he keenly looked into his phone to check the latest scores of the Augusta National tournament. He was a little miffed that I had chosen to leave home just as Tiger Woods was teeing off. If only he paid as much attention to me as he did to Tiger Woods' swing. "A birdie!" he reported. I shook my head. Some things never change. I went back to looking at my phone and checked the time. I had two minutes more until the recital so clicked on the Facebook icon. Fifteen notifications and seven updates? Already? My status update had already received twelve likes and three comments from around the world. Ooh, I felt loved and popular. I proceeded to the home page to check the news feed.

The first feed — a friend who had changed her profile picture. I was amazed. "Wow! Did she look hot! How could a mom of three young kids possibly find the time and energy to work out and stay in shape?" I felt lousy about myself.

The self-pity was quickly overcome with hope when I saw the next feed. Guess Facebook was reading my mind. Another friend had shared a blog post: "How to get rid of stubborn belly fat in ten days!" I would definitely have to read that when I got home.

Next post — 215 pictures of a friend vacationing in Bali. I was awestruck. Another vacation? The crystal blue waters and sandy beaches looked mesmerizing but I didn't have time to look through the entire album. Honestly, I was a little envious too. It was baffling that she could vacation in an exotic locale so often.

The next update was a post on a terror attack accompanied by photographs of orphaned children. How could people hate and kill in the name of God? I felt utter disgust and rage for the perpetrators of terror and violence.

Next was a post on the plane crash in the Alps. The article stated that it was a deliberate attempt by the co-pilot. Sadness for the innocent victims of these incidents filled my heart.

My husband nudged me gently to let me know the show had begun. I switched back to the video mode to record my daughter and quickly realized that I was no longer brimming with excitement. Too many emotions had made their way through my mind and heart in a matter of seconds. I mechanically turned on the red button and watched through the lens, all the time making sure I was getting the best angle. It didn't seem too clear. Maybe zooming in would help. I was still adjusting the zoom feature when the phone informed me that the storage capacity was exhausted. I was exasperated!

I glanced at my husband and saw that he had put away his phone to listen intently with his eyes closed. Rather than prod him to start recording I chose to put away my phone too. And that's when I experienced it... a soul stirring similar to what I felt when I heard church bells ring. Up until now I had watched the performance from behind the lens for the benefit of my Facebook audience and it had diluted the experience. It was only when I put the phone away that I engaged my senses fully in the experience. Only then did I notice my daughter's deft fingers flawlessly caress the piano. Only then did I pay attention to her intense expression, a reflection of her focus on the beautiful composition. Only then did I experience the joy she felt as the melody flowed from her heart to reverberate all through the chapel. It was a memorable experience that was captured by my heart, and not by a gadget. How apt that she had chosen to play "River Flows in You" because that day it truly did.

> *It was only when I put the phone away that I engaged my senses fully in the experience.*

~Vidya

74

The Last Meal
of the Month

It's not what you look at that matters, it's what you see.
~Henry David Thoreau

"What's for dinner, Mom?" I couldn't help the smile that broke out on my face upon hearing those words. The last-meal-of-the-month had become an eagerly awaited family adventure and I'll admit, I enjoyed the challenge.

"I don't know," I answered, "but I'm sure I'll come up with something."

My son watched as I gathered whatever I found lurking in the refrigerator and cupboards and placed them on the counter where my imagination would magically conjure up a dinner plan.

When we moved back east we simplified our lives. But along with simplicity came sacrifices. Out west I'd helped financially support our family, but now I was a full-time mother. With one meager income and five hungry mouths to feed, plus our pets, we needed a plan.

We didn't squabble about a monthly budget. After we paid the bills, we had two hundred dollars left and not a penny more for groceries, paper products, and pet food.

In a homesteading magazine, I'd read about a family that spent one hundred dollars a month for food. But I hated their suggested menus. Bacon gravy stirred with white rice and fried onions didn't sound appealing. And while beans and rice are nutritious, I wouldn't care for them night after night. I'd studied nutrition and insisted that my family would eat healthful meals without feeling as if they had gone without.

Of course it made sense that the more shopping trips we made, the more money we spent and so we shopped once a month, saving money as well as gasoline.

In order to shop the best sales we drove an hour away so that we had our choice of three competing grocery chains, all in the same vicinity. We made every penny count.

Getting the hang of this new system took a while, but if an item wasn't on the grocery list, we didn't buy it, period!

At the end of the month, when the cupboards seemed bare, I found we had plenty of food left once I figured out how I could "throw" it all together.

Buying in bulk became a necessity. We made sure we got the most nutritional bang for our buck by cutting out packaged and processed foods. Even the canned soups disappeared, replaced by rich homemade broths and creamy celery, mushroom, or bean soups. Homemade oatmeal, Cream of Wheat, whole grain muffins, or granola replaced boxed cereals. In the summer we gardened, preserving our bounty by canning or freezing our harvest. During the fall and winter I picked delicious greens from a simple cold frame crafted from an old sliding glass door the neighbor had thrown away.

We ate simple foods and only in season. When available, we purchased fruits and vegetables locally, such as potatoes or apples. Sliced potato fries drizzled with oil and seasoning made tastier, healthier fries than the frozen store-bought variety, and baked apples dotted with butter and sprinkled with a little cinnamon and sugar tasted heavenly.

At the end of the month, when the cupboards seemed bare, I found we had plenty of food left once I figured out how I could "throw" it all together. No recipes here. And while my family should have eagerly awaited that first meal of the month, when the house overflowed with freshly stocked groceries, the last-meal-of-the-month is the one that grabbed all the attention. It became an amusing guessing game as the family wondered what concoction I'd come up with next.

One evening I lovingly placed my last-meal-of-the-month masterpiece on the table. "What's that?" my kids asked, excitedly anticipating the mystery dinner. As I removed the lid from the casserole I heard, "What's in it?"

"Good stuff, that's what's in it," I carefully answered.

My husband's face perked up. "Not only does that look delicious, it smells incredible," he said, sniffing the air.

The dish looked sensational, with its gorgeous, thick, spicy-green Mexican sauce, sprinkled with shredded cheese, topped with tomatoes and garnished with shredded greens — almost too exquisite to eat.

But we did eat it. The family devoured the entire meal and insisted I make it again soon.

As we cleared the table, my daughter asked, "Mom, what was in that sauce?"

With a smile on my face I proudly answered, "I made it from the leftover green peas." Judging from my family's bulging eyeballs and upturned noses I knew I'd made a huge mistake. I promised myself I'd never disclose my secret ingredients again.

My children are all grown, but today I still grind my wheat, make bread, and buy staples in bulk, although now I can order them online and have them shipped. Out of necessity, we still budget. Today's food is more expensive and while we occasionally splurge on a few frivolous purchases, for the most part we eat simple, healthful food and spend far less than most people do on groceries.

Delicious homemade food is one of life's greatest pleasures and a family tradition, but we keep it simple in our home. And believe it or not, we still eat a few of our favorite last-day-of-the-month, thrown-together meals, including tortilla crumb casserole or deep-dish pizza. Simple doesn't get any better than that!

~Jill Burns

75

Slightly Bent Flugelhorn, Best Offer

*Men will always be mad, and those who think they can
cure them are the maddest of all.*
~Voltaire

Lord, please save me from garage sales.
Every time I see one, it just never fails.
I always have to stop and look around
at all the junk laid out on the ground.

Oh, the excitement! What might I find?
What treasures await? It boggles the mind!
It's usually worthless, but you just never know.
I might find an authentic Vincent van Gogh!

We've all heard the stories about some typical fool
who paid ten cents for some tacky, cosmetic jewel
then a week later, the same guy found out with a thrill
that it was Cleopatra's ring and it's worth twenty mil'!

Doesn't that make you just want to puke?
I mean, don't we deserve to have such a fluke?

It'll happen to me, though folks say it can't.
Someday, I'll score an original Rembrandt!

But so far, I've only bought stuff I don't need
like a mountain of books I can't find time to read,
old clothes that are already starting to fray
and old records that are too scratched to play.

I have tons of toys (though my kids aren't yet born).
I've got a stuffed iguana and a bent flugelhorn,
a velvet painting of Elvis that nobody can stand
and a baseball mitt that doesn't quite fit my hand.

I have a cymbal-banging monkey, an old tambourine,
a lava lamp, some hula dolls and *MAD* magazines,
a banged-up surfboard and a magic eight ball.
I've got enough stuff to start my own mall!

My den looks like the set of *Sanford and Son*.
I know I should stop but it's just too much fun!
Some people like neatness but I'd be in a funk
if I wasn't surrounded by cool, kitschy junk!

Searching through old boxes gives me such pleasure.
It makes me feel like a pirate searching for treasure!
It's probably wishful thinking, but I know that someday
I'll find something to sell for big bucks on eBay!

But half the joy of garage sales is passing the time
with old folks and children and neighbors of mine.
Just shooting the breeze like folks did in the past
is less common now that the world moves so fast.

I have no excuse. I guess I'm a hopeless case
but I run into garage sales all over the place!
My home's filled with junk. My family's in a huff.
I've got to have a sale to get rid of this stuff!

~Mark Rickerby

76

Happiness Is Raising a Roof

Never believe that a few caring people can't change the
world. For, indeed, that's all who ever have.
~Margaret Mead

The picture of my self-indulgent lifestyle sickened me. The speaker's words pierced my heart; I was horrified to discover that I was a middle age, successful and pampered woman. I needed more clarification so I leaned forward with interest as the conference speaker continued: "Many women in other parts of the world cannot get into their SUV and drive to the nearest medical walk-in clinic. They cannot run to the corner store or shopping centre to pick up fresh vegetables, toothpaste or a new outfit for their next social function. These women have time and no stuff. People in North America have stuff but no time."

I sat back in my comfortable chair and was jolted back to reality. I looked around at my beautiful conference room, the women in their exquisite outfits, and I knew in the next few minutes I was going to a local restaurant to enjoy a splendid meal with friends. I cringed when I realized I was one of those self-indulgent women.

Over the years I saw videos and heard numerous pleas for impoverished countries, children dying from AIDS, grandmothers raising their children and grandchildren. I have always done my part by adopting children in Africa and Haiti and sending money when I saw the need. But that part is easy for me. Pull out my chequebook and write a cheque to ease my guilty conscience. I've done my part; what more can I do?

This time I knew it wasn't enough. At the end of the day, as I drove across the bridge to my home in West Kelowna, British Columbia an outrageous idea hit me: *Heidi, until you see your own lifestyle as self-indulgent, you will never understand and experience the plight of these impoverished women. For the next four months don't buy anything for yourself or indulge in any luxury and see how this makes you feel.*

This was the middle of August, so that meant I had to do without any shopping, restaurants and any other indulgences until the middle of December. By the time I arrived at my home I was determined to do it and excited by the prospect. In fact, I was going to take it one step further. Whatever money I would have spent in those four months I would contribute to a worthwhile project.

Over the next two days, as the conference continued, I shared my story with my closest friends and asked if they wanted to join me. I was amazed at their excitement and eagerness to jump on board. Word spread and soon we had twenty-three women ready to sacrifice everything for the next four months and donate the money they saved to a worthy fund. It was interesting for me to hear what other women indulged in and what they had to give up:

"I'm not much of a shopper Heidi, but I do spend about $150 each month on specialty coffees."

"I don't spend money on clothes, but I sure do love to shop for kitchen gadgets."

"Gardening supplies, flowers and tools are my weakness."

"I watch too much TV, I am going to cut off my cable for the next four months."

"I spend way too much money on magazines each month."

We all indulge ourselves in different ways. I have the luxury of buying new outfits for my speaking engagements, and I love the challenge of finding just the right attire for each event. I was just going into my busiest months for speaking engagements and I would have to "make do" with what I already had. For the first time I was shocked and yet very grateful that my closet was already filled with beautiful clothes, scarves and shoes and all I had to do was get creative.

The next few months were a revelation. I discovered I had so much more time to spend on coffee dates with friends instead of stopping off at a mall or a favourite store. And I was able to go right home after work. I also found that I had shampoos, toothpastes and soaps tucked away that I had never used. Eventually when I did go into the mall with a friend, I found the atmosphere to be loud and confusing. I was quite disgusted with the frenzy of people searching for their next purse, shoes or unnecessary trinket. I saw the obsession of our culture with stuff and it saddened me. Finally I was able to "feel" and experience a smidgen of what women from an impoverished country might be feeling.

> *People in North America have stuff but no time.*

At the end of four months the twenty-three women handed me the money they would have spent. Some of the women had tears in their eyes when they gave me a cheque and said things like: *"Heidi, this experiment has changed me forever, thank you for allowing us to experience it. I don't know when I have experienced such joy."* When all the money was deposited I was amazed and delighted with the final amount. After some research, and by placing this money into trusted hands, we were all delighted to be able to put a roof on a church in Hermosillo, Mexico.

These four months of walking in someone else's shoes taught me truths that will affect me forever and have changed me. Here's what I learned:

1. Stuff does not bring me happiness.
2. Before I buy anything I re-evaluate the cost and need.
3. Nothing will change until my heart really wants it to change.
4. We are all on this earth to help one another and we all have to do our part.
5. When we pour out our lives for others, we are the ones who experience the happiness and feel fulfilled.

I am so grateful that a speaker had the courage to tackle some tough issues about the overindulgence of my lifestyle. Those words changed my behavior and put new happiness into my heart.

~Heidi McLaughlin

77

It's Still Too Much

If you live for having it all, what you have
is never enough.
~Vicki Robin

I t took all I had to fight back the tears that were beginning to trickle down my cheek. Crying was not allowed in my home growing up, especially over material things. We were to be appreciative and grateful for all that we had, because we didn't have much.

As the tears began to fall I found myself thinking what I had felt many times before: "Why can't I have what she has?" "Things" mattered to me. I wanted the latest designer jeans, the newest bike, the roller skates with stoppers on the toes. But my family didn't have much money. And even if we did, it certainly wouldn't be spent on such frivolous things. Yet it seemed that all my friends and neighbors had all the money they needed, and it made me so sad that I often cried myself to sleep.

I just wanted to be like all the other kids. In my mind, I needed these things in order to fit in.

Being the determined young lady that I was, if my parents wouldn't buy me the things I so desperately wanted, I would make them myself. I began designing clothes at the age of thirteen. As soon as I was old enough, I began to work. I loved making money. I could buy whatever I wanted, and that's exactly what I did.

To make matters worse, I discovered credit cards! I started

spending money faster than I could make it. It was wonderful—or so I thought—to live above my means and not have to worry about it until later. Or course, I would later discover that "later" always came.

After several years, the harsh possibility of bankruptcy woke me up. I had to get my act together or forever suffer the consequences. By this point in my life, I no longer liked myself. I had spent every penny I earned and more, and I had nothing to show for it. All of the friends that I bought things for were gone. Everything that I just "had to have" was already in the trash or worthless.

While I spent a good number of years improving my credit and reining in my spending, there was still a part of me that vowed, "When I earn more money I will get it all back." My desire for what I perceived to be the must-haves was keeping me from focusing on the bigger picture. I was always focused on what I didn't have, until the day when I walked into my closet, which was the size of a small bedroom, and I really looked. I rationalized that other women had even more clothes, but a little voice inside me said, "It's still too much."

> *"Can you do without this?"* *If my answer is yes, or if I have to think about it for a moment, I don't buy it.*

I was disgusted with myself. "This ends here," I thought.

I began to set aside all of the clothing and shoes that I hadn't worn in years. The pile was huge. That small voice rose up inside me and asked, "Could you have made do without these?" The answer was yes. I could have done without all of those clothes. I had barely worn them, and now I had no interest in them at all.

Then I added up the amount of money that I spent on those clothes. It came to $8,000.

That was my breaking point. I thought of all the good I could have done with $8,000. I began to look around at all the "stuff" in my house and asked myself the same question. Could I have done without all this stuff? The answer was a resounding "Yes!"

Even though I was a grown woman at this point, I was still trapped in that little girl mentality of needing to have it all. It was time to change.

I repented of my gluttony and asked God to help me through this transition. I wanted nothing in my life that wasn't needed. I wanted only what would bring me true and meaningful joy and not rob me of money and — more importantly — time. When I thought of how much time I had lost trying to acquire these expensive, wasteful things, it was painful, but it fortified me. This was a new day.

From that moment on, I have asked myself this question: "Can you do without this?" If my answer is yes, or if I have to think about it for a moment, I don't buy it.

My closet today is one-tenth the size it used to be and nowhere near filled. It brings me tremendous joy when I see how simple life can be just by looking in my closet. I love my clothes and I wear each and every piece. No longer do I look around at my life and think, "What a waste." Rather, I think, "What a blessing to be so free from the chains of STUFF."

~Kris Reece

78

The Most Valuable Lessons

Happiness resides not in possessions, and not in gold,
happiness dwells in the soul.
~Democritus

I f you work hard for your money you deserve to have fun spending it. And spend it I did — mostly on clothes. Long, floaty dresses in a range of colours, dangly earrings, and shoes for all occasions. High, low, pointed, patent, round — whatever the pair, or the price, there was always a reason to buy.

For a few moments, clothes brought me joy, and I firmly believed they were the means to a better life. With a pink silk dress I could capture the attention of my perfect man. A tailored suit would ensure I aced the job interview. From the moment I spotted an item in a shop, lifeless on its hanger, an image of a sharper, chicer me would appear in my mind and propel me towards the till.

Some years later, with a bulging wardrobe but still no closer to contentment, I was given the opportunity to work at a primary school in Nigeria. The pay was basic but the chance to help others and explore a new country was priceless. Within a month I'd made the move and started adapting to a new culture and lifestyle.

I know that some people have epiphanies — they are suddenly struck by an urge for less. However, I wasn't one of them. My transition to a more minimalist existence was a result of circumstance rather than intent.

It was inconvenient, and expensive, for me to get hold of the magazines and cosmetics I'd always bought in the UK so I was forced to forage for replacements. Instead of consuming one women's glossy after another, all regurgitating exactly the same empty promises, I switched to books and never looked back. Meeting with other volunteers once a week we'd swap paperbacks — biographies, short stories, spiritual tomes — the genre didn't matter but my rediscovery of reading did.

Cosmetics, which had previously given me no trouble in colder climes, suddenly seemed to react with the intense Nigerian heat and my skin became incredibly sensitive, causing an ugly, throbbing rash to spread across my face and down my neck. With the guidance of my new friends I replaced my large collection of beauty products, and my exhausting ten-step cleansing routine, with just two items: African black soap and coconut oil. They turned my skin around in less than two weeks and they're the only two products I continue to use to this day.

As I reduced my possessions, giving them away to the people who really needed them, the amount of pleasure I got from life increased.

I discovered that Nigerian women excelled at fashion, looking so much more stylish than their western sisters, and if they were on a limited budget it was never reflected in their attire. Gowns and dresses were chosen with unparalleled attention to cut and colour. Cool cottons and silks were selected in rich jewel colours to complement skin tones and carefully cut to drape rather than cling. The end result was two or three perfect outfits, tailored especially for the woman who was wearing them.

As I reduced my possessions, giving them away to the people who really needed them, the amount of pleasure I got from life increased. I no longer took hours to get ready, hunting for missing items or trying to salvage an ill-matched outfit. The constant hum of anxiety, which I'd dragged around with me since my twenties, began to abate and in its place I found freedom.

What I lost in possessions, I gained in experiences. The time I saved was put to good use. I travelled all around Nigeria — from the red stone villages of the north, smelling of dust and heat, to the hustle of Lagos in the south. I walked across the lushest most beautiful forests and played in waterfalls under dark, starry skies.

I spent three years in Nigeria, teaching underprivileged school children, and in return I learnt the most valuable lessons of all: possessions will not make you happy but people might; experiences are worth more than the world's most amazing dress; what you lose in clutter you'll gain in joy; don't choose trappings, choose life.

~Celia Jarvis

79

Setting the Place

Life is short. Use the good china.
~Author Unknown

For the past five years, I have been employed in the marketing department of an upscale retirement community. I view my job as a vocation because it taps into something I hold dear—I love working with seniors. Where some folks adore babies, kittens and puppies, I find the grace, wisdom and life experiences earned by those over the age of eighty-five a treasure trove.

Classified as a continuing care retirement community or CCRC to those of us in the business, my place of employment offers five levels of senior care. These include: independent living with supporting amenities; assisted living; sub-acute rehabilitation; skilled nursing; and memory care. The goal of a CCRC is to have seniors age in place, ideally entering the community as independent residents and then moving seamlessly through the continuum of care should the need arise.

Sounds like a plan? Perhaps to some, but for far too many, this scenario presents a major stumbling block—one that may extend beyond medical issues and financial challenges. To those of us in the field, it's the dreadful "D" word: downsizing. Though many retirement communities offer spacious apartments—featuring open floor plans, large bathrooms equipped with every safety feature, and huge closets with built-in devices for easy access—I know of none that can accommodate all the contents of a family homestead.

I will never forget one lovely lady, a widow, who lived in a magnificent Victorian mansion. I nicknamed her "Rapunzel," not so much for her thick white hair, neatly arranged in a long braid, but more so for the "tower" in which she lived. Her home was built with many deeply pitched staircases, diminutive bathrooms, and breathtakingly beautiful, but slippery, hardwood floors. She was quite frail, arthritic, and used a walker to navigate. Her mind, however, was razor-sharp. While her family was urging her to consider a move to a home that was more suitable for woman in her nineties, she was adamant about remaining "home, with all of my things." When I asked her what "thing" was most precious, she directed me to the breakfront in her dining room, a huge mahogany cupboard that housed English bone china, with place settings for forty-eight guests. "You see, my dear," she said to me, "how could I ever leave this home? No other place could ever accommodate my china like my breakfront."

> *At a time in her life when she was losing so much — family, friends, her health, and maybe her home — the contents housed in that piece of furniture represented the opposite.*

Looking at the furniture, I had to agree with her. At that moment, gleaming in the afternoon sunlight, it seemed larger than my living room! Then, she went on to reminisce about the parties, the dinners, and all of the celebrations whose memories were captured within that one piece of furniture. And at that moment, I have to say that I finally got it.

It didn't matter that the last dinner party she had hosted was thirty-five years ago, or that the last time that china was used Ronald Reagan resided at 1600 Pennsylvania Avenue. What mattered was that, at a time in her life when she was losing so much — family, friends, her health, and maybe her home — the contents housed in that piece of furniture represented the opposite. Whenever she looked at that china, she remembered a time when she was surrounded by family and friends, a time when she excelled at arranging dinner parties, and even more so, a time when she enjoyed presiding over these celebrations as one of the most sought after hostesses of the day.

A very bright friend of mine, a psychotherapist, once told me, "When patients come into my office, and tell me that they cannot stop thinking about what I call, 'blue elephants,' I cannot tell them to just stop it. Even though the 'blue elephant' may be bad for them, cause them pain, or make them sick, the mind does not work like that. To change their behavior, I have to provide them with what I call 'a pink giraffe,' something else, something positive, to replace the blue elephant."

The following week, I thought a lot about blue elephants, pink giraffes, and my ninety-year-old Rapunzel imprisoned in her "Victorian tower." Thinking about the upcoming Thanksgiving holiday, I had an idea, and convinced my Rapunzel to help me plan a special holiday luncheon for the forty-five residents living in our assisted living community. I needed her expertise in selecting the décor, the menu, the music, and the entire venue. That, in essence, was my pink giraffe.

To my surprise, she was immediately receptive to the idea, and agreed to spend several afternoons at our retirement community that week. While there, she worked enthusiastically with our dining and recreational staffs to organize the event. Without a doubt, it was one of the most elegant affairs we had ever hosted, with Rapunzel handling every exquisite detail.

Looking back, I wish I could report that planning the luncheon, selecting the entrees, and finally hosting the event, banished the "blue elephant" immediately — it didn't, but we did manage to make significant progress. In the coming weeks, my "Rapunzel" visited us regularly, and one day I was even able to show her a lovely apartment, with spacious rooms, each equipped with every possible safety feature. During these visits, while she did seem to enjoy the various activities, delight in the company of our residents, and appreciate the assistance from our staff, it would take nearly a year before she was ready to leave her Victorian tower.

I'll never forget that conversation. It went something like this, "You need my help in hosting another luncheon, and this one will be better than last year's. We'll use real china this time, but don't worry. I have service for forty-eight. I have a request, however: please have your dining staff make a permanent home for the china."

And without hesitation, she added, "Because after the luncheon, we'll both be moving in."

~Barbara Davey

This Little Piggy Came Home

Those gifts are ever more precious which the giver has
made precious.
~Ovid

A couple of years ago my husband and I decided to get new living room furniture. It was a huge decision. We were still using the same furnishings we had purchased twenty-one years before when our house was built. In fact, everything was the same — same pictures on the wall, same curtains, and the same clutter.

Our old décor was a country/farmhouse style, with a big emphasis on pigs, my favorite farm animal. I had spent years collecting anything that had to do with pigs, and people gave me pig gifts as well. We had everything from wall hangings to figurines, dishes, stuffed animals, stationery, and even Christmas ornaments. There were pigs everywhere.

We loved our new furniture but it made everything else in our home look dated. I decided we would have to update other items as well so I started removing things that didn't match our new décor, including a lot of pig items.

I tried to stash everything in the attic, but my husband convinced me that we should have a yard sale or take it all to Goodwill. So, we brought the boxes down and stacked them in the garage. And there they sat, in spite of my good intentions. There would be a yard sale one day."

I never did have a yard sale but I eventually sorted through the boxes again and started giving things away. I gave stuffed pigs to my grandchildren and a local women's shelter. Some of the knick-knacks and kitchen items went to a thrift store. I was happy that others might enjoy our old things that had been hidden away in boxes for so long.

Then our church announced a yard sale. I still had one box of things that I had decided to keep, but I decided that I could find one thing in there to contribute to the church. After much deliberation, I chose a blue pig planter that had sat on a shelf above our couch for twenty-one years.

> *I was happy that others might enjoy our old things that had been hidden away in boxes for so long.*

The afternoon of the sale I returned home from a meeting and started doing my weekend chores. My husband walked in, smiling. "I've got a surprise for you," he announced.

I quickly unwrapped the unexpected gift.

For a moment I could only stare in disbelief when I saw what it was. It was blue. It was a pig. It was a planter. It was the blue pig planter I had just donated to the church sale.

"Did you stop by the church on your way home?" I asked.

Yes indeed! He had spotted the pig planter and thought it looked like something I would like. What's more, he had paid three dollars for it.

"That's the one thing I donated to them!" I exclaimed. "Didn't you recognize it as an old relic of ours? After all, it sat on a shelf in our living room for the last twenty-one years!"

Needless to say, my husband was a bit embarrassed but we couldn't help but laugh!

Although this little pig no longer matched our décor I decided to keep it by the kitchen sink. It is just right for holding scouring pads, a dishcloth, and a unique memory.

When my children found out about their dad's special "gift" to me they practically rolled with laughter. They now joke about who should inherit the pig and say they will fight over it for sure. I doubt that, but I do think this little piggy is home to stay.

~Carol Emmons Hartsoe

Chapter 9

the joy of less

The Joy of Starting Over

81

From Tragedy to Triumph

*When I chased after money, I never had enough. When
I got my life on purpose and focused on giving of
myself and everything that arrived into my life,
then I was prosperous.*
~Wayne Dyer

etal crushing, glass shattering and the acrid gun-
shot smell of airbags deploying are all I remember
of the single minute that took me from an upper
middle–class life to poverty-level, surviving on
less than fifteen percent of what I previously made. For the first six
months after the accident, I spent every day curled up on my bed,
unable to move, and shocked at how much of my identity had been
tied to how much I made and how much I spent.

I finally faced the fact that although I had worked hard my entire
life, everything I had was gone. I now had to learn how to live on almost
nothing. Even if I did receive permanent disability, it would still be
less than twenty percent of what my six-figure income had provided.

At first I was angry, resentful and fed-up. I no longer had the
option to make any decisions about discretionary spending. There
simply WAS no extra money available. Everything had to be prioritized
so that only the necessary bills were paid. The rent was first, utilities
second. After that it became a game of spreading the money between
groceries, caring for the animals I had adopted, and medicine for me.
It was a miserable existence, and then two things happened in the

same week and broke me out of this rut.

The first was receiving a series of pictures showing how much people in various cultures got to spend on food in a week. When I saw a family in Africa making do with their single bag of rice and a few wilted vegetables I gained a new perspective on my own situation.

Then I had a conversation with a neighbor who was going through essentially the same process as me and I realized that I had already survived the worst of my debacle. I hadn't lost my home; my utilities hadn't been shut off, and although I hadn't eaten the sumptuous restaurant meals I was used to consuming while working two jobs, I also hadn't starved. I had, by sheer stubbornness, found ways to make the reduced income do double duty and survived.

> By not being able to buy myself whatever I want, I've learned how to develop deeper and richer relationships, networks and friendships.

The accident had taken away my purpose in life. But as often happens, what doesn't destroy us makes us stronger and wiser. I knew that finding a new purpose was mandatory, and that instead of feeling angry and resentful, I could begin to look at the need to live successfully on significantly less as a challenge. If I could win this game, I could help others do so too. That gave me a new focus.

I cut up all my credit cards and sent them back to the credit card companies. I paid them only what I could, when I could. I sold all the high-priced examples of over-spending I had accumulated over the years: fancy collectibles; expensive jewelry, too-expensive automobiles and anything else that had a value. By doing so, I was able to keep going and pay off much of the debt I had. A second benefit was that I began to have a lot less to clean, and began to truly find a lightness in my spirit that the weight of "stuff" had held down all those years.

Being freed from caring what anyone else had or did allowed me to become my own person. Instead of trying to keep up with anyone else, I got to concentrate on what really mattered to me. Amazingly, over a five-year period, I learned that living in the finest home, driving the newest car and/or having the latest gadgets were simply no longer important to me. Even when I got an increase in my disability check, I no longer desired to run out and replace any of the "things" I previously had found so important.

Little by little I cleaned out and downsized to the point where I now have a minimalist home that I can take care of pretty much by myself. Interestingly, if the dogs do something that creates a mess, it no longer stresses me out. There's nothing so important that it's worth having a meltdown about anymore. I also have so much more of that illusive item that most people running on the hamster wheel of ambition have almost none of — time.

I now focus on spending time with family and friends. We talk about the olden days, the days of lavish Christmas presents, of eating out every night, and of buying new clothes, toys and décor almost monthly. Amazingly, my kids don't remember most of what I gave them or they played with. Instead, their memories are of the days I couldn't attend their ceremonies or my coming home from work after they were already in bed asleep. Time with people can never be replaced by stuff.

Granted, there are still days I wish I had more income to accomplish a cherished goal or make a repair to my home. But I've found that if the goal is meant to be, eventually it will happen. God provides in interesting and unique ways, and helping neighbors with their problems has opened avenues for them to help me with mine. By not being able to buy myself whatever I want, I've learned how to develop deeper and richer relationships, networks and friendships.

And a lot of the resentment my children once felt at my quest for the best and brightest has gone by the wayside. We were recently all just talking over a simple salad and tea — realizing that we were closer now than many families who have much more materially, but spend no time connecting emotionally.

Would I have voluntarily gone through what happened? Possibly not, but since I was allowed to experience it, I have been able to help many others make wiser financial decisions and survive in the face of traumatic events. I am now at a place in life where I can truly say that I wouldn't exchange the life I have for my old one. Living on less allows you to truly live — a rare gift that many miss out on.

~Kamia Taylor

82

Small Blessings

*Sometimes the hardest part isn't letting go but rather
learning to start over.*
~Nicole Sobon

I was having my third cup of coffee and trying to force a piece of toast down my throat when I heard a light tapping at my front door. Sighing heavily, I rose to my feet. I didn't want to see anyone. I just wanted to marinate in my grief. Nobody could understand my misery anyway. Losing my husband, Wayne, was bad enough. The fact that we had just heavily mortgaged the house so he could pursue his dream of starting a business made his death even more unbearable.

I opened the door and tried to smile at my neighbor Mary who lived half a mile down the road. I knew her from my evening walks. When I passed her tiny house she was almost always tending her rose garden or the numerous flowerbeds in her small yard. Over the years we had gotten into the habit of exchanging a few words. Mary always looked like she was ready to burst into laughter, with her perpetual wide smile and sparkling eyes. Even though she lived alone in her small cottage she seemed more content than anyone I had ever known. This morning, though, her smile wasn't quite as bright and some of the shine had left her eyes. In her oven-mitted hands she held a steaming pot. "I know you aren't eating right," she said, coming into the house as I stepped aside. "I lost twenty-five pounds when my Bill died." She ran her eyes over my body. "At the rate you're going you might top that."

She followed me into the kitchen and put the pot on the stove. She turned to face me with hands on her hips and a no-nonsense look on her face. "Where are your bowls?" she said. "We're going to have some soup."

"I just ate," I said, shaking my head. The soup smelled delicious but I had no desire for food.

Mary scowled at the half eaten piece of toast and cold cup of coffee on the table. "Are you going to get the bowls out or do I have to scrounge around in your cabinets and find them myself?"

I got the bowls and spoons and poured us some tea. "I know you mean well," I said. "But I have lost my appetite since Wayne died."

"I know," she said, giving me a sympathetic pat on the shoulder. "But we're going to find it. Soup is the best thing in the world for perking up a poor appetite."

> "This house has become a burden that you have to let go. Find a smaller place and make it a home."

To my surprise, after a few bites I realized that I was actually feeling hunger again. "How did you know this would work?" I asked Mary, as she filled my bowl up again.

Her big grin was back. "A kind person did this for me when Bill died. I think eating with someone is the trick more than the soup is."

After we ate I told her of my predicament. "I don't know what I am going to do. I can't even make the mortgage payment on the house, not to mention the utilities and everything else."

Mary glanced around the room. "Honey, you really don't need this big house with all the upkeep."

I shook my head. "This is the home that Wayne and I made together. I expected to spend the rest of my life here. I don't want to lose it."

"You aren't going to lose it," she said. "You're going to give it up."

I looked up at her, shocked. "What do you mean?"

"Have you seen the big house with the huge lawn that is next to my cottage? Well, that used to be our home. When Bill died I tried for a while to hold onto it. But I was stressed out from trying to meet all the bills and keep up the place. I even told myself that Bill would be devastated if he knew I ever let the place go. Then I came to my senses. He would have been upset if he knew how hard it was on me to hold onto something that was draining my life of all joy. I woke up every day troubled and went to sleep every night troubled. I knew I didn't want to spend the rest of my life like that. I sat down one evening and asked myself what made me happiest in life. It came down to having peace of mind, a lifestyle I could maintain without stress, and my flowers. So I sold the big house and kept the guest cottage for myself. Without Bill the large house didn't really feel like home anyway. But the cottage does." She reached over and took my hand. "This house has become a burden that you have to let go. Find a smaller place and make it a home. Your home. Your life with Wayne is over but your life isn't over."

I rejected her advice at first, but at odd times her words would come back to me. The more often they invaded my thoughts the more sense they made. When I signed the final papers after the house was sold I didn't feel the pain I expected to feel. I was relieved to pass the responsibility for the house on to the beaming young couple who bought it.

I love my new home. Built in the thirties and located in a lovely old neighborhood, it is small but loaded with character. Mary and I have gone from being casual neighbors to very good friends. She is helping me put in some flowerbeds. I think there might even be room for a few rose bushes. Giving up the home I made with Wayne and making another home for myself was the best thing I could have done. Bigger isn't always better. Peace of mind and living stress free is better by far. I am learning every day how right Mary was.

~Elizabeth A. Atwater

83

Half Is More

Women usually love what they buy, yet hate two-thirds
of what is in their closets.
~Mignon McLaughlin

Being the mother of three active children, I enjoyed volunteering at their school and attending their music concerts and athletic games. That is why I was taken aback one morning at breakfast when my youngest son asked, "Mom, are you coming to my doo-wop concert tonight?"

"You know I am, so why are you asking?"

"Well, umm, please don't wear your clown blouse," he said.

"So what blouse are you talking about?"

Looking at the floor, he softly replied, "The bright blue one with the yellow confetti specks and it ties in a big bow at the neck."

He had just described my favorite blouse. Suddenly I started laughing and couldn't stop because I had to admit it did look a bit clownish. With tears running down my face and a big smile I promised him: "I will never wear that blouse again."

The look of relief on his face was unforgettable as he grabbed his books and ran out the front door to school. Reluctantly I went upstairs to get dressed for work. Since my favorite blouse was now definitely out, I had to choose another top to go with my navy blue skirt and heels. Stressed, I pulled on a red short-sleeve sweater that was too hot for the sunny September day, but there was nothing else that looked appropriate.

Off and on that day I couldn't stop thinking about all the clothes in my packed closet. After the birth of my first child I had started purchasing my clothes exclusively from clearance racks to save money. This plan had worked when I was a stay-at-home mother and for the past five years working part-time in the trade school's construction office. Jeans, T-shirts, and hoodies were my main wardrobe.

However, things had changed this school year. I had a new job working full-time in the school district's Public Information Office. This first week had been really stressful, between trying to get dressed each morning and learning my new responsibilities.

Knowing I had to make some major changes, I got up early on Saturday to take everything out of my closet, which I hadn't done in years. Methodically I tossed all the worn clothing and shoes, stretched out belts, and dusty purses into large trash bags. The items that were still in good condition, but didn't fit or I hadn't worn in a year, I put in boxes to donate to charity. I kept only the clothes and shoes that fit perfectly and were a solid color. Looking at the few remaining dresses, skirts, slacks, and blouses I could see there wasn't much left to wear to work.

She started off by instructing us to purchase a skirt, slacks, jacket, cardigan sweater, shoes, and a purse all in the same color like black, gray, dark blue, brown, or beige.

As I carried the trash bags out to the garage and loaded the boxes into my car, I decided to buy at least two new tops. That afternoon, I went to the shopping center and carefully selected a long-sleeved white blouse and a structured beige tee that would go with everything. Unsure of what to buy next, the following week I signed up for an adult education class that was offered in October. It was for women like me who wanted to learn how to dress professionally for the office. When the big day arrived, there were thirty women in attendance. The instructor welcomed everyone and promised, "In the next two hours, you are going to learn how to put together a simple and basic working wardrobe for the business world."

She started off by instructing us to purchase a skirt, slacks, jacket, cardigan sweater, shoes, and a purse all in the same color like black, gray, dark blue, brown, or beige. "Whatever your budget, try to buy these basic items from the same manufacturer so the dyes and styles match."

I had never thought about details like this before, but this was definitely the information I was looking for. Her assistant wore a matching black skirt and jacket to show us the many different looks you can achieve by adding a scarf, belt, or jewelry. At the end of the class, the instructor summarized, "Remember to limit the color in your outfits to your tops and jewelry; and keep an up-to-date wish list of clothing you need or want. By following this easy plan, you will always have something to wear that fits every occasion."

This simple wardrobe strategy changed my life completely. Over time I bought the basics in black, dark blue, and beige. Of course I still shop the clearance racks, but I only buy an item if it is on my list and in the right color. With half the clothes, I am always amazed and relieved that I have so many outfits to wear.

~Brenda Cathcart-Kloke

The Real Treasures

There are two ways to be rich: One is by acquiring
much, and the other is by desiring little.
~Jackie French Koller

Over the years I'd collected all sorts of things — unusual napkin rings, antique hatpins, beach glass, old crocks, glassware, rag rugs, brass and silver. But a number of years ago I noticed a heavy feeling whenever I looked at my collections. I wasn't sure why, but the fun had gone out of collecting.

"Why do I have so many things?" I'd ask myself.

Then, surprisingly, I'd answer right back. "They're your treasures. Keepsakes. Things to pass on to your children and grandchildren. Besides, they're fun to look at and display."

But something happened over twenty years ago that made me see my collections in a whole different light. I was in Louisville, Kentucky, visiting my brother and sister-in-law. One day we attended an auction… a little slice of heaven for a collector like me. The newspaper ad proclaimed it to be "The Lifetime Collection of Treasures!"

I wondered if the couple who owned the house and its furnishings were paring down their possessions before moving into a retirement home. I wondered if perhaps one of them had died recently.

What my brother, sister-in-law and I discovered when we pulled into the driveway was that the owners were very wealthy. Their house, on acres and acres of a perfectly manicured estate, complete with a huge in-ground pool and spa, had sold to the first looker for $650,000. And remember, this was back in the early nineties. All of their exquisite possessions were sitting on the front lawn under huge tents, waiting to be sold at public auction. Over four hundred items worth hundreds of thousands of dollars were cataloged on legal size sheets given to the many potential bidders on that hot June afternoon.

Items on that list included, a "Highly carved Chippendale mahogany king size four post canopy bed on claw feet. Superb Queen Anne burl walnut bookcase china cabinet with beveled glass doors, dated 1890. Mother of Pearl inlaid rosewood tea caddy with hinged box interior, circa, 1850. Rare signed Tiffany and Company coffee urn. Three piece Ansonia marble clock set with open encasement and mercury pendulum, circa 1880."

This wasn't your typical auction. The auction also included a Mercedes Benz in superb condition; a six-month-old snazzy red pickup truck; and an Audi 200 Quattro Turbo with heated seats. The couple was selling everything, including the wheels right out from under themselves.

"Why would anyone part with all their treasures?" I asked my sister-in-law.

Linda just shrugged her shoulders, obviously as mystified as I, and said, "Look at the china, candelabra and cut glass. Think of the parties these people had!"

I ran my fingers over the fine sharp edges of half a dozen huge cut glass vases and umbrella stands. As I walked around a dozen antique Persian rugs stretched out on the lawn, I tried to imagine why or how one could part with such exquisite beauty.

The auction began under another giant tent filled with folding chairs out on the south lawn. The pristine navy blue leather sofa sold to the highest bidder for just under two thousand dollars. The huge mahogany dining room table sold for $1500. The twelve matching chairs went for $265 each. This definitely wasn't a sale for folks like me.

Why, I wondered over and over… why would they sell it all? Don't they have children who would want these treasures? Certainly many of the antique items had been in their families for generations.

We left after three hours, before a third of the items had been sold. My brother managed to get a dandy oak workbench for fifty dollars. The next day, when we went back to the estate with his van to pick up the workbench, my curiosity got the better of me. I just had to know why these people were selling their home and all those exquisite furnishings, antiques and treasures.

When I rang the doorbell a pretty young woman with long, light brown, wavy hair, no make-up and simple clothes answered. Wow, they even have a maid, I thought to myself wistfully.

"Is the owner of this house at home?" I asked.

"I'm the owner," she said simply, flashing a warm smile.

"Oh, my goodness," I stammered.

Giving away my things slowly but deliberately is giving me a sense of freedom, a cleansing of sorts.

"Forgive me, I don't mean to intrude, but, well, I'm here with my brother. He's out in the garage loading the workbench he bought yesterday. I just had to meet you. I'm wondering if you would mind telling me why you sold all your beautiful possessions."

The young woman graciously invited me into their home and introduced me to her husband, who reminded his wife that they had to be at the house closing in forty-five minutes.

I repeated my question. "How could you sell all your beautiful treasures?"

The husband, a very good-looking, curly-haired man in his early forties smiled, put his arm around his wife's waist and said quietly. "Oh, I didn't sell my treasures. All that is just STUFF. My treasures are right here, my wife and daughter. Have you met our daughter? She's eleven. Yes, these are my treasures: my wife and my daughter. They are all I need."

The young woman explained that the previous April she had gone to the Bahamas for a week with a friend and fallen in love with a tiny island called "Green Turtle Cay" in Abaco. She called her husband and asked him to join her so he could see the beauty of the tiny island. He flew over the next day and together they explored the island, befriended the local residents and thoroughly relaxed in a world that had missed out on the twentieth century. After a few days the couple decided to change their lives. They agreed to sell their home and all their possessions and move to the Bahamas with nothing but their bathing suits and a few small personal items.

The young wife's eyes danced with excitement as she explained further. "We're leaving tonight; can you believe it? Tomorrow our address will be Green Turtle Cay. We're moving into an old, simple, one-story oceanside home with just four rooms; a kitchen, living room and two bedrooms. No phone or TV. In fact, there are only two pay phones on the whole island. It takes three weeks for mail to get from here to there.

"We're really looking forward to just spending time together. This life here, these things, the big house, all those furnishings and stuff, the Junior League, it's just not me. I don't like what happens to your life when you have money. Things somehow become more important than people. This house and all those expensive items are not important. What's really important is family, sunshine, wind and the sea and those will be the things we'll have every day on the island."

It was time for me to leave and let this amazing family get on with their lives. I shook hands with each of them and wished them a happy life. I left with a sense of awe, knowing these wonderful people had given me a valuable gift.

I came home from Louisville and started cleaning house. I gathered up hundreds of items for a rummage sale. I wrapped up a cherished silver casserole dish and two collectible green vases that my sister-in-law had admired and shipped them off to her.

I gift-wrapped a set of antique butter plates that had been in my family for three generations and gave them to my neighbors who had just gotten married. I gave my brass collection to my son for Christmas. I placed 150 books on my dining room table and insisted that my friends in my woman's group each take a handful of books home with them. I gave most of my silver collection to my four children. The next spring I put over a hundred items on a big table out by the street in front of my house with a huge sign that simply said FREE. Every month I clean out one closet or one drawer full of stuff and either give it away or toss it.

Giving away my things slowly but deliberately is giving me a sense of freedom, a cleansing of sorts. It's fun to see how much the people who receive my things are enjoying them.

But the best part is that now that I've stopped collecting and started giving away instead, I have less clutter around the house to dust, which means I have more time to spend with my friends and family. And those, as I learned earlier at the grand estate sale in Kentucky, are my real treasures.

~Patricia Lorenz

85

I Have Enough

We need much less than we think we need.
~Maya Angelou

A nother Monday morning. It was only nine o'clock, yet I felt like I had already put in a full day's work. The packed ferry and train meant I had to stand through the entire hour and a half commute into Manhattan's financial district. There had to be an easier way to earn a living.

I pulled out my calendar. Three management meetings scheduled for the morning and a working lunch to discuss how to announce impending budget cuts to the staff. The afternoon didn't promise to be any better — a three-hour training session to teach supervisors how to implement disciplinary action for poorly performing employees.

I liked my job most of the time. My undergraduate and graduate degrees were in business administration and I had been blessed to develop a career in my field of study. It paid well and I had worked my way up to vice president. However, as the years passed I found myself longing to do something more fulfilling with my life.

My heart was drawn to writing, teaching Bible studies, and mentoring. But it just didn't seem sensible to leave a profitable career to focus on something so idealistic. Besides, living in New York City meant struggling with a high cost of living, including steep mortgage payments. I also did not want to give up the perks of my job. I enjoyed the executive benefits and international travel. So for twenty years, I climbed the corporate ladder and dreamed of a time when I could spend my days doing the things I really wanted to do.

How do you know when you have enough? I struggled with that question until I remembered the quote from John D. Rockefeller. He was once asked, "How much money is enough?" He answered, "Just a little bit more." I decided I didn't want to be someone who spent her life chasing "just a little bit more."

When my husband retired, we decided to grab the opportunity to make a major change and simplify our life. We exchanged life in the big city to start over in a small town in Florida. Our goal was to trim our living expenses and try to live solely on my husband's pension. If we could manage it, then I would be free to write and teach. Clipping coupons seemed a small price to pay to follow my dream.

> *I decided I didn't want to be someone who spent her life chasing "just a little bit more."*

Still, I had reservations. While I was eager to give up the stress and pressures associated with my career, I wasn't eager to give up the status, travel, and benefits that accompanied it. And our move wasn't just about changing careers. I had lived in the same area for my entire adult life and would be leaving my entire support network of family and friends. Was I making too many changes at once?

It didn't help that I had received an abundance of conflicting advice from well-meaning people. One extended family member said I was making a big mistake in leaving the corporate world so soon. According to him, I had "at least another ten good years of work" left in me. From his perspective, I was foolishly throwing away a lucrative earning opportunity. Sadly, he could not comprehend that, although we weren't rich, we had enough.

Others shared the opposite view. They said I wasted those first twenty years trapped in the nine-to-five rat race. According to them, life is much too short to put our dreams on hold. The sooner I left my job and followed those dreams, the better.

We completed our relocation and pursued our initial plans. I'd be lying if I said it didn't require a major adjustment. But as I began teaching and writing, I came to the realization that both extremes of advice had been wrong for me.

I may have had at least "ten good years of work" left in me for the corporate workplace. That certainly would have been the more lucrative option. But it was indeed time to move on to follow the dream of my heart. It was time to stop chasing "just a little bit more."

Besides, those twenty years weren't a waste at all. The skills I acquired in the corporate workplace were just as useful in my new life. Writing position papers, memos, and corporate policies honed my writing abilities. Researching policy development prepared me to research the books I write. The exhausting daily commute provided the content for my first paid submission: "Not Just Another Rat" in *Chicken Soup for the Working Woman's Soul*.

I may have spent one thousand Monday mornings postponing my dream, but nothing is ever wasted... in work and in life. I've learned to appreciate the worth of all my experiences. I've also learned to be content with what I have.

Others may have more, but I have enough... and enough is just right for me.

~Ava Pennington

86

Recharged Without the Cards

Credit cards are like snakes: Handle 'em long enough,
and one will bite you.
~Elizabeth Warren

I was twenty when I got my first credit card. My dad said I might need it in an emergency while I stayed with my friend in Hawaii. My shiny blue Visa card remained untouched in my wallet throughout my trip; when I ran out of money, I returned home. What a concept: when you're out of money, you stop spending!

I can't remember the first thing I charged, but like the first puff of a cigarette, it was my line crosser. I'd entered the world of plastic and it became easier to rely on it with each new swipe. My charge card replaced old tires and covered costly veterinary bills. The minimum monthly payments seemed very reasonable to me and I worried less and less about saying, "Charge it."

Soon my wallet expanded as I accepted an assortment of department store cards. Each store enticed me with sizable discounts on the day I opened my account. They kept me coming back with mailers promising extra discounts or rewards for my loyal purchases. The more I bought, the more I saved… or so I thought.

A major vehicle repair maxed out my Visa but that didn't seem to be much of a problem. After all, I was receiving weekly invitations from other banks offering more Visa, MasterCard, and Discover cards.

Everyone seemed eager to help me obtain whatever I might need or want without any saving, waiting or planning on my part.

Interestingly, many of my charges were not for me personally. I gave wonderful gifts, especially to my mother. Each piece of jewelry I chose for her on Christmas, Mother's Day and her birthday cost as much as $500. My friend couldn't afford the surgery his cat needed, so I charged it. Three of my friends died within a two-year period. At each of the funerals, the extravagant wreath with the banner "Friend" was from me. Meals out with friends and co-workers usually ended with me picking up the tab. If they resisted, I'd say, "I'll just put it on my card." You would have thought I had an unlimited corporate expense account instead of the reality: every cent would eventually come out of the Bank of Marsha.

One Christmas I made everyone brownies and these were received with much more enthusiasm than my usual store-bought offerings.

Finally, my charging hit a dead end. I had thirteen well-worn cards and was making the minimum payment on each. Once the interest (18 to 22% annually) was added, the balances didn't decrease even on cards I'd stopped using. The principal stayed the same.

At this point, my minimum payments totaled $1,270 a month — exactly half of my take-home pay as a teacher. My mortgage took the other half. I thought I'd found my escape from debtors prison when I received a twenty-thousand-dollar book royalty check and I applied almost all of it toward my seventy-thousand-dollar credit card debt. Unfortunately, I'd forgotten to set aside money for my income taxes. At the end of the year, I couldn't pay my federal taxes. The IRS set up monthly installments at 12% interest.

This new monthly bill returned me to my credit cards, no longer maxed out, to pay for essentials like gas and food. About this time, I hit rock bottom. Standing in a grocery store line, I realized my shiny little addiction that had once bought tires, extended Buttercup's life and made my mom's eyes light up was now needed for eggs and milk. Like the habitual smoker who finally recognizes the source of that bad taste in his mouth, I was suddenly sick of my dependence on credit cards.

My sister Connie took me to Consumer Credit of Iowa to end the cycle. My counselor totaled my recent statements. Despite my royalty payment, I still owed over fifty thousand dollars.

"You can't reduce your balances by making minimum payments. The thirteen hundred a month you're paying isn't making a dent. Are you ready to give up the cards?"

I gulped. What choice did I have? Resigned, I muttered a barely audible, "Yes."

"Okay. You need to write to each of your creditors using our form. You will assure them that you intend to repay every penny and NOT use the card before you reach a zero balance."

"But I can't pay any more per month. How can I pay them off?" I protested.

"We'll contact each of your creditors and negotiate a lowered interest rate for you. If you're not charging and your rates have decreased, your balances will steadily be reduced."

"How will I know if they agree to lower my rates?"

"We handle all your payments. Each month you send us one check for thirteen hundred dollars and we disperse your payments to your creditors. In effect, they're making the agreement with us."

Once in the program, I learned that the lenders agreed to as little as a half percent to as much as a sixteen percent reduction in their interest rates. My monthly statements from Consumer Credit showed how much each account had received and my after payment balance.

The changes weren't dramatic until the smaller accounts began to be paid in full. When a zero balance appeared on an account, that monthly payment was applied to another account. I was finally making progress!

I continued writing to earn my bread and butter money. Obviously, my teaching money was tied up for the next five years.

After the last bill was paid off, my counselor congratulated me. He couldn't have been as surprised as I was that I'd made it without charging as much as a pack of gum. Was I cured?

During my five years without credit cards and a limited, irregular cash flow, I developed some of the traits of people who survived the

Great Depression. Forget about shopping for trendy new outfits. I now wanted to wear my clothes until they fell apart. Who was treating everyone to dinner now? It certainly wasn't me. My gifts became more thoughtful and less expensive. One Christmas I made everyone brownies and these were received with much more enthusiasm than my usual store-bought offerings.

When I was finally free to resume using credit cards, I didn't. For big purchases, I used my debit card and anything under $200 was strictly cash. If I didn't have the cash, the purchase could, and did, wait.

Weekly offers for store and bankcards still fill my mailbox. Each one has an introductory offer meant to lure me in. They won't find me signing up for a low introductory rate, discounts on merchandise or cash back rewards. I've already ridden on that merry-go-round and I know how hard it is to get off.

~Marsha Porter

87

Finding My Sparkle

I would rather be adorned by beauty of character than
jewels. Jewels are the gift of fortune, while character
comes from within.
~Titus Maccius Plautus

When I saw an ad for a jewelry auction in my town, I attended, excited about the prospect of scoring a great deal. After all, what woman can resist a beautiful bauble to make her feel special? It turned out that several baubles caught my eye that day, and I spent a lot more money than I had intended. I took most of the pieces home with me, but one, a bracelet, was a little too big, so the jeweler running the auction said he'd size it for free and mail it to me. When I learned that the estimated arrival date would fall during the few days I'd be out of town for Thanksgiving, I asked him to send it to my parents' house, instead of the address I had previously given him.

Returning home from the auction, I couldn't even find room in my jewelry boxes for my latest acquisitions, so I ended up tucking them into a drawer. As I stuffed the boxes behind my T-shirts, I felt a pang of buyer's remorse. Would I even have any occasion to wear such fancy pieces? If I had thought more about my purchases, rather than letting my bidding enthusiasm carry me away, I would have realized that they didn't go with my casual lifestyle.

The following week I made the long drive up north to spend Thanksgiving with my family. On the eve of the holiday, I was making a pie in my parents' kitchen when my father handed me the phone. It was my neighbor Sally, calling to say the police were at my house. Someone had broken in about an hour earlier.

I felt my insides clench and couldn't breathe. I could hear Sally giving me details of what had happened, but my mind couldn't process what she was saying. All that registered was that my home — my sanctuary — had been violated, and I was five hours away and helpless to do anything about it.

I set out for home early the next morning, less than twenty-four hours after I had arrived and without even eating Thanksgiving dinner — a ten-hour round trip just to bake a pie. I called a friend and asked him to meet me at my house because I was afraid to go inside alone.

> *I don't hold onto things as much as I used to. When they no longer serve me, I let them go.*

Once home, I talked with Sally and learned that when my security alarm had gone off, the monitoring station called her when they couldn't reach me. She came over to investigate and saw a broken window, so she called the police. She handed me a business card for the police officer assigned to the case, and after meeting with him, I inventoried what was missing. Coincidentally, the thieves went straight for my jewelry — they took it all, leaving my TV, camera, and computer untouched. It occurred to me that perhaps they had been at the auction, seen me buy several pieces, and overheard me tell the jeweler my address, along with the fact that I'd be out of town for the Thanksgiving holiday.

As I itemized the missing pieces and their estimated value, I was appalled by how much jewelry I owned... and had lost. Some items had sentimental value, like the necklace a boy had given me at my sweet sixteen party and a charm bracelet that marked every important event in my life. It was the loss of those that I felt most deeply. My insurance only covered a tiny fraction of what was stolen, so I didn't try to replace everything. Instead, I saw this as a chance for a new beginning.

I had received some of the jewelry as gifts and didn't care for it anyway. Other pieces had appealed to me when I bought them, but I had outgrown them; they were no longer me. I made a conscious decision to only buy the bare minimum: a simple pair of gold stud earrings, a pair of silver hoops, a plain gold chain necklace, and a strand of pearls (all costume jewelry, in case they were stolen again). This was all I really needed to accessorize.

After the shock and horror of being robbed wore off, I actually felt lighter, less encumbered, without all that "stuff." I was almost embarrassed to turn in my multi-page inventory of missing items to the police. They probably wondered; why does one woman need all this? Having only a few pieces of jewelry certainly made it easier to get dressed in the morning. If it weren't for the awful feeling of violation, I would have wished for someone to break in and take most of my clothes, too!

Years have passed since that angst-ridden autumn. I don't hold onto things as much as I used to. When they no longer serve me, I let them go. It's not wasting money or hurting the giver's feelings, as I once thought. I like to think I'm freeing them up for someone else who really wants them and will use them. Beautiful jewelry deserves to be worn, seen, and adored, not shoved in the back of a drawer and forgotten.

When I was younger, I loved to "try on" new things: new activities, new foods, new people... to see what suited me. Now that I'm older, I finally know myself. These days I'm simplifying my life; with fewer hobbies and commitments, I need less stuff. I can get rid of the dance shoes, athletic gear, and business suits that were part of my old lifestyle, as well as the home furnishings, beauty products, and even people in my life who are no longer right for me. And when it comes to jewelry, I've come to realize that I'm not the diamond tennis bracelet type. I had to lose all those sparkling things to find my own sparkle. As I'm paring down my lifestyle and possessions, I'm homing in on the essence of me.

~Susan Yanguas

88

What a Young Life Can Teach You

The best and most beautiful things in the world cannot
be seen or even touched. They must be felt
with the heart.
~Helen Keller

My husband and I were living the American Dream. We had two beautiful children, nice cars, great jobs and a big house with a pool, until one day four and half years ago, that all changed.

When our third child Bowen was born, we didn't know he had a fatal kidney disease. Bowen went to Heaven after living thirteen days.

After Bowen died, we tried to go on living our lives the way we had been. We thought building a house would help us "start over" without him. It didn't take long to discover, life without Bowen was going to be hard and a new house was not going to change that.

Most days were spent cleaning and taking care of all the stuff that went inside our new house. The more time I spent cleaning, the more I realized how much time it took away from what I really wanted in the first place, which was to be with my family and spend time with them. The more stuff that came into our lives the less time we had with each other.

After a year in our new house, my husband and I started having serious conversations about the purpose of our lives. Was making lots of money, owning a big house and all of these things what our lives were all about? Something was missing; there was more to life than taking care of that big house and maintaining all of our stuff.

At the time my husband was in a thriving oral surgery practice, at the peak of his career. Running his practice became more like running a rat race, keeping up with the competition, keeping the overhead low and the production numbers up. It was like running on a treadmill with no stop button. He desired to have more meaning and purpose in his career — to do something that was bigger than himself.

One January day in 2014, he came home and said, "I want to walk away from all of this and join the United States Air Force. What do you think?"

I said, "Yes! Let's do it!" On September 21, 2014 my husband became Major John M. Gillis of the United States Air Force. He would still practice as an oral surgeon in the Air Force, but be serving men and women who serve our country, serving something that was bigger than him, not running the treadmill of life. It took a lot of courage to walk away from a thriving nine-year oral surgery practice, and I am proud of him for doing so.

Life is focused now on what we are putting into our hearts and not what we are putting into our closets.

To the world, it didn't make sense that we walked away from a lucrative practice and the American dream. But some things in life cannot be bought. Walking away allowed a door to be opened for so much more. We were able to fill our lives with what mattered most, to live a life that was truly rich.

The day my husband was commissioned into the Air Force, we received our orders. We were moving from Arizona to Alaska. Right when my husband told me the news, a beer delivery truck wrapped in an Alaskan Amber ad passed right in front of me. It was like God had sent me a confirmation that our life was heading in the right direction.

Things fell into place quickly after that. We put our newly built house on the market and it sold in four days. We moved to a house half its size on the military base, so we donated fifty percent of our clothes and shoes to Goodwill, and gave away half of our children's toys and some furniture.

Our lives are so different now. We traded our travertine floors and granite countertops for a military house with white walls. Our children gave up their own rooms and bathrooms to now share a room and a bathroom. I sold my luxury vehicle to buy a Subaru, which I love! We traded in our resort vacations for camping trips in an RV. Trading in all of these things was the best decision we ever made. It helped us get back to our roots and become a tighter knit family.

We make less money, live in a much smaller house, and have a lot less stuff, but we are so much happier. Our lives are not focused on taking care of the house, making more money and acquiring more stuff, but building lasting relationships and making more memories. Life is focused now on what we are putting into our hearts and not what we are putting into our closets.

Losing our son was devastating, but his death taught us to cherish and treasure every moment that life has to offer and to live life with more intention. Bowen showed us what was really in our hearts and gave us the courage to move forward after his death with more clarity and purpose.

~Heather Gillis

89

My Kitchen in a Trunk

If you look at your entire house as one unit of junk,
you'll never do anything because the job is too
overwhelming. Take it one drawer at a time.
~Janet Luhrs

Kitchen remodels are not easy or fun, but sometimes they yield the most surprising benefits. Besides putting in a new countertop and sink, we were having our cabinets refaced, so I emptied all the drawers and cabinets.

By the time I was done, I was surrounded by boxes filled with dishes, glassware, gadgets and utensils. I had no idea where many of the things even came from, or what they were supposed to be used for. My kitchen had become quite the storage space.

I did what most sane people do at that point. I took a break and watched some television — not just any television, but one of the channels that dealt with home and garden issues. Episode after episode was filled with ideas for meals to prepare, renovations to complete and gardens to transform. When you are in the middle of renovations, I don't recommend watching others handling it better than yourself!

In the midst of these shows was nestled a little gem of an idea. The host talked about our obsession with utensils. Her advice was to eliminate all but the seven basic utensils that really are needed for cooking the majority of our meals: a slotted spoon, regular stirring spoon, spatula, tongs, measuring spoons, measuring cups, and peeler.

The idea made me sit up straight and bring out the boxes of assorted utensils I owned. I dug out the seven items and set them aside. I was overwhelmed by what was still in the box. Each item had a specific purpose, but how often did I really use them, and could I accomplish the task with one of the seven instead?

I closed up the boxes of utensils and put them in the trunk of my car. I was about to conduct an experiment — one that would keep these utensils and kitchen tools close enough to retrieve, but also far enough away to make me think twice about reaching for them.

> *I took every piece of clothing out of the closet and piled it on the bed. Next I put back into the closet the clothes that I truly wore.*

As I fit my seven surviving "essential" utensils into just one of my beautiful new kitchen drawers, I instantly felt lighter and freer. With that big step under my belt, I took the opportunity to lighten a lot of my other cabinets and drawers. Using the same thought process, I simply "put back" what I used on a regular basis, and left the rest in the boxes. Then I added the boxes to my trunk, which was now very full.

Over the next month my experiment yielded some very surprising and interesting results. First, I rarely faced a cooking project that couldn't be accomplished with what I had saved. Next, having my trunk handy allowed me to retrieve the few things that I needed to add to my streamlined kitchen drawers to keep me sane. Best of all, it was much more fun to cook without foraging in drawers and moving things on shelves to get to what I needed! And because it was more fun to cook, I was cooking more!

Having survived my kitchen experiment, I needed to decide what to do with the boxes in my trunk. Surprisingly, I kept coming upon people that were either in the process of starting out on their own, or in need of some odd kitchen item for a project. So, I would lead them to my car and watch them excitedly dig through the boxes like they were on a treasure hunt, holding up the items they found to take to their home. Little by little, news got out, and the boxes shrunk to nothing. What a fun time that was!

But it didn't stop there. At one point I decided to expand this newfound concept to my clothes closet and surveyed the crammed quarters. I took every piece of clothing out of the closet and piled it on the bed. Next I put back into the closet the clothes that I truly wore — yes the ones that fit and I enjoyed being seen in. The rest I placed in bags and took to the local thrift store. What an easy process that was, versus the normal mental anguish I went through as I evaluated and scrutinized each item in my closet!

Looking back over the whole episode, there is not much I would do differently. Occasionally I stand at the stove and miss a specific tool, but I only have to look at my orderly drawers and do some creative thinking to put the smile back on my face. It was a kitchen remodel that yielded the most amazing results ever!

~Joan Wasson

90

Embracing Black

I've been forty years discovering that the queen of all
colors was black.
~Pierre-Auguste Renoir

I walked into the same sporting goods store where I'd bought a
bicycle just a few days earlier. "I need some bike shorts," I told
the sales clerk. "With lots of padding."

She nodded sympathetically and led me to the cycling department. "Here they are," she said, waving her arm toward a two-tiered
clothing rack. "Lots of different lengths, lots of different styles, lots of
different sizes." I stared in disbelief. There must have been a hundred
pairs of shorts hanging there. And every single one of them was black.

"Don't they come in colors?" I stammered.

The clerk shrugged. "Some manufacturers offer other colors. But
we never order them. Everyone seems to want black."

I bought two pairs of shorts that afternoon — one pair that hit
me just above the knee and one pair that hit me just below, both in
black. As I rode my bicycle in the days that followed, I made a happy
discovery. Every single T-shirt I owned, no matter the color, looked
good with black bike shorts.

Not long afterward, my co-worker Ruth and I attended a weeklong
conference. I took three pairs of slacks — brown, navy and khaki.
Naturally, I packed tops, belts and shoes that coordinated with each
outfit. Ruth took one pair of slacks (black), one belt (black) and one
pair of shoes (black). And three tops.

"Everything goes with black britches," she said. "I don't own anything else."

Yeah… but, I wanted to say. I love my blue jeans. And my pink-and-white gingham capris. And my neon green running shorts. And my brown wool skirt. But when I thought about all the clothes I "loved" that were crammed in my closet and stuffed in my dresser drawers, I had to admit it was frustrating and time-consuming to put together an outfit every day.

Could I embrace black like Ruth had done? It was worth a try.

I pulled all the skirts that weren't black out of my closet, folded them neatly and put them in a box. I did the same with slacks and shorts that weren't black. But I wasn't going to be hasty about this radical wardrobe change. It was too early to give these things away. So I taped the boxes shut and carried them to the basement.

I tried on the few black items that remained and found that many of them were out of style or didn't fit well. Into a "donate" bag they went. Then I went shopping, vowing not to purchase anything that wasn't comfortable, flattering and well made.

> *I've discovered that an overstuffed closet is more than a hassle and a headache—it's a thief of time and of joy.*

These days, my closet is home to one pair of black jeans. A pair of black corduroys. A black wool skirt and a black polyester-blend skirt. A pair of black dress pants and a pair of black capris. In my bottom dresser drawer are black yoga pants, black running shorts and black biking shorts.

That's it.

I also boxed up all my shoes that weren't black. I won't say it wasn't painful, but I did it. My shoe rack now holds one pair of black heels, one pair of black flats, black athletic shoes, black sandals and black flip-flops. Next to it is my beloved pair of black cowboy boots.

What did I do with the taped-up boxes in the basement? A few months after I stowed the boxes away, I gave them to a used clothing drive without ever opening them. And you know what? I've never missed a single thing that was in them. Not once. I've discovered that an overstuffed closet is more than a hassle and a headache — it's a thief of time and of joy.

I cherish the day I decided to embrace black. And I'll never go back.

~Jennie Ivey

91

My Father's Watch

*Oh, my friend, it's not what they take away from you
that counts. It's what you do with what you have left.*
~Hubert Humphrey

O n the tenth anniversary of my father's death, I awoke at 3:30 a.m. to deafening fire alarms. Alexis, my older daughter, was standing in the hallway with her cell phone and a blanket wrapped around her younger sister, Sierra. We ran down the stairs to the main floor. The girls stood by the front door while I checked for the cause of the alarm.

When I opened the door to my living room, I could see the carpets were smoking. My house really was on fire.

I yelled to the girls, "Get out! Get out! The house is on fire!" They turned and ran out the front. Because there was no smoke in the hallway, I ran upstairs two times to drag our terrified dogs outside. On my third trip, to find our cat Biscuit, the smoke curled up the stairs like a black menacing snake. Dreading Biscuit's fate, I abandoned him and ran.

Explosions were shattering glass everywhere. The cars in the garage were exploding along with the lawnmower and snowblower. The fire burst out of the garage doors and crawled up the wall like deadly reptiles slithering up to the main floor. The heat shattered the windows, allowing the fire to climb back inside to continue its advance.

We ran through the woods to our neighbor's house. Alexis was carrying Sierra and I was pulling both dogs by their collars as we climbed over limbs and stumbled over rocks. I pounded on my neighbor's front door as police cars with their sirens blaring passed by.

Later, I was told it only took eight minutes for the fire trucks to arrive. The firefighters immediately started containing the fire. They saved a lot of our things and most importantly, Biscuit.

Standing outside my burned and smoking house the next day, I struggled with dozens of questions. I had no ID or cash. How was I going to pay for anything? I didn't have a car so I couldn't leave. Where would we sleep? Where would we live? What would happen to my house now? I didn't even know where to start.

I was sleep deprived as I stood in my burned-out kitchen wearing my neighbor's shoes, pants, and robe. My throat ached with unshed tears as I stared at my home in ruins. Everything was covered in burned wood, broken furniture, glass, soot, water, chemicals, and insulation. Everything smelled like smoke.

Despite the loss of valued mementoes, the fire did burn away a lot of needless clutter from my home and my life.

During the first weeks I wasn't thinking clearly, eating, or sleeping. I was afraid of everything: loud noises, unusual smells, electricity, fire alarms, and being away from my girls. In our new rental, the girls and I slept huddled together in one room, even though we had separate rooms.

What I didn't anticipate was how it would feel to have no personal items from our old house. Nothing was mine. I was sleeping in someone else's house, wearing someone else's clothes, and driving someone else's car. The fire not only burned our possessions, it seemed to strip us of our identities.

Every day, I visited our burned house to search through the debris. It's interesting how you learn what really matters to you in those circumstances. I found myself primarily searching for my late father's watch. I found other treasures as I searched for his watch, including the ring my mom gave me when I left for college, a watch my grandmother gave me for high school graduation, and my daughter's unworn prom dress, which was ruined. I found the last shirt I remembered my father having worn before his hospital stay. We had taken a cruise after his second course of chemo. It was the last vacation we would take before his death.

For sentimental reasons, I wanted to make sure my dad's watch wasn't thrown in the Dumpster. After weeks of searching, in the corner of the study underneath a pile of destroyed books, I found my dad's watch. I wept with relief.

The lessons my daughters and I would learn from this experience were numerous. One of the greatest gifts we received was experiencing firsthand the kindness and thoughtfulness of our community. Friends and acquaintances, school counselors, teachers, principals, supportive contractors and thoughtful neighbors dropped by with food, clothing, furniture, and money. Others came by to help me sort through the debris for salvageable items. We had no idea how amazing people could be until our house caught fire.

Two years later, I feel differently about the fire. Despite the loss of valued mementoes, the fire did burn away a lot of needless clutter from my home and my life. I discovered that life is much easier with fewer items and less "stuff" to clutter the journey. I didn't replace many of the things that I thought were necessities before the fire. My newly built home is cleaner and has more open space, as do I.

My dad's watch is on my bedside table now. It is a physical reminder that time matters. Anyone or anything can be lost without warning. My desire is to find a sense of serenity, compassion, and strength within myself, model those qualities for my daughters, and share those qualities with others.

Since the fire, my girls and I keep watch for those who experience loss. It is important to us to repay the many kindnesses we received. My family experienced the genuine love and assistance of a community and the warmth it provided. That feeling was priceless. We will forever be profoundly grateful.

All in all, the fire gave us more than it took away.

~Paula Sherwin

Chapter
10

the joy of less

Lessons in Less

92

The One Thing We Didn't Have to Unpack

A memory is what is left when something happens and
does not completely unhappen.
~Edward de Bono

It was two days before we had to leave our large four-bedroom house and move out of state. I loved this house and all the memories we had made in it. I thought back to raising our son and daughter there. We had brought them home from the hospital to this house. This was where they learned to walk and to talk. This was where we watched them play on the lawn as we rocked on the welcoming porch on beautiful spring and autumn days. I had picked apples from the trees in the back yard and learned to make apple pie from scratch in this house.

And now we were saying goodbye.

My husband announced that our things would not all fit in our POD. I stood in our driveway while the cicadas screeched like a car alarm. "What's not going to fit?" I asked.

"The sage couches, the kitchen table, the coffee tables, the treadmill, the rocking chairs…"

"We have to take the porch rockers!" Thunder was starting to rumble in the distance, and the wind was picking up, only adding to my sense of urgency. "I nursed our babies in those! We sat in those and counted the fireflies every summer."

"Honey," my husband continued patiently, "they're not going to fit. And even if they did, we're not going to have a porch in California."

We lived east of the Mississippi and all our family was out West, so we were moving out there to be with the people we so desperately missed. We needed our children to be surrounded by people who loved them unconditionally the way only grandparents can. We needed to know that someone had our back and would move heaven and earth to be there if we called. We had flown solo for five years, and although we had made dear friends, there was just no substitute for our parents, Grandma and Grandpa for our kids.

When an opportunity came for my husband to transfer west (to a town that was just a few hours from my parents and a day's drive from his), we knew it was time. We were excited. We would be living in a house half the size of this one, but we didn't care. We would never have to spend Thanksgiving or Christmas alone again. Our children would be able to grow up with grandparents, aunts, uncles, and cousins in the picture.

"Could we get a bigger POD?" I asked, still trying to bring everything along with us.

Jason sighed. "Amy, this is as big as they come."

"But I love the kitchen table," I said.

"Do you want to bring that one instead of the dining room table?"

I thought a moment. "No."

"Honey, we can't take both!" My husband took off his work gloves. He wiped the sweat from his forehead and locked the doors to the POD. The wind was blowing the branches of our pear trees sideways. The thunder boomed. "We have to wait until the storm passes before we can load anything else in the POD. Okay? You think about what you want to take with us." He slipped quietly back into the house.

I stood in the garage and watched the rain run off our driveway. I felt like the sand was running out of our hourglass. We had to say goodbye to the home I loved and the furniture I loved, too.

I sat down on the bumper of my car and called my mom.

"Hello?"

"Hi, Mom. It's Amy."

"Hi, honey. What's new? How's the packing going?"

"It's not all going to fit," I said, trying to keep my voice steady and not burst into tears.

"What's not going to fit?"

"The treadmill, the kitchen table, the couches, the porch rocking chairs." I felt hot tears spill down my cheeks. "And I know it's just stuff, and I know stuff doesn't matter, but it's hard! I sat in that rocking chair and read stories to Azure when I was pregnant with Seamus. And I lost the last thirty pounds of my baby weight walking on that treadmill at night after the kids went to bed. And I've sat at that kitchen table every night with my family since we moved into this house…"

"Amy, honey. The stuff isn't the memories. You don't need the rocking chairs to remember reading books to Azure on the front porch when she was small. You don't need your

> *You will always have those memories, whether the stuff comes with you to your new house or not.*

kitchen table to remember family dinners. You will always have those memories, whether the stuff comes with you to your new house or not. And you don't have to worry about losing the memories when you leave your stuff behind. Those you take with you, and you don't even have to worry about boxing them up. Okay?"

"Okay," I said.

"How's your weather?" my mom asked.

"We're having an afternoon thunderstorm." I looked up at the skies. The clouds had thinned and bright blue sky bent around them. "But it looks like the rain has stopped."

"Yeah. You are going to be just fine. Moving is tough, but we are so excited that you are going to be closer."

"We're excited too."

My mom was right.

We've been very happy in our new home, half the size of our old one. We have half as much stuff as we did before. We don't miss it, and we have not lost the happy memories of our old home. Those came with us, and they were the only things we never had to box up or unpack.

~Amelia Hollingsworth

93

The Rule of Twenty

To manifest something in your life it is wise to first
clean out your closets.
~Author Unknown

M y eyes narrowed as I pawed through a tumbled mountain of shoes. They were once stacked in two neat lines across the floor. Now the closet looked as though an earthquake had shaken a shoe store. It took me more than five minutes to find a mate for the navy blue pump clutched in my hand. Being late to work again wouldn't be beneficial to my performance appraisal. I could no longer avoid my need to organize.

Later that morning I grumbled to a co-worker about the mess my closet had become. She grinned before giving me a sound piece of advice.

"The best thing I ever did was buy a shoe rack. One glance and you can find what you need in a snap."

Her suggestion made sense. The idea of bringing order out of chaos appealed to me so much I drove straight to a discount store after work to see what they had available. I browsed up and down aisles until I found the shoe rack jackpot. A multitude of choices included racks that held as few as six pairs of shoes all the way up to seventy. I calculated my needs. Only six pairs of shoes would be impossible. Yet I knew I didn't have anywhere near seventy pairs of shoes in my closet. I scanned the options until I noticed a tiered portable shelving unit that held twenty pairs of shoes. Twenty would be perfect. I even felt a little smug. I'd only need to get rid of a few pairs for the new system to work.

At home I assembled the shoe rack and then sipped a cup of hot tea while staring into my closet. The first step would be to see exactly what I had accumulated. I began to pull out shoe after shoe until my bedroom floor was completely littered with them. There were flats and pumps and boots and sandals and tennis shoes and flip-flops.

> *I decided to get rid of any shoes that hadn't been worn within the past eighteen months.*

Once I'd emptied the closet I counted shoes and couldn't believe my eyes. Sixty-three pairs were on the floor. They looked like a sorrowful, drab rainbow in shades of black, blue, and tan.

My brow furrowed. I didn't spend lavishly. Buying shoes wasn't one of my guilty pleasures. In fact, I hardly ever visited the shoe department. I tried to analyze my unexpected excess. True, in the Midwest, wardrobes are more complicated. Four seasons require different types of shoes. You can't wear sandals to trudge through snow or fleece-lined boots when it's hot enough to fry an egg on the sidewalk. Yet I finally had to admit changing weather couldn't hide an obvious fact. Somehow I had collected way too many shoes.

Twenty pairs of shoes ought to be enough for anybody. I set my lips in a firm line. I only needed to figure out a way to reduce sixty-three pairs to twenty. At first the sea of shoes overwhelmed me until a ragged and scarred pair of brown leather boots I'd owned for nearly twenty years caught my eye. Then I spied dingy gray tennis shoes used in the days when we'd gone on float trips. Next to the tennis shoes sat a pair of rhinestone-studded sandals I'd worn to a wedding ten years ago, but never again because they hurt my feet. Perhaps the problem wasn't how many shoes I had added to my closet. It was how few I subtracted. This realization provided my strategy.

I decided to get rid of any shoes that hadn't been worn within the past eighteen months. If a shoe looked like it had been fished from a dumpster, it would have to go, too. With a plan in place, I armed myself with two enormous trash bags. In one bag went shoes too beat up to save. Gently worn shoes suitable for donation went into the other. I would keep the remaining shoes.

At times the process pained me. How could I get rid of the shoes I wore to my daughter's wedding or the run-down-at-the-heels loafers I grabbed because even though they looked ragged, they fit me like a glove? Yet I realized if I had any hope of staying within my twenty pair target, I had to forget sentimentality. I squared my shoulders and stuck to the plan.

Two hours later, the bags were bulging. A count of the surviving shoes revealed twenty-three pairs still standing. I resisted the urge to shove the extra shoes under my bed and with a single deep sigh, selected three more pairs for the donation bag.

Finally I filled the new shoe organizer and stepped back to admire my handiwork. The closet hadn't looked so good in years. I could see every shoe I owned with no need for digging. Fewer choices gave me an added bonus. It would take less time to decide what to wear. By taking control of my closet, life became a little easier. I decided never again to own more than twenty pairs of shoes.

I've kept to my rule though there are occasions when I find myself gazing at a snappy pair of shoes marked down to nearly nothing. But there's truth in numbers. My twenty-pair rule shapes the parameters of my shopping. I can't add new shoes without subtracting old ones. This formula helps me think a lot harder before succumbing to temptation and making a purchase.

Spending money just because you discover a good deal makes no more sense than holding on to something you don't need. There are fewer shoes in my closet, but like old friends, they're the ones I really want to keep.

~Pat Wahler

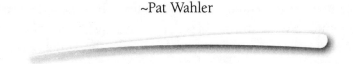

94

The Yard Sale Party

*People coming together as a community can
make things happen.*
~Jacob Rees-Mogg

We have a real estate agent who markets our neighborhood and gives us a great gift each year — he sponsors a "Neighborhood Yard Sale!" He buys ads in the local paper and puts up signs to direct traffic into our neighborhood. We simply need to open our garages, haul out our unwanted stuff, and reap the financial benefits.

One year, I decided to make a real party out of the neighborhood yard sale. I got busy on the phone and asked several friends to join in by hauling their own offerings over to my driveway. As the time grew closer, we kept each other accountable as to our progress and challenged each other to release more and more of our unnecessary possessions. Why is it so hard to part with things you haven't used in years? I realized it was also getting quite competitive! But with the added energy and support, it seemed just a bit easier to release your once "prized treasures" into the hands of others.

We decided that we would all meet on Friday night with our boxes of sale items so we could semi-arrange them before the sale started early Saturday. What an array of stuff arrived at my doorstep — kitchen items, clothes, sports equipment, books, music, office supplies, camping gear, artificial Christmas trees, dishes, jewelry, and garden stuff. There was even a bathtub, remnants from a recent remodel! Over pizza, we talked about the game plan for the morning and shared laughs about the memories attached to so many of the items.

The next morning arrived way too early but strong coffee and donuts got us motivated and we started hauling our assortment on to the lawn and driveway, each lady carefully displaying her wares in her designated zone. As we all sat down to await the arrival of our first customers, we took in the splendor of the view, realizing that it was more of a confusing mess than splendor at all. We also had a friend arrive with one last item — a box of kittens!

As we sipped more coffee and munched more sugary treats, one by one we started to offer some ideas on how our display could be improved. Within thirty minutes we had transformed our mess of merchandise into a mini retail outlet! We had our clothing, sports, housewares, holiday, and garden departments each neatly displayed along with a small music and bookstore. We put the "pet store" near the cashier so that any potential buyers could be properly interviewed to assure the kittens were going to a good home.

> *We have a real estate agent who markets our neighborhood and gives us a great gift each year — he sponsors a "Neighborhood Yard Sale!"*

As the morning moved along, we needed to consolidate areas as sales were made and more space opened up. It was like a perpetually renovated store that took on new dimensions with each passing hour! So many people lingered just because of our friendly banter and discussions over prices and new ideas for arranging our mall. Some shoppers even offered their own ideas of how to make the remaining items more appealing!

By the end of the day, we were exhausted but filled with such joy. Not only were we each getting some much needed cash as well as less congested homes, but we had enjoyed a day of laughter, creativity and time to talk with friends and neighbors. Our yard sale party was a gift to treasure for years to come!

~Joan Wasson

95

Clearing Out the Clutter

*It is preoccupation with possession, more than anything
else, that prevents men from living freely and nobly.*
~Bertrand Russell

I recently completed my grand summer cleanout, an ambitious home project I started in July. My goal was to have a place and a purpose for every single item in each drawer, cupboard, cabinet and closet. It was a lofty ambition to be sure. This cleanout, born of necessity, was a project on which to focus in the midst of personal heartbreak. For a year prior, enduring family stress and illness, I sustained an injury that damaged my vocal cords. I couldn't speak or sing. Eventually the disability found me barely able to arise from my bed each morning.

Not only was the loss of my voice a career destroyer for me, a singer and voice teacher for twenty-five years, but it caused me to question my true purpose in this world. I viewed it not simply as the quitting of a job, but also as a shift in my worth. I was a woman at sea without a life jacket, that which I generally wore in the form of a worthy vocation. I was devastated. Months later, after surviving a period of vocal mourning, I knew I needed something to pull me out of the doldrums. I turned my attention to home.

"Closets and cabinets and cupboards, oh my!" was my Oz-inspired mantra. I had been daunted by the overwhelming task of organizing my house for almost a decade. As an admitted project-starting enthusiast without the discipline to complete my ventures, I had continued to purchase and plan, cram and pile designs into every crevice without completing most of them. Now, there's a saying about what happens when the going gets tough. Yes, as the truism states, I "got going" when things got tough. I wish I meant moving with resolve. Instead, I mean I would literally GO — out the door — on my way to the next idea, all without seeing my original plan through. Thus the sheer volume of "stuff" jammed into every nook and cranny of our home had gotten overwhelming.

I started small and cleaned out a drawer. A slight weight lifted, then I felt a tickle of pride. So I cleaned out another, then another. Next I tackled a kitchen cabinet. I was breathing easier already. The stress of the previous months began to abate, coupled with a sigh of relief that only ridding one's life of excess can produce. "Okay," I thought, "time to rope the kids in." As my son watched the Little League World Series, I would hand him a drawer full of pens and markers with a request, "Will you test each of these on a piece of paper? Toss anything that doesn't work." Forever my happy helper, especially if he can work while watching sports, he would grab the drawer and say, "No problem, Mom!" My daughter was a harder sell but was eventually converted. Though she may deny it, I think she secretly enjoyed the time we spent together getting organized. Side by side, the kids cleaned out our movie cabinet, discovering video compilations along with hours and hours of family events recorded but never enjoyed. We loved watching these precious finds. Little did I know, however, the intangible treasures would continue abundantly as we furthered our mission.

> *I began to view the contents of my home for what they truly were. They attempted to fill a void in my heart.*

For somewhere in the midst of days, then weeks, spent cleaning and organizing, a familiar thread began to surface. I began to view the contents of my home for what they truly were. They attempted to fill a void in my heart. They were a bandage, a temporary fix of an illness. So many years of craving and purchasing passed by without the desire to address the real issue. I was not living life. I was not valuing my role as a mother and wife. I was dreaming and spending my way through it. I had been covering up lack of purpose with material possessions just as my injured vocal cords were now covering up the ache of our family issues. Only when everything ground to a halt was I able to see clearly what I had been camouflaging. What a blessing in disguise.

We worked diligently for three months, and as I cleared the dark recesses of my closets, I recognized I was also clearing the pain, sorrow and insecurities from the past year and beyond. The empty spaces on the shelves signified new spaces within me to fill with an openness of heart and mind: new beginnings, new goals, and new healing. As I straightened each cabinet and drawer, I was straightening out my priorities. Family was once again at the forefront, and even though we weren't having a summer vacation, we were spending hours of quality time together, helping one another and laughing all together. My children and I were never closer.

Lastly, I grasped the importance of completing this monumental project — step by tiny, necessary step — as a final resolution to my self-indulgence. For years I had longed for a bigger home, newer furniture, more space, and more fashionable things. I longed to be accepted for my personal savvy rather than the beauty of sacrifice in raising my family. In finishing all of my tasks, I finally understood that I had been longing for all of this as a way to fill a thirst in me that objects could never quench. I was longing to run from those personal qualities I didn't want to face. Starting small, I finally completed my grand summer cleanout of both my living spaces and my head spaces. Now that I have faced my fears, my regrets, and my skeletons in the proverbial closet, I look forward to each day in my home, free of clutter, free of disorder, and free of distraction. I am focused on life. Best of all, my heart is free once again to be filled with the good things it has to offer… hope, faith and family. It was the greatest summer of my life.

~Cynthia McGonagle McGarity

96

How a Clean Closet Changed My Life

If you want to improve your life immediately,
clean out a closet. Often, it's what we hold onto
that holds us back.
~Cheryl Richardson

I looked at the bed in our room in amazement. It appeared that a very large, very colorful volcano had erupted. Instead of spewing lava though, the duvet was covered in mounds and mounds of clothes. My clothes. Skirts tangled with button-down shirts and jeans, while T-shirts peeked out between the cracks. Belts coiled like snakes among the hems and sleeves of dresses.

How had this happened? I had always excused my "retail therapy" habit. After all, it more closely resembled recycling than outright consuming. Sure, I might "binge" at tag sales or thrift shops, but I always brought bags of other clothes and accessories to donate weeks later. The process, in my mind, cancelled itself out. Was I living in dreamland?

I've always had a romantic view of life. I grew up, in fact, thoroughly convinced that I'd been born in the wrong century. I was a Laura Ingalls Wilder wannabe, an Anne of Green Gables devotee. I longed to live in a simpler time: when women held quilting bees, and poetry readings were entertainment in place of television. When women had one "good dress," and took pleasure in making butter by hand, tatting and making beautiful quilts. Honestly, I'm still not sure what "tatting" is, but it sounds industrious.

Those pioneers lived in the moment. I dreamt of being whisked back in time, living in a sunny cabin on the outskirts of town, talking with my neighbors instead of dashing off hurried e-mails, and enjoying extended family dinners on Sunday afternoons instead of trying to keep my son entertained on rainy days.

Nowhere in my childhood daydreams did I imagine the stress of maintaining a career, caring for a house and family, and performing all the other tasks that adulthood demands. If I had, my daydreams of living in the early nineteenth century would have been even more impassioned. Was modern-day stress what fueled my desire to shop?

> *More important than all the physical changes though, are the emotional ones.*

I sighed and returned to the closet to survey the results of the last hour's decimation. Empty hangers swung from the clothes rod, but other than that, and a row of shoes and boots neatly lining the floor, my half of the closet was empty. It looked so big! Spacious. It hadn't looked like this since we first moved in.

Stretching my back, I returned to the bed and sat down. Or tried to. Instead I slid off the mound of clothes and onto the floor. Why had I ever thought this de-cluttering challenge would be "fun?"

For months I'd been scouring the Internet and reading blogs and articles on minimalism and intentional living. The premise of the idea wasn't new to me: in my early twenties I'd called a timeout on credit cards and cleaned up my financial act. Eventually my husband and I had paid off more than $5,000 worth of credit card charges. I never wanted to do that again.

I'd even run a class on simple living and written articles on the topic. I'd learned though, that one can live "simply" and still accumulate "stuff." And that's why I'd decided to join a closet-reformation challenge I'd found online. Project 333 (www.theproject333.com), founded by Courtney Carver, entices would-be minimalists to live with only thirty-three items in their wardrobes for three months. Sound impossible? I thought it would be easy.

Sitting here now though, I wasn't so sure. I took a deep breath and walked over to my pile of trash bags. First sort, then pile. It took hours of brain-numbing decisions to decide what to keep and what to let go of. In the end I hauled three bags of clothes and accessories to the garage for my next donation run. I stuffed another four bags under my bed. These were the "maybe" clothes. As in "maybe I'll need this again, maybe I won't." According to Ms. Carver this was allowed as part of the challenge. I was grateful for that.

With the clothes making up my new "capsule wardrobe" selected, I hung them carefully, then stood back to survey the results.

"Wow," I said, a shiver running down my spine. "This looks amazing."

I could clearly see everything that was available. Rather than a mishmash of shirts, skirts, dresses and pants coordinated only by color, I could now easily see each item. There was even a slice of beautiful space between each hanger.

Now the real test began, though. I bit my lip as I shut the closet door and flicked off the light. Would I be able to create stylish outfits from such a small number of items?

Weeks later I noticed something: getting ready for work in the morning was a snap. Plus, I hadn't worn the same outfit in the exact same way since the closet metamorphosis. Because I could see (and actually like) all the pieces left in my wardrobe, it was much easier to put a stylish ensemble together in much less time. I loved the lightness and airiness of my side of the closet, too; so much that I often paused after choosing my clothes for the day and drank it in.

It's been more than a year since that closet cleanout. Do I still maintain just thirty-three items in my closet at all times? No. I still have a lot of room between hangers, though, and the clothes there are items that I love and wear frequently.

Something else interesting happened: my closet became an impetus in other areas of my home and even my life. I've lost track of the number of bags and boxes I've brought to Goodwill over the past year. The kitchen counter is nearly bare. I love it. I've given away more than half of my book collection and a recent rearranging of rooms in our house gave me the opportunity to sort our young son's toys and share or sell a good portion of them.

More important than all the physical changes though, are the emotional ones. I find myself asking, "Is this really going to make my life better?" before buying a new piece of clothing. And before I enter a commitment into my calendar, I say, "What will I say no to in order to make time for this?"

I'm certainly not perfect. Occasionally, I bring home an item of clothing or something for the house because I need a lift or a change of scenery. More and more, however, I'm finding that the real key to living a life that resembles the nineteenth century is being content with what I have. Doing so helps me slow down and focus my attention on making memories… and enjoying a clutter-free closet each morning.

~Joy Choquette

97

The Lesson of the Mandala

*It's usually quite hard to let go and move on, but once
you do, you'll feel free and realize it was the best
decision you've ever made.*
~Author Unknown

I pushed and shoved then I pushed some more. When did my closet get so full? I looked down at the two shopping bags of clothes purchased on my latest spree. Maybe it was time to admit I had a problem.

Like many women, I always loved to shop. In my teen years, I was what my girlfriends and I affectionately called "a mall rat," a girl who hung out at the mall every weekend, checking out the current fashions while simultaneously checking out other teenagers of the male persuasion. Fast-forward twenty-five years. After the death of my mother, I once again found pleasure in walking the mall. No longer bound by caregiving responsibilities, I could spend as much time there as I pleased, have a pleasant lunch in the food court and get a bit of exercise in a temperature-controlled environment. It was the perfect activity. And now I even had something I didn't have as a teenager — credit cards.

Armed with my plastic and fueled by the sugar and caffeine of a tall mocha latte, I could shop for hours, returning home with incredible bargains. I'd hold up a sweater for my husband to see. "Can you believe this was only eight dollars?" I'd proclaim proudly. "And this one," I'd say while lifting a pair of slacks, "cost only slightly more — and it has a designer label!"

Oh, I was quite the shopper all right. It didn't matter to me that my sweater drawer overflowed and caused me to annex the extras to a storage container shoved under the bed. Nor did I mind when an excess of accessories was required to be housed in a plastic box atop my dresser. It had been so long since I did anything special for myself, I rationalized. I deserved some new things.

Yet now I was forced to take a closer look at my situation. I poked around my overstuffed closet and pulled out a few of my more recent purchases: a poncho emblazoned with butterflies, two pair of leopard leggings, two blue blazers and several sets of T-shirts in duplicate colors. Clearly, I had gone from a bargain shopper to a shopping warrior whose battle cry was "one if on sale, two if on clearance!"

Cleaning out my closet and drawers created a domino effect of benefits.

I slowly pulled a few more articles out of my closet and laid them on the floor in a careful circle, creating a sort of textile mandala. Long ago, when I still had time to read, I recalled reading about the Buddhist monks of Tibet who painstakingly created mandalas, a circular design created with colored sand, only to disassemble them upon their completion, signifying the impermanence of life. The letting go, they feel, is as important as the act of creation itself. It is only through the letting go, they believe, that growth and healing can take place. Yes, nothing is forever, I thought, looking back on my mother's long illness and her ultimate passing. It was time to let go.

I pulled each piece of clothing out of my closet and sorted them into several piles. Clothing with tags still attached would be returned to the store for a refund. Worn out clothing would go directly into the trash. Anything still in good condition but in a wrong size, style or color for me would be donated to an organization that helped women in need. The remainder would be returned to my closet. After that, I vowed, there would be no more shopping for a long, long time.

This act, which took all of about an hour, was exhilarating and freeing in a way I could have never imagined. Cleaning out my closet and drawers created a domino effect of benefits. Dressing each morning became a much simpler task since it was easier to both find and select outfits in a closet that had room to spare. Housecleaning became less of a chore once I no longer had to move boxes and bags of clothing to accomplish the task. Weekends were much freer, as well, once I wasn't spending so much time at the mall bargain hunting. No longer did I have to reconcile charge bills, file away receipts and run to the bank to transfer money for department store payments.

Now, with my newfound spare time, I make frequent trips to the library and catch up on my reading. I took up knitting again and committed to making two sweaters a year for a worldwide organization that distributes them to needy children. I renewed old friendships that had been put on hiatus during my caregiving days, and if I want to take a walk I lace up my sneakers and pound the pavement in the fresh air regardless of temperature. My life is varied and full again, all because I let go. It's true really, I think, what the Tibetan monks say. The real healing comes from the letting go.

~Monica A. Andermann

98

Waste Not, Want Not

The more you have, the more you are occupied. The
less you have, the more free you are.
~Mother Teresa

I reached up to grab a spare blanket from the top shelf of the closet and was immediately pelted by additional covers, spare pillows and assorted quilts shrouding me like a tent. "I have GOT to get my act together," I muttered.

I was never "neat" or "organized." My closets were jammed with clothes that fit, might fit one day, or would never fit but gave me hope. My important document storage consisted of one empty accordion file surrounded by bulging bags separated by year. My bathroom contained expired or partially used creams, shampoos, toothpaste, deodorants and other hygiene products that I kept in case I ran out of my usual items. I even had three junk drawers instead of the customary one. Meanwhile, my kitchen utensils sat crammed in jars on the counter or in a jumbled mess in one top drawer.

I'm not a hoarder, but I did grow up in an environment where we didn't discard things simply because they were outdated or worn out. My parents repaired what was broken and improvised with what we owned, finding different uses long after a cold cream jar or sturdy box was empty. The tip of a broken shoelace from a skate could easily be dipped in wax and reused on sneakers, while a ratty, torn dishtowel became a useful dust cloth. We recycled long before it became a "green" thing.

I extricated myself, kicked the pile of bedding aside into a heap and went to pour a cup of coffee.

"I need to make changes," I mused, sipping the hot brew, but the task seemed monumental.

I didn't even know where to begin. A tour of the house was unnecessary. I knew what I'd find. A mental inventory of the flotsam and jetsam of my life ran through my head, and it all boiled down to one thing — unnecessary clutter. Every nook and cranny of our adequately large home was filled with what I often deluded myself into believing were "prized possessions."

For starters, I had six shelves of knick-knacks — three for teapots and three filled with ceramic cats — all covered with a film of dust. I never actually intended to collect either, but once I had two of each, well meaning friends and relatives assumed I wanted more and I was inundated with them for Christmas and birthdays.

Family photos dotted the walls, and loose, curled snapshots were tucked into the corners awaiting more frames that I "eventually" planned to buy.

I had sufficient stemware and other assorted crystal to provide toasts for everyone in Times Square on New Year's Eve. Enough pots, pans, plates, bowls and dishes to open a soup kitchen were wedged into my cupboards, and three complete sets of cutlery — services for eight — jangled every time I pulled open the drawer. At least twenty unused mugs with cute sayings sat on shelves; we only used our two favorites. Unmatched glasses, their companions long shattered, were mixed in with newer full sets I couldn't resist buying on sale.

My office was a mess, too. Bookcases were tightly packed with notebooks, steno pads, copy books, stationery and multiple packs of notebook paper from my son's school days that ended more than a decade before, many still in their original plastic wrap. Pens, many of them already dried up, were crammed in jars, jugs, cases and boxes. Rulers, pencils, erasers, and markers I never used lay stacked and forgotten in caddies. Two old computers sat in a corner for one of those "you never know" days.

Even the guest room bulged with junk — outdated video games, a broken TV set, board games we never played. The dresser was filled with memorabilia dating back to my son's birth more than thirty years ago. Drawings yellowed from being stuck on the fridge, childishly scrawled notes, handmade greeting cards — even his hospital bracelet from the day he was born — all items I intended to catalogue when I had time. Another contained his baby blankets and stained christening suit.

"Why am I holding on to so much stuff?" I asked myself out loud.

Just then, the dog wandered in with the stuffed rabbit he carried everywhere. He had at least twenty toys, yet he favored this mangled little bunny, ignoring all the others.

"I need to be more like you, Jack," I told him. He wagged his tail and lay at my feet with a contented sigh.

As I watched him, I realized that I could, in fact, be like him — satisfied with only my preferred items. With a sudden burst of energy, I decided to begin right away.

> *As I suspected, I never even missed what I'd packed away all those months ago.*

I started with the living room. I carefully sorted through all the items, placing those I didn't like or use into boxes, dating them for exactly one year later. I stored duplicate stuff in bins for a garage sale, and planned to put the profits in a separate account, earmarking it to replace anything that broke at a later date. "Someday" and "in case" possessions went directly into the trash or, if in good condition, to a pile for donations.

The souvenirs of my son's childhood, along with all the loose photographs, were scanned and saved on a disk to be stored in a safety deposit box. I had long ago bought scrapbooks and photo albums, and vowed to begin categorizing the originals that same week.

I managed to go through four rooms that day. My bathroom was spotless, containing only what we used. I couldn't believe how much more spacious the house was beginning to look. Shelves held only the things we loved.

I allowed myself only one storage case for sheer sentimental value. Surprisingly, it was only half full, even with two of those favorite blankets. The christening suit was discarded. I had plenty of photographs immortalizing it. By the end of the week, I'd managed to organize most of our belongings. The dog didn't even notice that the toys I donated to the local animal shelter were gone.

A year later, I parted with my final hoard. The contents of those dated, unopened bins earned me several hundred dollars at yet another garage sale. As I suspected, I never even missed what I'd packed away all those months ago.

Not only did I de-clutter my home, but an added bonus was that my mind was now de-cluttered as well. By staying on top of mess, I no longer panic over disorganization and hurried cleaning when company drops in — well, except for my office. That door still remains closed, but I'm working on that. Maybe next year...

~Marya Morin

99

What a Birthday Should Look Like

We worry about what a child will become tomorrow,
yet we forget that he is someone today.
~Stacia Tauscher

We just celebrated my son's ninth birthday. If you had asked me ten years ago what my future son's ninth birthday would look like, I might have described the perfect summer pool party. Something rambunctious and loud and perfectly planned. Water balloons and cannonball contests and twenty sun-kissed kids clamoring around a cake shaped like a surfboard. Hot dogs and music and drinks in red plastic cups for the adults.

My son's ninth birthday looked absolutely nothing like that.

This is what we do, we special needs parents. We compare what we think a childhood should look like to what our kid's experience actually is. I play this game a lot, and it's like Tic Tac Toe — nobody wins.

This birthday, I stopped myself from creating the day I thought my son *should* want. I didn't plan a thing. There were no invitations and no guests. I told my autistic son to plan his perfect day, and I sat back and followed his lead.

His plan involved sleeping in my bed on his "birthday eve" so he could "wake up really early to a birthday hug." He wanted me to decorate the chandelier over the kitchen island so he "could feel happy all day." He wanted waffles; he wanted his therapist to make him a card; he wanted Hailey, his long-time sitter, to take him to see his favorite airplane; he wanted a funny video from his uncle; and he wanted to eat cheese pizza with candles on it with his mom and dad.

> *My son's birthday was simple and easy, and pared down to only those things that were important to him.*

There was no fanfare, no plethora of presents, no big to-do. My son's birthday was simple and easy, and pared down to only those things that were important to him.

As I tucked my son into bed at the end of the day, his eyes half-closed with exhaustion, I asked him how his ninth birthday was. He smiled. "It was so awesome, Mom. I sure am loved."

I sure am loved.

My son has such a difficult time in so many areas, but he knows exactly how to make himself feel happy and loved. It makes me wonder who is really teaching who here.

My son's ninth birthday was nothing like I would have planned. But for the first time, it was everything it was supposed to be.

~Rebecca Smith Masterson

100

Fifty-Two Weeks

You can't lead anyone else further than you
have gone yourself.
~Gene Mauch

I kept complaining that my grown children wouldn't clean up their rooms in my house, even though they've both had their own homes for years. I even wrapped up some of their things and gave them their own stuff for Christmas! My husband Bill was also tired of hearing my snide remarks about his "souvenir T-shirt" drawer and all his college books that occupy valuable, shared bookshelf space. I call him the Territorial Imperialist. If you aren't sure what I'm referring to, please ask Bill for one of his college books and you can look it up… and please don't return the book.

In a rare fit of self-awareness at the beginning of the year, lacking a New Year's resolution that I believed I'd keep, I had an epiphany. How could I justify telling my husband and children to clean up when I was just as guilty?

It's not that anyone can tell. The house looks neat and organized, but behind those closet doors and inside those cabinets and drawers, hides twenty years of excess stuff, most of it mine.

I had also just finished reviewing the 300 finalists for this *Chicken Soup for the Soul* book, and I was confronted with my own poor behavior after reading these motivational stories. So I sat down at my computer during New Year's week and made a list of fifty-two de-cluttering projects to do in 2016, some big and some small.

I tried to make the projects as non-daunting as possible, cutting them into tiny bite-size pieces to the extent that I could. I also decided I can do them in any order I want. I can even leave the most difficult ones till last. They range from the mostly easy — "clean out sock drawer and throw away the gross ones" — to the occasionally awful — "go through basement with Bill and justify every single thing in there or get rid of it."

It's early February as I'm writing this and I've done six of the fifty-two projects. By the way, they don't get crossed off my list until whatever I've disposed of has actually left the house... and the back of my car. That means I've already made two trips to the thrift shop, two trips to the clothing recycling bin, and one trip to the consignment shop, to truly get rid of the stuff.

This past weekend I cleaned out the cabinet in which I store pantyhose. That was one of my fifty-two projects, and it was an eye opener. I had at least thirty pairs of white pantyhose, two-thirds of them never opened. I can't even remember when white pantyhose were last in style except on Snow White. And I found twenty pairs of navy pantyhose, too, that I have no use for now. The only survivors of any utility were the black pantyhose and tights and the skin-colored pantyhose (those may also be out of fashion right now, but if you had legs as sickly white as mine you would understand). To think that I've been carting around more than one hundred pairs of pantyhose for twenty-five years, moving three times!

> *How could I justify telling my husband and children to clean up when I was just as guilty?*

It took me three hours to sort out all the pantyhose and tights. And I must confess I've wasted an additional thirty minutes in the last twenty-four hours opening the cabinet and admiring my newly labeled and organized boxes every time I go by.

One of my big motivators, besides earning bragging and complaining-to-the-family rights in 2017, was that many of my excess possessions could be of value to someone else. The longer I hold onto them, the less valuable they will be to the next person, witness my twenty-years-out-of-style white pantyhose. It's just selfish to hold onto these things that may be of benefit to someone else.

The cold weather got us thinking and we cleaned out our coat closets over the weekend, too. I had already given away my excess coats in prior years, but my husband found more than a dozen men's coats and jackets — his and our son's — that he can share with people in our community. We don't need two of everything. It's a bit of a thrill now to open those doors, see everything with one glance, and not worry about throwing out my back stuffing a heavy coat onto a crowded rack.

Another impetus for this project is the thought of leaving this for our children to manage. We don't expect to die for three or four decades, but what if something were to happen? I spent three backbreaking months cleaning out my grandmother's apartment a few years ago, and I wouldn't wish that on anyone.

I'm quite excited about my year of projects, and I have to restrain myself from doing even more of the projects now. After all, I have a job and other responsibilities, so my fifty-two projects will have to be spread out over fifty-two weeks. In the meantime, my husband and my children won't be hearing any complaints from me. They get a whole year off.

~Amy Newmark

Controlled Chaos

In about the same degree as you are
helpful, you will be happy.
~Karl Reiland

Recently, I decided to partner with chaos and de-clutter my life in a BIG way. We decided as a family to return to one of our rental homes, and it meant downsizing by about two-thirds!

We needed to get rid of LOTS of stuff and we only had a few weeks to pull it off. You can imagine how much work that was with four children, but I turned it into a beneficial learning experience. I wanted them to take control of their own clutter and understand the value of getting organized and letting go of excess things they didn't need. I placed boxes inside each of their rooms and encouraged them to make three piles: things to give away, things to gift, and stuff to throw out. What survived the cut got to go back to our old house with us.

What is the difference between giving and gifting? For us, "giving" meant donating to a good cause for people we didn't know. "Gifting" meant seeing the value in something special for family and friends. We called the process "Gift/Give/Garbage."

It's amazing how much stuff one family of six can accumulate. And loads of it is *good* stuff! I love going through my closet and sharing some of my favorite fashion pieces with girlfriends who will enjoy them more than I do. And I always know I can find treasures in another friend's closet. Unorganized spaces stress me out so I try to keep only what I use. This is what I have always tried to teach my children, so this move was a HUGE teaching opportunity.

I knew that space and storage were going to be a challenge as we moved back into our old home, one-third the size of this one, so I threw out as many damaged goods as possible, donated bags of outgrown clothes and shoes to charity bins, and packed most of my extra kitchen stuff for future use. My kids did pretty well at separating what they loved, liked and didn't need.

I tried to sell most of our old furniture on the Internet, but no luck, so I called resale stores to try to make a few deals and had no luck with them either. Then I remembered Habitat for Humanity and discovered they would pick everything up and give me a tax write-off for my donation. What a win-win! They actually did me a favor by clearing out my crammed garage that looked like a swap meet, and allowed me to experience the joy of knowing I had participated in helping many families in need.

> *It was so much easier to let go of the clutter when we could imagine how it would help this unfortunate family.*

Then my e-mail chimed and the subject read "family lost home." A family in our temple community had lost everything when their house burned to the ground. The e-mail said they needed anything and everything. I read on to learn that their three children were close in age and size to mine and the father was the same size as my husband.

This awful news gave us even more motivation to give away our things. I quickly called for a family meeting and each of us went back to our rooms to revisit anything and everything we could part with to help out this family in need. With that message in mind and held close in our hearts, we easily parted with many more wonderful things and gave Gift/Give/Garbage a new meaning.

It was so much easier to let go of the clutter when we could imagine how it would help this unfortunate family. Sometimes someone else's tragedy becomes a lesson for another. My kids learned a great lesson — when it comes to charity, you get back as much as you give.

We managed to make it through the move, and it was a pleasure to reacquaint ourselves with our old house, accompanied by only the most meaningful of our possessions. I hope that we can all implement Gift/Give/Garbage on a regular basis now and continue to live a less cluttered life in which generosity plays a big part in our everyday thinking—without having to move again to remind ourselves!

~Brooke Burke-Charvet

Meet Our Contributors

Monica A. Andermann lives and writes on Long Island where she shares a home with her husband and their little tabby, Samson. Her work has been included in such publications as *Woman's World*, *The Secret Place* and *Guideposts* as well as many other *Chicken Soup for the Soul* titles.

Jema Anderson left Minnesota in 2011 for the open road as a full-time traveler in an RV. Jema shares a humorous and raw perspective of life through writing, photography, and video. Jema weaves stories of travel, adventure, and community through her authentic storytelling of the people she meets to the places she visits.

Mary Anglin-Coulter majored in English and Communication and received her Bachelor of Arts degree from Bellarmine University. She is a freelance writer living with her wife and their three daughters. They lovingly refer to their home as the Estrogen House.

Elizabeth Atwater lives on a horse ranch in a small town in North Carolina. She enjoys writing, gardening, the out-of-doors, and volunteering with senior services and hospice. Most of all, though, she enjoys the love and devotion of her husband Joe who is her soul mate.

Katie Bangert's stories have appeared in *Chicken Soup for the Soul: Find Your Inner Strength* and *Chicken Soup for the Soul: Thanks to My Mom*. She lives in Texas with her husband, three children and many family pets. Katie finds those many hours spent waiting in carpool line provide great literary inspiration. Read more at katiebangert.com.

Denise Barnes unfortunately sold her estate agency business to two conmen, resulting in her book, *Seller Beware*. She has since published *Annie's Story* and *Juliet's Story* in *The Voyagers* trilogy. She has a B.A. (honors) in the Arts and is crazy about her rescued white cat. E-mail her at denisebarnesuk@gmail.com.

Brianna Bell is a writer from Canada. She is married to her college sweetheart Daniel, and has two young children, Penny and Georgia. E-mail Brianna at briannarbell@gmail.com.

Bruce Black, the author of *Writing Yoga* (Rodmell Press), received his MFA degree in writing from Vermont College. When he's not practicing yoga or writing, he's taking photographs of the plants and flowers that blossom in his front yard or that he discovers on his morning walks. He lives in Sarasota, FL.

Veronica Bowman is a poet and writer who aspires to inspire others with her writing. She lives in North Carolina with her husband and a menagerie of pets.

John P. Buentello is an author who has published essays, fiction, poetry and nonfiction for adults and children. He is the co-author of the novel *Reproduction Rights* and the short story collections *Binary Tales* and *The Night Rose of the Mountain*. E-mail him at jakkhakk@yahoo.com.

Jill Burns lives in the mountains of West Virginia with her wonderful family. She's a retired piano teacher and performer. She enjoys writing, music, gardening, nature, and spending time with her grandchildren.

Christopher E. Cantrell has several diplomas from the Tennessee College of Applied Technology. He teaches Industrial Maintenance in Middle Tennessee and was in the maintenance field for twenty-four years.

He and his high school sweetheart started dating at sixteen and have been married since 1991. They have two children, and love to travel.

Brenda Cathcart-Kloke is a retired school district administrative assistant in Thornton, CO. She enjoys spending time with her family, oil painting, reading, and writing short inspirational stories.

Joy Choquette has been writing professionally for the past eight years and loves to find new ways to de-clutter her life to focus on what she loves. In her spare time she makes junk art, upcycles, and enjoys spending time with her family outdoors. E-mail her at joywriter55@ gmail.com or read her blog at www.joy-creates.blogspot.com.

Maril Crabtree lives in the Midwest and enjoys writing about her far-flung and amazing family. Her award-winning poetry and creative nonfiction have appeared in numerous journals and anthologies. More of her work may be seen at www.marilcrabtree.com.

Priscilla Dann-Courtney is a writer and clinical psychologist living in Boulder, CO. Her columns have appeared in a number of national magazines and newspapers. Her book, *Room to Grow: Stories of Life and Family*, is a collection of her essays. Yoga, meditation, running, writing, family, and friends light her world.

D.S.A. enjoys her career as a wordsmith and believes everyone should have a favorite word, one that brings a smile and serenity upon hearing it. Hers is "lovingkindness," chosen for what it represents. She hopes every life is graced each day by moments of both receiving and bestowing lovingkindness.

Barbara Davey is the Director of Community Relations at Crane's Mill in West Caldwell, NJ. She received a B.A. and M.A. from Seton Hall University, where she majored in English and journalism, and is an adjunct professor at Caldwell University. She and her husband live in Verona, NJ. E-mail her at BarbaraADavey@aol.com.

Gwen Daye is a wife, homemaker, dog rescuer, parent of two teenagers, and is thrilled to have her second piece accepted into the *Chicken Soup for the Soul* series.

Mary Dempsey, a former teacher and bookstore owner, resides in Bluffton, SC. Her writing has appeared in newspapers, magazines and five *Chicken Soup for the Soul* books. She is a freelance writer for a local newspaper and has recently published a book of short stories. Mary enjoys traveling and is an avid cycler.

Katie Drew is a retired lawyer, enjoying her slower-paced life and the chance to do the things she never had time for before. Less really *is* more — more breathing space for the things that matter. E-mail her at kidsbookwrighter@gmail.com.

Aimee DuFresne is a writer and coach for women ready to embrace their true power. After publishing her book, *Keep Going: From Grief to Growth*, Aimee and her husband packed up their Prius in 2014 and have been traveling the country speaking, housesitting and petsitting ever since. They continue to spread joy wherever they go.

Danica Favorite loves the adventure of living a creative life. She and her family recently moved to their dream home in the mountains above Denver, CO. She writes inspirational romance and can be reached via her website at www.danicafavorite.com.

Sally Friedman is a longtime and proud contributor to the *Chicken Soup for the Soul* series. Her work has appeared in *The New York Times, Ladies' Home Journal, Family Circle,* and national and regional magazines and newspapers. She writes about real life, with her own family as her favorite material. E-mail her at pinegander@aol.com.

Robyn Gerland is the author of *All These Long Years Later*, a book of short stories; a past editor of the internationally distributed glossy, *Hysteria*; a frequent author in the *Chicken Soup for the Soul* series, and a contributor and columnist for several magazines and newspapers, including the Federation of British Columbia Writers' *WordWorks*.

Heather Gillis is a military wife, mother and nurse. She is a blogger, speaker, and author of *Waiting for Heaven*. She is founder of Bowen's Hope, a ministry that helps "Kidney Disease Kids and Their Families." To learn more about Heather or to read her blog, visit www.heathergillis.com.

Bracha Goetz is a Harvard grad who loves to write about the deepest topics in a simple and delightful way so children can understand them. Her more than thirty spiritual picture books can all be seen at www.amazon.com/author/spiritualkidsbooks-brachagoetz.

Kelti Goudie has a Bachelor of Arts degree, with honours, in Spanish and a major in English with a concentration in creative writing. She enjoys listening to music and playing with her cats. She is looking to become a professional freelancer and work with her own writing on the side.

Carol Hartsoe is a retired teaching assistant and former newspaper columnist. She stays busy with writing, visiting schools to share her own children's stories, and spending time with family.

Jill Haymaker is an attorney and author of Western contemporary romances. She lives in Colorado and has three grown children and three granddaughters. This is her fifth story published in the *Chicken Soup for the Soul* series. Contact her at jillhaymaker@aol.com or www.jillhaymaker.com.

Miriam Hill is a frequent contributor to the *Chicken Soup for the Soul* series and has been published in *Writer's Digest*, *The Christian Science Monitor*, *Grit*, *St. Petersburg Times*, *The Sacramento Bee*, and Poynter online. Miriam's submission received Honorable Mention for Inspirational Writing in a Writer's Digest Writing Competition.

Maggie Hofstaedter is a freelance writer who tries to find inspiration in everyday life and express it through her writing. She works from her home in Lansdale, PA where she lives with her husband Dan, their kids Molly and Zach, and their dog Casey.

Amelia Hollingsworth wishes everyone could have a friend like Lois Thompson Bartholomew. When Amelia told Lois that she was interested in writing, Lois encouraged her. She mentored Amelia, and even sent her the submission guidelines that led to Amelia's first publication in *Chicken Soup for the Soul: Just for Preteens.*

David Hull was a teacher in upstate New York for twenty-five years before joyfully retiring to do more writing, reading, watching old movies, gardening and spending time with his nieces and nephews. David writes a monthly column in a local newspaper and has stories published in other *Chicken Soup for the Soul* books.

Jennie Ivey lives in Tennessee. She is the author of numerous works of fiction and nonfiction, including stories in several *Chicken Soup for the Soul* books. Learn more at jennieivey.com.

Jeanie Jacobson is on the leadership team of Wordsowers Christian Writers in Omaha, NE. She's been published in seven *Chicken Soup for the Soul* books, and is writing a Christian-slanted fantasy series. Jeanie loves visiting family and friends, reading, hiking, praise dancing, and gardening. Learn more at jeaniejacobson.com.

Tanya Janke has worked in three schools, two shopping malls, a theatre, a market research company, and a berry patch. She now spends her days writing. Her first play, an adaptation of *The Little Prince*, was produced in Toronto in 2010.

Celia Jarvis is a trained journalist with a love for both exotic food and travel—ignited after her trip to Nigeria. She currently lives in

London, where the weather is often bad but the culture is always good, and makes her living copywriting.

Debby Johnson lives in Southern California with her husband Ron, and youngest child, Christopher. Her four older children have flown the coop enjoying life's adventures. She has published one book of poetry and two illustrated children's books. She is also an artist, showing her art in various galleries.

Terri Kafyeke is a Canadian tree hugger and traveler, currently based in the German capital where she works as a researcher. She studied environmental biology and environmental impact assessment in Montreal. Terri enjoys reading, writing and exploring the world while cultivating a popcorn addiction.

K.D. King is a freelance writer who specializes in holistic health and wellness articles. She is also busy working on her first novel. When she's not writing, she enjoys gardening, traveling and knitting.

Suzannah Kiper is a graduate of the University of Louisville and has been married to her high school sweetheart, Tim, for over eighteen years. She is the mother of two amazing kids and two Maltese dogs. She is a seventh-generation Kentuckian and enjoys reading, singing, crafting, and traveling. She often blogs about her adventures.

This is **T. Jensen Lacey's** thirteenth story in the *Chicken Soup for the Soul* series. In addition, Lacey has published fourteen books and/or novels and, as a freelance journalist, has published more than 800 articles for newspapers and magazines. She enjoys reading, hiking, being outdoors and cooking. E-mail her at TJensenLacey@yahoo.com.

Ruth Lehrer retired from her fifth grade classroom thirty years ago, began writing Personal Essays and became an Elderhostel coordinator. Her memoir, *My Book of Ruth: Reflections of a Jewish Girl*, is dedicated to her two grandsons. She conducts a writing workshop at the Bay Club in Queens, NY. E-mail her at ruthartl@gmail.com.

Susan Leitzsch, a retired microbiologist, lives and travels full-time across the United States with her husband Tom. She has two grown children (twins), and one grandson. Her many interests include traveling, nature, hiking, knitting and several other creative outlets.

Kate Lemery earned an undergraduate degree in English literature and a master's degree in art history. She worked for the National Gallery of Art and Smithsonian Institution for fifteen years before resigning to be a stay-at-home mom. She's finishing her first novel and lives with her family in suburban Washington, D.C.

Sydney Logan is an elementary school librarian and the best-selling author of six novels. A native of East Tennessee, she enjoys playing piano and relaxing on her porch with her wonderful husband and their very spoiled cat. Learn more at www.sydneylogan.com.

Barbara LoMonaco has worked for Chicken Soup for the Soul as an editor since 1998. She has co-authored two *Chicken Soup for the Soul* book titles and has had stories published in numerous other titles. Barbara is a graduate of the University of Southern California and has a teaching credential.

Patricia Lorenz is a frequent contributor to the *Chicken Soup for the Soul* series with stories in nearly sixty of them. She's also the author of fourteen books, her latest being *57 STEPS TO PARADISE: Finding Love in Midlife and Beyond.* E-mail her at patricialorenz4@gmail.com to contact her as a speaker for your group.

Shehfina Mamdani has a passion for teaching and hopes to make a difference in the world and the lives of her students through her teaching. She loves to capture every moment with her amazing family and friends through pictures and has been lovingly encouraged by them to internalize these memories through "mental selfies."

Rebecca Smith Masterson lives in Phoenix, AZ, where she is a litigation attorney, special education consultant for parents, and most importantly, a mother to her adopted son. Rebecca has been featured in numerous publications, including *The Huffington Post*, Scary Mommy and Autism Speaks.

Though her career as a teaching artist for The Walt Disney Company and The Young Americans keeps her very busy, **Cynthia McGarity** has a large following for her blog, *God's Daily Message for the Terminally Dense*, and has been published in several anthologies. Her app, Branching Out in Faith, is available at the iTunes store.

Phyllis McKinley has one house, two citizenships, three step-grandchildren, four children, five grandchildren, and soon-to-be six books published. She has lived in seven houses in eight years and nine cities in ten years. She collects books, quotes and friends wherever she goes. E-mail her at leafybough@hotmail.com.

Heidi McLaughlin is an international speaker and author of five books. She inspires women to become beautiful from the inside out. Heidi lives with her husband Jack among the beautiful vineyards of Kelowna, British Columbia. She loves her eclectic family of five children and nine grandchildren. Learn more at www.heartconnection.ca.

Dee Dee McNeil, educator/singer/songwriter/poet/journalist/producer and playwright has received several national commendations and awards for her journalism and music contributions. She has a column at www.musical.memoirs.wordpress.com and has contributed to www.lajazz.com for the past six years. Learn more at www.deedeemac.co.

Marybeth Mitcham holds a B.S. degree in biology, is completing her MPH in nutrition, and currently works as a community educator. A contributor to The Mighty website, she is a freelance author whose writings have been published online, in *Celebrate Life Magazine*, and in several printed and e-book anthologies.

Geri Moran is a technical writer and craft artist who lives in New York. She loves to make people smile with the handcrafted products she sells at EmeraldGreetings.com. Geri is thankful daily for her wonderful friends and family, and is especially grateful for her son, Paul.

Marya Morin is a freelance writer. Her stories and poems have appeared in publications such as *Woman's World* and Hallmark. Marya also penned a weekly humorous column for an online newsletter, and writes custom poetry on request. She lives in the country with her husband. E-mail her at Akushla514@hotmail.com.

Nicole L.V. Mullis is the author of the novel *A Teacher Named Faith* (Cairn Press 2015). Her work has appeared in literary magazines and anthologies, including the *Chicken Soup for the Soul* series. Her plays have been produced in New York, California and Michigan. She lives in Michigan with her husband and three children.

Kaitlin Murray loves to travel, write, and volunteer. She was born in Holland and has also lived in Germany, France, the USA, and Italy. For the past two years, Kaitlin has been traveling full-time and volunteering all over the world. She also founded a charity called Kids Unite 4 Hope to help children in need. Read her blog at travelinkait.com.

Leah Shearer Noonan is a two-time cancer survivor, writer and wife who has worked both in non-profit and education. Leah graduated from St. Bonaventure University in 2000 and has worked with teens with disabilities for over a decade. She speaks nationally on behalf of young adult cancer survivors.

Cindy O'Leary has been in education for thirty years. She is married to her college sweetheart, has three daughters and three grandchildren. Cindy enjoys spending time with her family, traveling, scrapbooking, and painting. She has also written a children's chapter book, *Leprechauns on the Loose*.

Nancy Panko is a retired pediatric RN who has had the honor of contributing to the *Chicken Soup for the Soul* series several times. A member of the Cary Senior Writing Circle and The Light of Carolina Christian Writers group, Nancy plans to publish a novel, *Guiding Missal*, in 2016. She lives with her husband in beautiful North Carolina.

Ava Pennington is a writer, speaker, and Bible teacher. She authored *Daily Reflections on the Names of God*, a devotional endorsed by Kay Arthur. Ava has written for magazines such as *Today's Christian Woman* and Focus on the Family's *Clubhouse*, and contributed to twenty-one *Chicken Soup for the Soul* books. Visit www.AvaWrites.com.

Mary C. M. Phillips is a caffeinated wife, working mom, and writer. Her essays and short stories have appeared in the *Chicken Soup for the Soul* series, *Cup of Comfort* series, *Bad Austen: The Worst Stories Jane Never Wrote*, and various other anthologies. She blogs at CaffeineEpiphanies. com. Follow her on Twitter @MaryCMPhil.

Connie Pombo is an inspirational author, speaker, and freelance writer. She is a regular contributor to the *Chicken Soup for the Soul* series and is currently touring South America with her husband. When not traveling or writing, she enjoys spending time with her granddaughter. Learn more at www.conniepombo.com.

Marsha Porter co-authored a movie review guide for twenty years and taught a class on foreign films. She's published hundreds of articles and written a monthly column. Her attempts to finish a great American novel have repeatedly failed but left a variety of short stories in their wake.

Kris Reece is a licensed counselor, speaker, and author of the book *Build a Beautiful Life Out of Broken Pieces*. Kris devotes her time to helping others heal from brokenness and become all they were created to be. She lives with her husband and their three children in New Jersey, and loves cycling and animal rescue.

Natalie June Reilly is an author and a mother of two good men. She is also an empty nester who graduated *cum laude* from Arizona State University with a Bachelor of Arts degree in Communication. She has written two children's books: *My Stick Family: Helping Children Cope with Divorce* and *Pax the Polar Bear: Breaking the Ice*.

Mark Rickerby is a writer, singer and contributor to multiple *Chicken Soup for the Soul* books. His proudest achievements are co-authoring his father's memoir, *The Other Belfast: An Irish Youth*; and *Great Big World*, a CD of fifteen original songs he wrote and sang for his daughters, Marli and Emma. He's currently writing a children's book series.

Louisa Rogers has been an international business trainer, workshop leader and writer for thirty years. She divides her time between California and Mexico. Her articles on personal/professional development have appeared in over 200 publications, including *Glamour*, *Entrepreneur* and *Yoga Journal*. E-mail her at louisarogers51@gmail.com.

Liz Rolland lives on a small farm with her husband, two daughters, and two rescued Akitas. Her blog, *Balance Salad*, features healthy recipes, weight loss tips, spiritual musings, and occasional restaurant reviews. She collects sea glass, shark's teeth, and unpublished novels.

Kimberly Ross earned her Master of Divinity from Saint Paul School of Theology. After a career in ministry, she enjoys sharing her gifts as an intuitive, teacher, writer and energy healer. She recently moved from the Midwest to Arizona, where she enjoys delightful times with her small grandson and the warm winters.

Julie Sanderson has focused her career on helping people. She taught fifth grade before becoming a police officer. She is involved with a church camp and foster care. She now works with alcoholics and veterans on probation. She loves to hike and snowshoe with her black Lab, Brady. E-mail her at juliesanderson70@gmail.com.

April Serock earned an M.A. degree in writing from Seton Hill University. She lives with her husband and son where she can see the sun rise over the Appalachians each morning. She's published romantic short stories with *Woman's World* magazine and writes nonfiction articles for money-saving websites.

Paula Sherwin received her Master of Education degree from Utah State University. She adores her two adopted daughters, three cats and dog. Paula enjoys traveling, illustrating, and writing. She is currently writing and illustrating several children's books.

Selena Singh earned her Bachelor of Science degree, with honors, from McMaster University in 2014. When she isn't writing, doing crafts or baking, you can find her traveling and spending time with family. She plans to write children's science books and become a healthcare professional. E-mail her at selena.singh9@gmail.com.

Gene Smillie received a bachelor's degree in three stages at Wheaton College, with intervals of several years in between. Then, master's degrees at Princeton and Wheaton, and after years of missionary work in Africa, South America, and Europe, a Ph.D. at age fifty-one. Since then he has alternated between pastor and college professor.

Sheila Sowder and her husband Jimmy still live in an RV, but they recently traded in their small RV for a really large model with lots more storage room, which they immediately filled up with things they don't need. She continues to write about their experiences while living on wheels.

Diane Stark is a wife, mother, and freelance writer. She loves to write about the important things in life: her family and her faith. She is a frequent contributor to the *Chicken Soup for the Soul* series. E-mail her at Dianestark19@yahoo.com.

W. Bradford Swift has written several true-life stories for the *Chicken Soup for the Soul* series. He and his wife co-founded Life On Purpose Institute in 1996 (www.lifeonpurpose.com). He also writes speculative fiction under the pen name of Orrin Jason Bradford. Learn more at www.wbradfordswift.com.

Kamia Taylor is a real estate paralegal who changed her life by moving from Los Angeles, CA to a small organic farm in the Midwest. She began writing professionally and doing large black dog rescue after becoming disabled because a drunk driver hit her truck head-on at 70 mph. E-mail her at bigblackdogrescue@gmail.com.

Stacy Thibodeaux lives in San Antonio, TX, where she writes a weekly column for the *Hill Country Weekly*. She enjoys running, reading, wine tasting and spending time with her husband and four children. This story is dedicated to all those who asked Stacy: "What in the world are you going to do with a degree in English?"

Author **Julia M. Toto** shares stories of hope, forgiveness, and second chances. Both *City Sidewalks* and *Wait for Morning* (Pelican Books) have earned five-star reviews on Amazon. "A Letter to Daddy" appeared in *It's a God Thing* (Worthy Publishing), and "Home Free" in Family Fiction's *The Story 2014*. Learn more at www.juliamtoto.com.

Miriam Van Scott works in a variety of media ranging from magazine articles to television projects. Her books include *Song of Old: An Advent Calendar for the Spirit*, *Candy Canes in Bethlehem*, *Encyclopedia of Hell* and the *Shakespeare Goes Pop* series. For clips, photos and more information, visit miriamvanscott.com.

Vidya lives in Charlotte, NC with her husband, two children and her octogenarian father-in-law. She enjoys writing, dancing and cooking for her food-loving family. She is currently learning to be a Reiki practitioner and hopes that someday she will be able to touch plenty of lives through her healing and inspirational writing.

Pat Wahler is a retired grant writer and proud contributor to eleven previous *Chicken Soup for the Soul* books. Pat resides in Missouri and draws writing inspiration from family, friends, and the critters that tirelessly supervise each moment she spends at the keyboard. Visit her at www.critteralley.blogspot.com.

Joan Wasson received her Bachelor of Arts degree, with an emphasis in Accounting, from California State University, Fullerton in 1979. She lives with her husband Charlie in Orange, CA and enjoys teaching children.

Marjorie Woodall works as a freelance copy editor and lives in the Sierra Nevada foothills with her husband. E-mail her at marjoriewoodall@hotmail.com.

Dallas Woodburn is a writer, editor and teacher living in the San Francisco Bay Area. She has contributed to more than two dozen *Chicken Soup for the Soul* books. Connect with her at her blogs DayByDayMasterpiece.com and DallasWoodburn.blogspot.com.

Following a fifteen-year career in nuclear medicine, **Melissa Wootan** is finding her joy by exploring her creative side. She enjoys refurbishing old furniture but is most passionate about writing. Her stories have appeared in the *Chicken Soup for the Soul* series and *Guideposts*. Contact her at facebook.com/chicvintique.

Susan Wright lives (and writes) in an old farmhouse, along with her husband, a dog, three cats, and the current foster dog. Learning to want less has opened the door to a beautiful life, filled with the things money can't buy. E-mail her at wereallwright@gmail.com.

Susan Yanguas is a five-time contributor to the *Chicken Soup for the Soul* series. She plans to embark on a major purge over the next year to simplify her life and make room for new opportunities. Susan hopes her de-cluttering campaign will result in more time for writing her mystery series.

Meet Amy Newmark

Amy Newmark is the bestselling author, editor-in-chief, and publisher of the *Chicken Soup for the Soul* book series. Since 2008, she has published 125 new books, most of them national bestsellers in the U.S. and Canada, more than doubling the number of *Chicken Soup for the Soul* titles in print today.

Amy is credited with revitalizing the Chicken Soup for the Soul brand, which has been a publishing industry phenomenon since the first book came out in 1993. By compiling inspirational and aspirational true stories curated from ordinary people who have had extraordinary experiences, Amy has kept the 23-year-old Chicken Soup for the Soul brand fresh and relevant.

Amy graduated *magna cum laude* from Harvard University where she majored in Portuguese and minored in French. She then embarked on a three-decade career as a Wall Street analyst, a hedge fund manager, and a corporate executive in the technology field. Her return to literary pursuits was inevitable, as her honors thesis in college involved traveling throughout Brazil's impoverished northeast region, collecting stories from regular people. She is delighted to have come full circle in her writing career — from collecting stories "from the people" in Brazil as a twenty-year-old to, three decades later, collecting stories "from the people" for Chicken Soup for the Soul.

When Amy and her husband Bill, the CEO of Chicken Soup for the Soul, are not working, they are visiting their four grown children. Follow her on Twitter @amynewmark and @chickensoupsoul.

Meet
Brooke Burke-Charvet

Brooke Burke-Charvet is above all a wife, mother, and philanthropist. She is one of social media's most influential moms and a constant source of information regarding health and fitness, with an outreach of almost four million followers via Twitter, Instagram, and Facebook. Her blog is published on the ModernMom.com website. *Forbes* recognized her as one of America's top ten moms to follow. She has also written an autobiography: *The Naked Mom, A Mother's Fearless Revelations.*

Brooke is recognized for first winning, and then going on to co-host eight seasons of *Dancing with the Stars.* Last year Brooke joined the CBS Dream Team to host the educational Saturday morning show, *Chicken Soup for the Soul's Hidden Heroes.*

Brooke also co-created, produces and stars in *Breaking Bread with Brooke Burke,* a food-oriented lifestyle talk show with celebrity guests. She is a contestant on the 2016 *Celebrity Apprentice,* as well as being a frequent guest and host on a variety of other television shows.

Brooke has a fitness DVD series with Sony Home Entertainment, a line of fitness clothing, and she even teaches classes in her hometown of Malibu. She has graced the cover of every major fitness magazine.

Brooke beat cancer in 2013, and she continues to bring awareness and inspire people to support a variety of cancer organizations. She became the face of the American Cancer Society's "Bucket List" campaign in 2014, and she continues to share her story through speaking engagements across the country. She sits on the boards of cancer related charities as well. Brooke is also a "Smile Ambassador" for Operation Smile.

Brooke enjoys her blended family life in Malibu with her beloved husband David Charvet and their four beautiful children, dogs, cats, lizards, and other creatures.

Thank You

We owe huge thanks to all of our contributors and fans, who shared thousands of stories about decluttering their lives. We loved reading all the submissions and choosing the 101 that would appear in the book. We have perhaps never turned away so many excellent stories. All of us on the editorial staff were so inspired by the stories that we all began our own cleanup projects.

We owe special thanks to Ronelle Frankel, who read all the submissions. She narrowed it down to more than 300 finalists for Amy to choose from. Assistant Publisher D'ette Corona then did the initial editing of the stories and picked the wonderful quotations that appear at the top of them. This paved the way for Amy to edit them, choose the "pop-up" phrases that we highlighted (a first for us) and shape the chapters. Our editors Barbara LoMonaco and Kristiana Pastir, along with outside proofreader Elaine Kimbler, jumped in at the end to proof, proof, proof. And yes, there will always be typos anyway, so feel free to let us know about them at webmaster@chickensoupforthesoul.com.

The whole publishing team deserves a hand, including Executive Assistant Mary Fisher, Director of Production Victor Cataldo, and our graphic designer, Daniel Zaccari, who turned our manuscript into this beautiful book.

Sharing Happiness, Inspiration, and Wellness

Real people sharing real stories, every day, all over the world. In 2007, *USA Today* named *Chicken Soup for the Soul* one of the five most memorable books in the last quarter-century. With over 100 million books sold to date in the U.S. and Canada alone, more than 200 titles in print, and translations into more than forty languages, "chicken soup for the soul" is one of the world's best-known phrases.

Today, twenty-three years after we first began sharing happiness, inspiration and wellness through our books, we continue to delight our readers with new titles, but have also evolved beyond the bookstore, with super premium pet food, a line of high quality soups, and a variety of licensed products and digital offerings, all inspired by stories. Chicken Soup for the Soul has recently expanded into visual storytelling through movies and television. Chicken Soup for the Soul is "changing the world one story at a time®." Thanks for reading!

Share with Us

We all have had Chicken Soup for the Soul moments in our lives. If you would like to share your story or poem with millions of people around the world, go to chickensoup.com and click on "Submit Your Story." You may be able to help another reader and become a published author at the same time. Some of our past contributors have launched writing and speaking careers from the publication of their stories in our books!

We only accept story submissions via our website. They are no longer accepted via mail or fax.

To contact us regarding other matters, please send us an e-mail through webmaster@chickensoupforthesoul.com, or fax or write us at:

Chicken Soup for the Soul
P.O. Box 700
Cos Cob, CT 06807-0700
Fax: 203-861-7194

One more note from your friends at Chicken Soup for the Soul: Occasionally, we receive an unsolicited book manuscript from one of our readers, and we would like to respectfully inform you that we do not accept unsolicited manuscripts and we must discard the ones that appear.

Chicken Soup for the Soul

Changing your life one story at a time®
www.chickensoup.com